A Learning Community in the Primary Classroom

D0147292

Jere Brophy
Michigan State University

Janet Alleman
Michigan State University

Barbara Knighton
*Waverly Community Schools &
Winans Elementary School*

Routledge
Taylor & Francis Group

NEW YORK AND LONDON

First published 2010
by Routledge
711 Third Avenue, New York, NY 10017, USA

Simultaneously published in the UK
by Routledge
2 Park Square, Milton Park, Abingdon, Oxon OX14 4RN

Routledge is an imprint of the Taylor & Francis Group, an informa business

© 2010 Taylor & Francis

Typeset in Sabon by RefineCatch Limited, Bungay, Suffolk

Library of Congress Cataloging in Publication Data
A catalog record has been requested for this book

ISBN13: 978–0–8058–5573–9 (hbk)
ISBN13: 978–0–8058–5574–6 (pbk)
ISBN13: 978–0–203–85182–1 (ebk)

A Learning Community in the Primary Classroom

This richly detailed description and analysis of exemplary teaching in the primary grades looks at how a teacher establishes her classroom as a collaborative learning community, how she plans curriculum and instruction that feature powerful ideas and applications to life outside of school, and how, working within this context, she motivates her students to learn with a sense of purpose and thoughtful self-regulation. The supporting analyses, which ground the teacher's practice in principles from curriculum and instruction, educational psychology, and related sources of relevant theory and research, are designed to allow teacher-readers to develop coherent understanding and appreciation of the subtleties of her practice and how they can be applied to their own.

Resulting from a lengthy collaboration among an educational psychologist, a social studies educator, and a classroom teacher, the aspects and principles of good teaching this book details are widely applicable across elementary schools, across the curriculum, and across the primary grade levels. To help readers understand the principles and adapt them to their particular teaching situations, an appendix provides reflection questions and application activities.

Jere Brophy was University Distinguished Professor of Teacher Education and Educational Psychology, Michigan State University. Jere passed away shortly after completing this book.

Janet Alleman is Professor of Teacher Education, Michigan State University.

Barbara Knighton is an Early Elementary Educator, Waverly Community Schools & Winans Elementary School, Michigan.

This book is dedicated to our dear friend and co-author, Jere Brophy.

Shortly after our manuscript was sent to the editor, Jere Brophy sadly passed away. Jere was a dedicated husband, a proud father and grandfather, and a world-renowned educator. His unwavering commitment to excellence and his thoughtfulness inspired everyone who knew him. Jere was humble, kind, exhibited a dry sense of humor, expressed equity and equality in all his actions, and was truly brilliant! He was an amazing researcher, teacher, colleague, and friend.

Contents

Preface

This book is a product of years of collaborative research, development, and reflection on teaching conducted by a team consisting of a researcher on teaching, a social studies educator, and a primary teacher. It describes in rich detail and illustrates with excerpts from recorded lessons how primary teachers can establish and maintain their classrooms as collaborative learning communities and teach subject matter in ways that focus it around big ideas and personalize it to their students' prior experiences and home backgrounds.

The team's collaboration culminated in the kind of research that produces findings of most interest and value to teachers and teacher educators: fine-grained analysis of exemplary teaching. The work began with development of instructional units that were suited to the developmental stages and prior knowledge levels of primary students, yet much more coherent and powerful than what was found in the major publishers' textbook series. The next step involved audiotaping and observing an exemplary primary teacher who adapted the units to her students' personal backgrounds and taught them in her classroom. The resulting sets of transcripts and supporting field notes, compiled over several years, then were analyzed by team members to elaborate what occurred in detail and induce principles of good teaching.

These analyses were unusually penetrating, including not only rich description of the teacher–student interaction that occurred during lessons, but detailed information about how and why the teacher adapted the lesson plans to her students' needs and background experiences, how and why she adjusted these plans to take advantage of teachable moments or react to other events that developed during teaching, and what all of this might imply concerning principles of practice.

As the collaboration developed, the two professors became increasingly impressed with the teacher's practice, not just in social studies but across the curriculum, and not just in how she taught subject matter but in how she addressed her students' affective and social needs. She shaped each new class into a coherent learning community in which members shared responsibilities to one another and to the class as a whole, including learning collaboratively and interacting supportively.

The ways that she reached out to include her students' families were especially noteworthy. She took pains to establish collaborative relationships with them and to learn things that would enable her to personalize her curriculum by incorporating connections to her students and their family members. She also displayed impressive classroom management skills (in her classroom, very little time is lost from lessons and activities to accomplish transitions or deal with behavioral issues), and infused a remarkable volume and variety of motivational elements into her teaching.

She was consciously goal-oriented in planning and implementing lessons and learning activities that "brought home" the curriculum by connecting it to her students' lived experiences. She also was reflective and analytic as she assessed each day and planned adjustments for the future. She consistently communicated learning goals and strategies to her students, modeling the self-talk involved in active and self-regulated learning, and in other ways helping them to remain metacognitively aware of their learning goals and strategies and prepared to make adjustments if necessary (even though they were still in the primary grades).

Eventually, our collaboration accumulated more than enough lesson transcripts, observational field notes, interview material, and analytic summaries to provide a basis not only for writing the originally intended book on the teacher's curriculum and instruction in social studies (Brophy, Alleman, & Knighton, 2008), but this volume as well. It describes and analyzes how she establishes her learning communities at the beginning of each new school year; maintains learning community norms through her daily classroom management throughout the rest of the year; incorporates motivation, modeling, and metacognition into her teaching in ways that encourage her students to become active and self-regulated learners; adapts or elaborates her basic instruction to meet the special needs of individual students; and plans and implements coherent teaching of literacy, mathematics, science, and social studies. The book concludes with a chapter on how she sustains her own professional motivation and remains reflective and growth-oriented, always seeking to find ways to improve as a teacher.

This book focuses on how an exemplary teacher establishes her classroom as a collaborative learning community, and working within this context, motivates her students to learn with a sense of purpose and thoughtful self-regulation. The supporting analyses ground her practice in principles from curriculum and instruction, educational psychology, and related sources of relevant theory and research. They are designed to develop coherent understanding and appreciation of the subtleties of her practice, synthesized in enough detail to allow preservice and inservice teacher-readers to understand it well enough to be able to apply it in their own teaching—not just by rote imitation, but adapting it to their own students and teaching circumstances.

The teacher worked in a school serving primarily working-class and lower-middle-class students of mixed racial and ethnic backgrounds, so the principles of practice derived from research in her classroom are likely to be applicable in most elementary schools in the United States. In addition, as will be seen when reading the details, most of the principles developed from this work are applicable to teaching across the curriculum and across the elementary grades (not just the primary grades).

Although not written as a textbook, the book should be useful as a text for courses in preschool and primary education, as well as courses in general elementary education. It is rich with explanations and examples relating to both the content (structured around powerful ideas) and the processes (engaging students in thoughtful participation in authentic learning activities) involved in creating powerful learning experiences for young learners. To help readers understand the principles and adapt them for application to their particular teaching situations, it concludes with an appendix that features reflection questions and application activities.

Acknowledgements

We wish to thank the colleagues, students, and teachers who have collaborated with our work and enriched our understanding of classroom teaching and learning. This includes the faculty and staff of the College of Education at Michigan State University, an institution that exemplifies the concept of learning community and nurtures groundbreaking and collaborative work such as ours.

We also wish to express our appreciation to two individuals who provided vital text processing support to the project. June Benson was our secretary throughout most of the years of our collaboration. She consistently handled manuscript preparation and other normal secretarial tasks with efficiency and good humor, but in addition, produced remarkably complete and accurate transcriptions of observational field notes and audiotapes of classroom lessons. Her successor, Amy Peebles, has continued to provide us with very high-quality text processing support, including preparation of the manuscript for this book.

Although this book is dedicated to Jere Brophy, who passed away suddenly shortly after this manuscript was sent to the publisher, we want to acknowledge Arlene Pintozzi Brophy and Janet Alleman's spouse, George Trumball, for their unwavering patience and support.

We also wish to thank the administrative staff of the Waverly Community Schools for supporting our research and work together, especially Ruth Foster, the principal who first suggested and supported our collaboration. We also thank the families of Barbara's students over the years who agreed to allow their children to participate in our research.

Finally, Barbara would like to thank her husband, Keith, for being the one to say, "You should be a teacher if that's what makes you happy," and also for allowing his life to be an ongoing social studies lesson, complete with photos, vacations, and innumerable conversations devoted to developing big ideas with young learners.

Chapter 1

Introduction

This book is about teaching in the primary grades (K-3). It offers a detailed analysis of effective primary teaching, illustrated with excerpts from audiotapes recorded in first- and second-grade classrooms. It demonstrates the importance of molding a class of diverse students into a collaborative learning community. It also reveals that primary students can learn with enthusiasm a much more substantive and coherent curriculum than they usually receive, when a skilled teacher connects this content to the students' prior knowledge and home cultures and develops it with emphasis on understanding, appreciation, and life application. Finally, it shows how this kind of powerful and challenging teaching can be embedded within a supportive environment that attends as much to the students' affective and social needs as to their learning needs.

This is one of two books developed through a unique collaboration between two university professors and a primary-grade teacher. Jere Brophy was a developmental and educational psychologist whose work prior to the collaboration focused on teachers' expectations and attitudes as they related to their patterns of interaction with their students, classroom management, student motivation, and generic aspects of effective teaching that cut across grade level and subject matter. Janet Alleman is a social studies educator whose previous work focused on curriculum, instruction, and assessment in elementary social studies and the teaching of undergraduate and graduate courses in social studies education. Barbara Knighton is a classroom teacher who has worked with primary students for 15 years and recently shifted to fourth grade. She enjoys a reputation for being a very successful teacher.

Our Partnership

Collaborations between professors and teachers are likely to be challenging but potentially productive because these two groups of educators often hold contrasting views about best practice (Brophy, Prawat, & McMahon, 1991; Hinitz, 1992; Marker & Mehlinger, 1992). Professors tend to criticize teachers for relying too much on textbooks, teaching isolated facts and skills without enough emphasis on coherent structures and application opportunities, being overly accepting of textbook content as valid, and being unjustifiably pessimistic about what students are capable of learning. Teachers tend to criticize professors for being too academic and middle class in their orientation, overemphasizing generalizations from the disciplines while underemphasizing humanistic or value elements and content that is important in the students' lives or currently in the news, underemphasizing the need for direct teaching to develop a strong base of concepts and factual information before undertaking problem solving, and overemphasizing experimentation, inquiry/discovery, or other approaches to teaching that often are either impractical for classroom use or not worth the time and trouble they require (Leming, 1989; Shaver, 1987; Stanley, 1985).

Our collaboration bridges these tensions in ways that address the concerns of both professors and teachers and lead to powerful instructional programs for young students. It had its origins in the 1980s, when Jere and Jan conducted fine-grained analysis and critique of several elementary social studies textbook series, looking comprehensively at their instructional goals, content selection and representation, questions and activities suggested as ways to develop the content, and assessment components. Then, after working inductively to identify effective practices, they developed a teacher education textbook (Brophy & Alleman, 1996, 2007) and many articles on improving elementary social studies curriculum, instruction, and assessment.

Textbooks and teachers' manuals are just resources, however; it is teachers who determine the curricula that students actually experience in their classrooms (Thornton, 2005). Recognizing this, Jere and Jan shifted their focus from analyses of instructional materials to analyses of ongoing classroom instruction, based on field notes recorded during observations and subsequent analyses of audiotape transcripts. Their intention was to analyze powerful social studies teaching in detail, and then induce models or sets of principles that captured the essence of this teaching and could be incorporated into teacher education programs.

To provide a content base for such powerful teaching, Jan and Jere produced full-scale instructional units (with detailed resources), in which not only the goals and big ideas but the content to be developed and the associated learning and assessment activities were elaborated at length. These units focused on cultural universals, the same topics emphasized in the textbook series and in most states' elementary social studies guidelines, but they were much richer in content and much more clearly structured around big ideas than conventional units. Jan and Jere eventually produced nine of these units, on food, clothing, shelter, communication, transportation, family living, childhood, money, and government. The units were published as a three-volume series designed for use by elementary teachers (Alleman & Brophy, 2001, 2002, 2003).

Barbara Joins the Team

While developing the units, Jan and Jere searched for collaborators who could teach them at high levels of effectiveness and would allow us to observe and collect data in their classrooms. Gradually, our search focused on Barbara Knighton, who appealed to us for several reasons.

First, people familiar with her work led us to believe that she was an unusually good teacher, and our own early contacts with her and observations in her classroom reinforced this impression. She was warm, nurturant, and sensitive to the needs and interests of her students, but also concerned about developing their knowledge and skills and systematic in her efforts to do so. The clarity and detail with which she was able to talk about her teaching suggested that she would provide unusually observant and detailed feedback as she field-tested our units.

Second, although she had never participated in a similar collaboration, Barbara felt ready and willing to do so because she viewed it as an opportunity to improve the weakest aspect of her teaching. As an experienced teacher who had received a lot of positive feedback, she had come to view herself as a skilled professional and was generally well satisfied with most aspects of her curriculum and instruction, but she knew that she did not have a clear vision of social studies.

Third, she taught in the public schools of a bedroom suburb of Lansing, Michigan, in a district that served a racially and ethnically diverse but socioeconomically midrange population. Most of her students lived in modest homes or apartments. Many came from traditional and intact families, but typically half or more lived with a single parent (divorced, separated, or never married), were members of reconstituted families, were being raised by grandparents or other relatives, or lived in adoptive or foster homes.

Within this district context, there was nothing special about the school in which Barbara taught (it was not a magnet school or a school that did anything special in social studies). Nor was there anything special about Barbara's assignment (she was a regular classroom teacher) or students (classes were not grouped by ability). If anything, she was likely to be assigned a few more of the most challenging students (e.g., autistic, behavior disordered) because of her reputation for good management. These classroom setting aspects appealed to us because they meant that what we observed in her classroom would have much broader generalizability than it would if we observed in a school near the university, where most of the students were achievement-oriented children of unusually well-educated parents.

As it happened, over the next several years Barbara's teaching context shifted in ways that allowed us to observe her working under varying conditions. She taught a self-contained first-grade class for several years, then collaborated with a second-grade teacher in a multi-age teaming arrangement for two years, then taught self-contained first- and second-grade classes within a looping arrangement for several years, then returned to teaching self-contained first-grade classes. When looping, she taught a new first-grade group one year, retained the same students the next year for second grade, and then started over with a new class of first-graders the following year.

Finally, Barbara understood and found appealing our emphasis on structuring curricula around big ideas. She was familiar with the problems implied by terms such as emphasizing breadth at the expense of depth, trivial pursuit curriculum, and mile-wide but inch-deep, so she immediately recognized the potential power of structuring curricula around big ideas developed with emphasis on their connections and applications.

Negotiating Understandings and Inducing Principles

Jan and Jere's instructional units supplied Barbara with a content base structured around major goals and big ideas, along with suggestions for activities and assessments. Barbara then applied her professional experience and her knowledge of pedagogy and her students to adapt and elaborate on these plans in preparation for teaching the units in her classroom.

Whenever Barbara taught one of our units, Jan would come to her class to tape record and take notes. Her notes described how the day's instruction went and identified where and how Barbara did anything more or different than what our unit plans called for. Jan also noted any other information that might be needed later to add context to the verbalizations that would appear in the transcripts (e.g., use of books, photos, or other instructional resources; involvement of special education teachers or any other adults who were present during the lesson). As soon as possible following the instruction, Jan also would get Barbara's impressions of the day's activities.

Once the tapes were transcribed, the three collaborators analyzed them in exhaustive detail. Prior to a half-day meeting each week, Jere, Jan, and Barbara independently studied and made notes on copies of the transcripts. Then, during the meetings, we worked our way slowly through the transcripts, raising questions, making observations, and offering interpretations.

These analyses included two levels: clarifying specifics and inducing generalities. *Clarifying specifics* involved filling in gaps or correcting any misinterpretations about what had occurred. This included such things as filling in missing words or making corrections in places where the transcriber had rendered a word incorrectly, noting that Barbara had been pointing to a photo at a certain point in the transcript, or clarifying whether she had stayed with the previous respondent or had called on a new one when she asked a follow-up question. These clarifications ensured that all three of us shared a common understanding of what was happening at each point in the lesson.

Induction of generalizations occurred as we discussed the potential implications of these events: What had worked very well and what had been less successful, and why? Which content explanations, question sequences, and activity segments were very well implemented, and which might have been improved (and how and why)? We did not always develop clear and confident answers to these questions, but frequently we did, and many of these conclusions about specific lessons provided bases for inducing principles that have broader ranges of application.

As Jere and Jan became more familiar with Barbara's teaching, they began to raise questions about issues that went beyond social studies, such as how she set up and maintained a productive interpersonal climate in her classroom, her approaches to classroom management and student motivation, and how she developed knowledge about her students and their families and then used this knowledge to personalize her curriculum.

Summaries of the understandings and generalizations that we negotiated in our meetings were preserved in meeting notes, and these were later revisited for potential alteration or elaboration. Over several years, we accumulated a volume and variety of notes (along with the transcripts they were based on) that went well beyond what we had envisioned when we started. Also, Jan began to visit Barbara's classroom to tape record and take notes at times when Barbara was doing things other than teaching social studies. Those visits focused in particular on the beginning of the year (when Barbara was connecting with families and socializing her new students into their roles as members of her classroom learning community), the end of the year (synthesis and culmination activities), and key lessons in literacy, mathematics, and science.

Over the years, Barbara became a more complete partner in our collaboration, and we often spent time developing models and principles of good teaching of primary-grade children in general, not just in social studies. We ended up with more than enough material to write not only a book on powerful teaching of primary-grade social studies (Brophy, Alleman, & Knighton, 2008), but also this companion volume on building a learning community in the primary classroom. It deals mostly with generic rather than subject-specific aspects of good primary teaching.

Focus of the Book

This book focuses on principles of best practice in planning and implementing primary teaching. Its analyses are more fine-grained and extended than those found in methods texts, because the material is drawn from thick description data collected over several years in the classroom of a talented teacher. Many of the principles are elaborated within the context of existing theory and research on best practice. However, the instruction documented here goes well beyond these existing guidelines, both by elaborating what is involved in implementing them and by suggesting additional guidelines that break new ground. The book exemplifies the subtleties involved in teaching at a very high level, based on collaborative analyses that surfaced many of these subtleties and developed guidelines for implementing them.

We believe that Barbara's teaching would be judged as highly effective according to just about any commonly accepted criterion, and that it is far more coherent and powerful than what is offered in most primary classrooms. We do not mean to suggest that it is the only or even necessarily the best way to teach primary students, but we can say that it worked well with her students, and given the diversity of the students she teaches, it should work well in most schools in the country.

We offer a coherent view of Barbara's teaching that reflects the consensus we developed over several years of frequent meetings. To simplify the presentation, we have personalized it around Barbara as the central actor (e.g., talking about Barbara's goals, how Barbara motivates students, and so on). However, these passages also reflect Jan and Jere's ideas. Therefore, except in a very few instances where the text explicitly states otherwise, it should be assumed that Jan and Jere support Barbara's approaches to teaching and her underlying rationales as described in this book, and endorse them as models of exemplary teaching practice.

As we elaborate on Barbara's teaching, we identify its major features, place them into context by reviewing relevant theory and research, and illustrate them with examples drawn from lesson transcripts, field notes, and our frequent interviews with her. These examples illustrate Barbara's teaching of first- or second-graders. Many are paraphrased or embedded in the text as brief quotes, but some are edited transcript excerpts. Most of the editing was done either to: (1) delete or change the names of students, teachers, or other individuals (to protect their anonymity); or (2) delete material that was tangential to the flow of the lesson around the points selected for highlighting in the excerpt (e.g., interruptions that occurred when the principal broadcast an announcement or a special education teacher came to pick up or return one of Barbara's students).

In this first chapter, we have explained the rationale for our work and described how our collaboration developed and functioned. In

Chapters 2, 3, and 4, we back up, broaden our lens, and analyze what she does to establish the classroom as a collaborative community, how she communicates with families, and how she manages her classroom on a day-to-day basis.

In Chapter 5, we introduce Barbara's teaching style, highlighting her storytelling approach to introducing new content to her students. Because she works in the primary grades, much of what she teaches is new to her students, and much of the rest is currently available to them only in the form of experience-based tacit knowledge (they have not yet thought about it systematically or articulated clearly-formulated understandings of it). Consequently, storytelling lessons like those illustrated in Chapter 5 occur frequently in Barbara's classroom, and incorporate many of the most salient features of her approach to teaching.

Chapter 5 also appears (as Chapter 4) in our companion volume on Barbara's social studies teaching (Brophy, Alleman, & Knighton, 2008). It is reproduced here (with additional examples drawn from the other core subjects) because the narrative style that Barbara uses to build content bases in social studies is the same style that she uses to build content bases in the other subjects. It also is among the most striking and characteristic features of her teaching, so we introduce it early in the book as a way to give readers a richly descriptive and professionally absorbing introduction to her practice—the same kind of introduction you would get if you visited her classroom on a typical day.

Chapters 6 to 8 describe and analyze how Barbara implements some of the qualitative aspects of her teaching, such as motivating students to learn, modeling the self-talk that guides learning, and meeting special needs within her inclusive classroom. Chapters 9 to 12 explain how she approaches instructional planning and her teaching of each of the major school subjects.

In the final chapter, we provide highlights of Barbara's inspiring philosophy of what it means to constantly renew oneself and grow as a professional.

Chapter 2

Establishing the Classroom as a Collaborative Learning Community

This chapter describes Barbara's techniques for establishing her classroom as *a learning community—a place where students come primarily to learn, and succeed in doing so through collaboration with her and their classmates*. Studies of workers' satisfaction and productivity have found that workers' motivation is affected by their job environment, social relationships with co-workers, and especially, their feelings about their boss. Even workers who do not derive much intrinsic satisfaction from their work will put forth reasonable effort if they like their boss. Classrooms follow the same pattern.

William Glasser (1990) urged teachers to act as lead managers rather than boss managers. Lead managers motivate by showing rather than telling, empowering rather than overpowering, reinforcing rather than punishing, and emphasizing cooperative work toward shared goals rather than rule enforcement. They elicit their students' cooperation and empower them to assume responsibility for controlling their lives at school.

Complementary ideas about establishing caring and collaborative relationships with students and their families have been advanced by James Comer and his colleagues (1999) in *Child by Child*, by Nel Noddings (2005) in *The Challenge to Care in Schools*, by Robert Pianta (1999) in *Enhancing Relationships Between Children and Teachers*, by William Purkey and John Novak (2004) in *Inviting School Success*, and by Carl Rogers and H. Jerome Freiberg (1994) in *Freedom to Learn*. These authors all advocate creating a school environment in which students feel comfortable, valued, and secure. This encourages them to form positive emotional bonds with teachers and peers and a positive attitude toward school, which in turn facilitates their academic motivation and learning.

Many emerging ideas about productive social contexts in classrooms center around the concept of *learning community* (Baker, Terry, Bridger, & Winsor, 1997). This term points directly to two key features of optimal classroom environments. First, it emphasizes *learning*. It reminds us that students come to school to acquire important knowledge, skills, values, dispositions, and appreciations, and that their learning is supposed to be enriching and empowering.

Second, it reminds us that this learning will occur within a *community*— a group of people with social connections and responsibilities toward one another and the group as a whole. The learning will be collaborative as community members encourage and support one another's efforts and feel comfortable asking questions, seeking help, and responding to questions when unsure of the answer. Members share the belief that "We're all learning together," so confusion and mistakes are understood as natural parts of the learning process. The teacher is a learner too, and models this fact frequently (Brophy, 2010).

Barbara's Approach to Learning Community

Barbara's approach to establishing and maintaining a collaborative learning community reflects the training she has received in applying William Glasser's ideas about quality schools. Glasser emphasizes guiding students to articulate and reflect on their class's most important learning goals, to envision the kind of high-quality learning environment and interpersonal climate that would best support progress toward those goals, and to commit themselves to making it happen by accepting their own personal responsibilities and cooperating with the teacher and their peers. There is heavy emphasis on personal responsibility and self-evaluation, so that once students understand learning community goals and commitments, the teacher's management interventions often involve asking them to evaluate whether their current behavior is supportive of the group's goals, and if not, to adjust it accordingly.

Barbara has found that even first-graders can understand and follow through on the roles and responsibilities associated with concepts such as learning community and quality classroom, provided that she allows sufficient time to establish norms and expectations at the beginning of the school year. Consequently, she spends a lot of class time in the first few weeks working to make sure that her students begin to know and trust one another and to collaborate as members of a coherent learning community. This heavy early investment in socializing students to learning community norms sets the stage for smooth functioning throughout the rest of the school year (Cameron, Connor, & Morrison, 2005). Visitors to her classroom commonly note its high rates of student attention to lessons and engagement in learning activities, as well as its almost continuous curricular focus (very little time is spent getting organized, making transitions between activities, or dealing with behavioral issues).

Wish List and Quality Indicators

To help her students articulate and develop commitment to learning community goals and norms, Barbara begins the year with a wish list activity in which she co-constructs with her students a list of things that they hope to experience in her classroom. For example, the wish list that one class generated included: learn, great class, safe place for everyone, playing, coloring, place where people listen, nice kids, and nice teacher lets us have fun. As she always does when constructing such lists with her students, Barbara not only wrote down their suggestions but contributed some of her own. This allows her both to model attentive and active participation in the activity and to make sure that certain desired items are included on the list if they are not mentioned by students.

The next day, Barbara follows up by reviewing the wish list with her students and then introducing the word "quality," defining it as "something really, really great." Then she asks, "What do you need to be a quality student?" As her students respond to this question, she begins to generate a list. When feasible, she uses the students' own words. At other times, she negotiates a revision that converts a specific example to a more general rule or incorporates key phrases that she intends to use as cues or reminders throughout the year.

One year, this process produced a list that included the following quality student indicators: listen to everybody, do things carefully, do your work, remember to follow routines, share things, play together, and no hurting. Once the list is complete from Barbara's point of view (i.e., it contains all of the guidelines that she wants to include), she reviews it with her students and begins to elicit their individual assent to it ("Does this sound like a great class? . . . Thumbs up if you think these things will work."). Eventually, she asks each individual student to focus on the list and then affirm that, "I can be a quality student."

Whenever Barbara wants to shift or broaden something that a student says before adding it to the list, she asks permission. The students give this permission routinely, but she continues to ask anyway, as part of a larger emphasis on modeling respect for her students as individuals. This emphasis on *honoring her students' thinking and creations* reflects not only Barbara's professional training but the resentment she experienced as a child when she did not receive such respect from an art teacher. To this day, she vividly remembers this teacher declaring her clay hippopotamus to be too fat and pinching it, as well as arbitrarily changing the background of one of her drawings. Although still a young child, Barbara experienced this treatment as violation, and she has resolved that she will not do anything similar to her students. A small ceramic hippopotamus sits on her desk as a reminder of this resolution.

The Class Pledge

Besides developing ideas about what is involved in being a quality student, using the language associated with quality on a regular basis, and maintaining a quality classroom, Barbara expands the ideas in the pledge that the school asks all students to affirm into a *classroom pledge*: "Today I am respectful, responsible, ready to learn and safe." For example, she unpacked the safety concept during an activity that included a puppet named Franklin that she often includes in start-of-the-year socialization activities. She finds Franklin useful not just because young children enjoy puppets but also because he makes it possible for her to convey socialization guidelines through an alternative source at times, rather than always doing so in her own voice. Franklin is especially useful for demonstrating how not to do things. As Barbara puts it, he "messes up a lot," and by correcting his mistakes and restating and modeling the desired procedures, she "doesn't have to rag on the kids so much."

For the pledge activity, she asked each student in turn to hold Franklin and "Share one thing you do at school to be safe." This yielded the following list: walk carefully, stay with teachers, no biting, stay with your class, sit flat, listen, don't walk out of class, stay calm, use kind words, take turns in the bathroom, be patient, keep your body to yourself, eat your own food, shoes stay on, no arguing, no hurting, no shoving, go to the end of the line.

These ideas then became the basis for a poster about safety that was constructed and displayed in the classroom. Ultimately, four posters were developed to spell out the meanings of the four general principles mentioned in the school's pledge:

> *Respectful*: Treat people right, be nice, share, use kind words, let everyone play, take care of other people's things, clean up your mess, take turns, use polite words (please, thank you), no bullies

> *Responsible*: Do the right thing, finish homework and bring it back, follow our pledge, get all your work done, take care of school things, remember our routines, follow directions, listen to all teachers

> *Ready to Learn*: Be quiet, silent, sit pretzel-leg flat, look in the right place, thinking, listen to everyone, help our learning, share your ideas, calm body, do your work, no playing, no interrupting, no noises

> *Safe*: Calm body, be careful, keep your hands off people, ask them to stop, walk frontwards, help each other, watch the line, find a teacher, follow recess rules, no hurting, no teasing

When the classroom pledge is complete, the students and other individuals who spend time in the room (aides, the principal, college interns, etc.) sign the pledge during a special ceremony. After completing the classroom pledge, Barbara invites *all* school personnel who will be working with her class to come and talk about their expectations for the year. Part of that time includes having the teachers and staff read the class pledge, promise to follow it, and sign it. This becomes a natural segue for engaging in conversations with the "specials" teachers about the classroom community. It also provides an opportunity for extending the community beyond the four walls of the room. This enables Barbara's students to benefit from greater consistency across the teachers they encounter throughout their day. It also is celebrated by the staff for greatly reducing the time they need to spend on disciplinary matters.

Class Names and Identities

Each year, Barbara creates a name for her learning community, such as the Peaceful Pond Family or the Fabulous Frozen Family (she notes that it is not advisable to allow the children to select the name, because their ideas often do not match the teacher's vision). The first word in the name (peaceful, fabulous) is chosen because it connects to important dispositional outcomes that Barbara will emphasize during the year. Peaceful connects with ideas about harmonious and collaborative interactions with peers, and fabulous (e.g., "What does it mean to be fabulous at something? ... Who is fabulous at _____?") connects with efforts to develop her students' self-efficacy perceptions (recognizing and appreciating growth in their own knowledge and skills).

The second word in the name (pond, frozen) is chosen because it connects with a significant strand in the curriculum. Pond connects with some of the plant and animal life that the students will be studying in science, and frozen connects with ideas about climate and about food preservation that will be taken up in social studies. Concluding with the word "family" underscores Barbara's expectation that all members of the learning community will identify with one another and with the group, thereby feeling positive connections similar to the ones they feel with their families at home.

The themes identified in the class names are emphasized in the physical appearance of Barbara's classroom and in many of the activities that occur throughout the school year. The Fabulous Frozen Family, for example, entered a classroom decorated with photos of animals that live in cold places and found their student numbers displayed on bits of paper cut to resemble snowflakes. The Peaceful Pond Family periodically visited the pond located near the school, where Barbara led them in observing and talking about the plant and animal life there.

The First Few Days

On the first day of each new school year, Barbara greets her students outside of her classroom, welcoming them and making individualized comments ("Oh my, how you've grown," "Wow. You've lost two teeth since I last saw you," "We're so glad to have you in our class this year," "Oh, I've been waiting for you," "I heard that your mother would be bringing you this morning."). Then, as students enter the class, she shows them where to hang their coats, how to find the things labeled for them with nametags, and so on. Once everyone is assembled, she begins by dealing with immediate concerns (lunch, drinking fountain, toilet, seating options, care of personal belongings, etc.). Then she distributes a worksheet on basic addition facts, both to provide her students with a probable initial success experience and to provide her with some assessment information about their mathematical knowledge.

Students come to school on the first day already knowing the class name and their own magic number. They find that many objects around the room are labeled with their number. They also can see posters supporting motivation and character development ("Welcome to our class," "All ye who enter must wear a smile," "Mrs. K's classroom creating lifelong learners," "Keep up the good work," "Go for it," etc.). There is a calendar that includes notation of birthdays occurring during the month, a spelling chart (100 top spelling words), an updated number of the days left in the school year, a weather chart, a posting indicating which students have lost teeth as the school year progresses, the schedule for the day, a lunch chart, and several others.

New entries or changes in these charts are discussed each morning at a meeting that kicks off the school day. Data entered on some of the charts (e.g., lunch choices or answers to questions of the day such as "Did I ride a bus to school today?") may be graphed periodically for public display and discussion. Also displayed are visuals drawn by last year's students, focusing on learning community guidelines (e.g., "Think," "We solve problems by talking").

In the first few days of the school year, Barbara focuses on *establishing her classroom as a safe and comfortable place in which her students feel that they belong and know how to operate.* During community-building activities, she makes sure all of them are in the classroom. She launches new routines by explaining and modeling what she wants her students to do and then having them practice doing it. If it is important for them to learn a particular process for accomplishing some routine, she makes sure that they learn and follow it. Some of the most important routines need to become habituated quickly (e.g., taking home the white envelope to parents each night and bringing it back the next morning), so she makes sure that her students understand the importance of the routine, makes sure that they follow it (reminding them to take their envelopes with them when they leave at the end of the day), and follows up to insure account-ability when necessary (checks to make sure that they have returned the envelope the next morning).

When possible, she connects with and builds on the knowledge of school routines that her students developed in kindergarten. She makes reference to their kindergarten experiences, includes games and activities they experienced in kindergarten, and draws helpful comparisons and contrasts. For example, she notes that a calendar and daily schedule will be posted in her first-grade room just as they were in last year's kindergarten room, but calls attention to the ways that this year's schedule is different from last year's.

Learning One Another's Names and Personal Information

Many of the activities in the first few days focus on learning classmates' names and personal details. In one activity, for example, Barbara gave each student a flash card with another student's name on it. She then called on a student to stand, read the name on the card, and then take the card to the named student. Then that student repeated the procedure with another card, and so on. The name cards also were used for curriculum-related activities (such as identifying and sorting by the first letters of the names). Another example was "Who's Missing?" For this game, the child who is "It" hides his or her eyes while Barbara designates another student to hide in the coat room. Then the child who is "It" looks at the remain-ing students and tries to name the missing classmate (three guesses if necessary).

Many of the sponge activities (short, five- to ten-minute activities to "soak up" time in between lessons or before something like lunch begins) that Barbara uses in between lessons are designed to elicit information about her students (e.g., their leisure activities and favorite things to do). She eats lunch with her students and interacts with them at that time and for the first month she goes to all recesses with them. She uses indoor recess times (both indoor and outdoor) to play *community-building games*. In the Four Corners game, for example, Barbara names four alter-natives (e.g., places where students have been or would like to go on family vacations) and has her students move to the corner that best repre-sents them. In That's Me, a student states a fact about herself (such as the kind of pet she has at home) and classmates say "That's me" if this is true of them as well. In Two Truths and a Lie, a student states two true things and one false thing about himself, and the class tries to determine which statements are true and which is false. Besides giving Barbara information about each individual, these activities are enjoyable ways for her students to learn about one another and form connections. To ensure that all students are connected, she assigns every child a recess buddy. She has observed that nothing is more scary and uncomfortable to a child than to find him/herself alone on the playground.

The most elaborate of Barbara's get-acquainted activities involve creating what she calls *Name Stories*. To begin, she calls on a student to come up and sit in front of the class and be interviewed. Initially she does the interviewing herself, using a standard set of questions. As the children become familiar with the questions, she turns the interviewing over to them. Questions include:

> What is your whole name?
> What is your favorite color?
> Do you live in a house or an apartment?
> Who lives with you?
> Do you have any pets?
> What do you like to do after school?
> What is your favorite thing to eat?
> What movies do you like?
> What TV shows do you like?
> Are you on a team?
> Do you have a favorite sport?
> Do you like to collect anything?
> Do you take any kind of lessons?
> Are you in a club?

During the first few interviews, she notes any similarities that have emerged among students interviewed so far. Then she instructs the class to begin listening for things they have in common with the current interviewee (tug their right ear if they hear something that is the same). At the end of the interview, she leads the class in developing a "story" about the interviewee. She makes sure that this child's name is included several times (to familiarize the rest of the class with the name and its spelling), that the story includes personal information that classmates are likely to find interesting or memorable, and that it includes sight words that she wants her students to learn early in the year (e.g., he, she, to, brother, sister, mom, dad).

When the story is completed, Barbara leads her students through reviewing it a few times on the spot. Then she laminates it for inclusion in a collection of literacy artifacts that she keeps available for her students to read and reread. Copies of these stories, accompanied by two pictures of each child, also are collated into a book about that year's learning community that is distributed to each family. Before doing so, however, Barbara sends each story home and asks the parents to verify the accuracy of its content and signify their willingness to share it with other families.

Another important activity in the first few days is taking photos of the students. Barbara makes immediate use of these photos to create a poster showing each child's name and photo. In addition, these photos (or others taken later) often are used in classroom displays relating to the curriculum.

Creating Predictability to Support Self-Regulation

Barbara's socialization in the first few days also emphasizes making her classroom an understandable and predictable environment for her students. At the beginning of each day, she goes over the day's schedule, which is kept displayed for easy reference. She tries to keep most aspects of the schedule constant from day to day, and she helps her students to see that this predictability can help them to regulate their own activities and be prepared for each transition as it occurs. If special events have forced a change in the daily routine, she points this out and explains the reason for it. As she goes through the day's schedule, she foreshadows what will happen during each activity, in ways designed to stimulate student interest.

Barbara's students quickly learn that certain activities occur on certain days of the week, and at certain times of the day. Her predictable schedule helps them to know what their jobs are at any given time, even if unusual events arise (e.g., substitute teacher, Barbara busy with an individual student, principal needing to speak to her, and so on). At the end of each day, Barbara and her students revisit the day's agenda to appreciate what has been accomplished. At this time, she also provides reminders about what needs to be taken home or what will be occurring the next day.

Barbara also builds predictability into the socialization that she communicates to her students, especially concerning rules and routines. She explains and demonstrates procedures for: making transitions; getting out, appropriately using and replacing equipment items; and storing and retrieving personal belongings. Her students quickly learn that storage spaces (envelopes, cubby holes, coat hooks, etc.) are all marked with their magic numbers, so they know where to go to get out or replace assignment sheets, hang their clothes, and store and retrieve personal belongings. They learn when and how to line up when getting ready to leave the room, following rules that prevent potential squabbles (e.g., the second person in line holds the door; if you get out of line, you go to the end when you come back). They also learn to make transitions quickly and quietly (e.g., moving from their table seats to gather together on the rug in the social studies corner).

As students internalize and automatize these rules and routines, Barbara's classroom becomes a focused learning community in which a very high percentage of the students' time is spent engaged in lessons and learning activities. Her students are seldom seen milling around without particular purpose, confused about what they are supposed to be doing, or creating disruptions.

In addition to her student numbering system, Barbara frequently uses color coding to provide cues that her students can use to regulate their behavior. For example, the tables at which her students sit in small groups are color coded, so she can conveniently refer to them as "the red table" or "the green table." This takes on special importance in her class because many of her activities are done with *ad hoc* groupings, so students are not always seated at the same tables. Typically, students are allowed to sit wherever they want as long as it doesn't interfere with their learning. Each table has a designated monitor for the week who distributes supplies. When they go to the lunchroom, her students carry colored sticks that they will exchange for their preferred lunch item (e.g., a red stick for pizza, a green stick for a corn dog). Whenever she is going to post something that involves a lot of printing or writing, Barbara will use space and coloring to make it easier for her first-graders to follow (by beginning each new phrase or sentence on a new line, separating the lines clearly, and rendering each new line in a new color).

Teaching and Reinforcing Learning Community Norms

Throughout the school year, but especially during the early weeks, Barbara systematically follows up on the learning community norms and expectations established during the first few days. She frequently explains or models appropriate attitudes and behavior.

For example, many of her activities are done in small groups. Sometimes she will assign these groups herself, but sometimes she will ask selected individuals to pick several peers to form a group. At these times, she emphasizes the value of using these picking privileges as opportunities to get to know all of one's classmates. She reminds students that if they always just pick their recess friends, "everybody loses, because some kids are always left out."

She also socializes students on the receiving end. For example, one day she observed a child pouting because he had not been selected for a game. She said, "We need to be good sports. That makes us want to play more games." Then she modeled more and less appropriate responses to not being picked.

Barbara reinforces desired attitudes during lessons as well. For example, when apple pie came up during a social studies lesson on food, she asked students to indicate (by tugging on their right ears) if they liked to eat apple pie. Noting that some did but others did not, she observed that,

"Different people like to eat different stuff." Similarly, whenever differ-ent careers arise during lessons, she will ask her students which of them might like to have such a career when they grow up. Typically there is disagreement, leading Barbara to observe that some students want to do certain kinds of jobs and some want to do other kinds of jobs, and that's fine. In large and small ways, she routinely models and reinforces valuing of *respect for individuals* and *appreciation for diversity*.

Similarly, she teaches the value of *generosity* early in the year and regularly takes advantage of opportunities to reinforce this idea and pro-vide examples of it in action. For example, her social studies lessons on food, clothing, and shelter include discussion of soup kitchens and other safety net services for indigent people, and Barbara uses these lessons as occasions for praising the "kind" and "generous" people who volunteer their time or donate goods or money to these services.

If students behave in ways that violate the pledge they affirmed at the start of the year, Barbara will revisit the pledge with them. Through ques-tioning and other scaffolding, she will lead them to see that they have not been fulfilling this pledge, and to reaffirm their commitment to do so.

Learning community norms are also reinforced when Barbara assigns jobs or helper roles for which students are "hired" for two weeks at a time (seeking to match the jobs to what the students want to do). Besides being a creative way to get students to help with classroom man-agement and housekeeping tasks, these jobs engage students in providing services for the learning community as a whole. Barbara makes sure that they are discussed in ways that *encourage those serving the community to take pride and satisfaction in doing so, and those being served to express appreciation for the services.* The classroom responsibilities fulfilled by individual students include: personal assistant (to Barbara), time keeper, duck handler, gardener, supply clerk, lunch supervisor, librarian, coat checker, expert assistant, mailbox stuffer, musical director, head meteor-ologist, recreation director, seating host, table sanitizer, chair wrangler, water bottle organizer, and interior designer!

Barbara always speaks of jobs rather than work when talking to stu-dents about their roles and responsibilities, because the term includes not only writing or other physical tasks but intangibles such as listening during lessons or using a kind voice with peers. As part of her emphasis on students taking responsibility for regulating their own behavior, she uses questions to remind them of their responsibilities when they are not fulfilling them. In these instances, she cannot ask, "What is your work now?" if the student's job is to be listening, but she can ask, "What is your job now?" Another advantage to the "job" term is that it typically is not applied to children, so she can define it as she wishes. Finally, job is a positive term for children (they aspire to have jobs), whereas work already has a negative connotation.

Barbara also takes pains to establish that *everyone's voice is important* and that participating in lessons involves paying attention not only to her as the teacher, but also to classmates. She typically addresses questions to the whole class, then calls on one or more students to respond. However, she does not have them raise their hands. All students are expected to be ready to respond to all questions. When they are not able to respond, she will help them. Onlookers are expected to pay attention to the resulting discourse, not seek to be called on to supply the correct answer. This approach produces a more conversational, less authority-projecting and distracting, form of discourse than what results when students are encouraged to raise their hands and compete for response opportunities. Barbara seeks to project the expectation, "I want to know what you think about _____," as opposed to, "I want to see if you know the right answer."

Teaching Self-Regulation

With respect to both their general classroom conduct and their engagement in lessons and assignments, *Barbara socializes her students to monitor and assess themselves, then take appropriate action.* With regard to progress on assignments or classroom responsibilities, for example, rather than just check students herself and give feedback and directions, she asks students to tell what they have and have not done, assess whether this is sufficient (e.g., "Is this a quality picture?" "How do you know?"), and identify any implications for subsequent action. The idea is to develop self-monitoring and assessment as ongoing dispositions. This helps to ensure that her students take ownership of their responsibilities and feel good about their progress, rather than feeling bossed around or completing tasks just because she tells them to.

These interventions are adaptations of William Glasser's WDEP technique, as developed by Robert Wubbolding (Glasser, 1965; Wubbolding, 1988, 1991, 1996), in which the leader first asks people what they Want to accomplish (what are their goals?), then asks them to identify and analyze what they are Doing, then asks them to Evaluate whether what they are doing matches their goals, and then calls for a Plan to improve the situation. This gives students a chance to own their own misbehavior and take the initiative in correcting it. Barbara notes that in the classroom, the W part often is pre-established and she simply states it as an assumption (such as, "We want to be safe for everyone" or "We need to become better readers").

In the early weeks, Barbara is very patient and persistent in teaching basic expectations and routines, but once her students understand what they are supposed to be doing and how to do it, she shifts emphasis from explanations and demonstrations to cues and reminders. For example, when table groups of students complete their math papers, they can interact quietly or play a game together. If these interactions should become disruptive, Barbara will go to the table and ask, "How can you help our class?" If necessary, she will shift students' seat locations to break up groups of recess friends or chatting students or to counteract distractions that develop when friends start fooling around instead of doing their jobs. ("Recess friends" is a term introduced early in the year to help her students identify people with whom they chat or get distracted too much during class time.)

Similarly, she will approach individuals and say, "Show me what a learning body looks like," or ask, "Are you helping our class?", "Are you helping us learn?", or "Are you watching and thinking with your head and your heart?" The latter question reflects *Barbara's socializing of her students to engage with both their head* (think about the meaning of what is said) *and their heart* (think about how it connects to their feelings or about their personal reactions to it, such as, "I never knew that," or "I never thought of that before.").

During the early weeks of school, Barbara frequently can be heard *restating expectations or providing cues and reminders* designed to socialize her students to regulate their own behavior:

> When passing out and gathering materials: "Watch the other kids so you will know what to do."

> When a student wants to go to the bathroom during her teaching of basic content: "Can you wait to do this later so I can get my job done? . . . If it gets to be an emergency, you know what to do."

> When a student appears to want to ask a non-task question during work time: "Is that a question I can answer later, or do I need to answer it now?"

> To call attention to desired behavior: "Are you sitting near a recess friend and still getting your work done?" (Student answers yes). "And I'm not fussing at you, am I?"

> To reinforce work expectations: "Here's the deal. I have to trust that you are really going to do your jobs—thinking, reading, writing. If not, you aren't helping your brains, are you?"

> Reinforcing the expectation that students will listen carefully: As students are getting snacks, one asks if they are going outside during recess. Barbara replies, "You'll need to ask a friend. I already gave that answer."

> Barbara is speaking with someone and a student starts to interrupt with a question: "Is this something that I need to handle right now? Is

it something that you could ask a friend about? Or is it something that you can just get? Probably your best guess will be good enough."

On frequent occasions: "Are you doing your job?" "Are you helping me do my job?" "Are you helping or hurting?" (The answers might be yes or no, helping or hurting, because Barbara will ask such questions in both situations, not just when a student is behaving inappropriately.)

When a student bemoans the fact that he did not get a turn: "Do you get a turn every time?" (Student answers no). "So it's no big deal!"

When things get a little noisy: "Check yourself out—if you are calm and quiet, you are doing your job."

Discouraging tattling: "Tattling is not helpful. I'll take care of it. You just need to do your job."

Barbara will provide special consideration and help to students who need it, but only as much and so long as appears really necessary. Meanwhile, she makes it clear to students who are immature or whiny, or students who attempt to garner unwarranted special treatment, that the rules apply to them, too. For example, one year on the first day of school, a student who was not on the free breakfast list declared that he had not had breakfast and was hungry. Barbara checked with his mother and ascertained that he had eaten breakfast at home that morning, and would be eating breakfast at home every day before leaving for school.

Another student began crying when she couldn't do one of the raps that Barbara had taught the class earlier. Barbara told her to sit at a table, calm down, and "Come on back when you are calm. This isn't an important thing to fuss about." The child did so and soon returned to the group. A child who had been reprimanded for calling out answers sought special treatment by asking, "How can I be quiet if I have a headache?" Barbara simply responded, "You will need to do that if you want a turn."

One day, a student started to become upset at the prospect of reading aloud. Barbara stuck with him, both pushing him and reassuring him, and he was able to read the words successfully. Shortly thereafter, the principal came into her class, and Barbara asked her students if they would like to read for the principal to show her what they were learning. The student who had started to become upset just a few minutes earlier was the first to volunteer.

Whenever Barbara finds it necessary to "fuss at someone," she makes a point of personally reconnecting with that student the first chance she gets. She draws an analogy to withdrawals and deposits in banking. "If I have to point out something that students are doing that might make them feel bad, I try to get back to them very quickly with something really positive. If I have to caution students about something, or make a soft reprimand, or give them a look, or whatever, I have made a withdrawal. Then I need to get back to them quickly, point out something positive or bring them into the conversation quickly, to make them feel really connected. That would be a deposit."

She likes to use short signals to re-energize her students if they start to become fatigued or inattentive. She wanted to use a variety of these signals but was not pleased with some of the more common ones, such as clapping hands or flashing lights. These are overly distracting and have connotations of teacher control rather than student self-regulation. One common signal is "Give me five," in which the teacher holds up and spreads five fingers as reminders of five ideas that apply in the situation.

When Barbara went to construct her own version, she quickly settled on look/eyes, listen/ears, and calm/body as three of the ideas, but was not sure what to include for the other two. She wanted to emphasize active learning rather than just passive listening, so she settled on thinking (use your head to figure out what this means) and responding personally (using your heart to care about it, make connections to it, and note your personal reactions). She emphasizes all five of these elements as contributors to good learning, but especially the head and heart. Consequently, she uses this intervention not only with students who are clearly inattentive, but also with students who have become passive and perhaps disengaged. When such students point out they were looking or sitting quietly, Barbara explains that she can get this level of response from her dog and expects more from her students.

After teaching her students to self-monitor and assess their work on assignments, Barbara subsequently cues them accordingly. For example, she teaches them to use the following checklist to determine if a story they have written is complete: 1) there are pictures and words on every page, 2) look to see if you can read the story (legible), 3) the story has to make sense, and 4) the story is easy to read. If a story passes these criteria, it goes into the folder on the side marked with a red dot (stop), but if it is not finished yet, it goes on the side marked with a green dot (still going).

When she inspects students' stories and gives feedback, she frequently refers to these four criteria. If a child has used a word inappropriately, for example, she will ask, "Does this make sense?" If necessary, she refers students to sources such as the word wall or their personal quick word dictionary where they can go to find letters or words that they do not know. She also does each assignment herself and posts her paper as a model for students to consult. As they develop early drafts of stories or compositions, she encourages them to cross out mistakes and move on rather than take time to use an eraser. Eventually, however, the draft placed into the folder as the final version should be reasonably neat and legible. If it is not, Barbara will ask, "Is this your best work?"

Socializing through Modeling and Role Play

Barbara routinely creates a series of resources to support her students' learning and use of self-regulation routines. Initially, she models the routine herself, then calls on individual students to perform it (providing feedback or correction as needed), then monitors while all of the students practice it (guided practice), and finally releases them to work independently (independent practice). She also posts reminders for easy reference. To support work on assignments, she typically produces her own version and posts it as an example of completed work. In addition, she makes it clear that her students are welcome to ask her or consult with one another if they need help with assignments (although she emphasizes the importance of getting help to make sure that you know what to do and how to do it, not just to insure that your paper contains correct answers).

To teach principles for behavior and decision making in social situations, she embeds rules of thumb within situational vignettes (e.g., "If situation _____ arises, you can respond by doing _____."). Finally, for interpersonal behavior problems that require special attention, she creates "social stories" that depict appropriate behavior and indicate why it is desired.

The process begins with modeling, role play, and practice of the new routine. For example, after initially presenting and explaining the morning routine, Barbara leads the class in reading it together, then doing it as a rap. Next, she asks individual students to respond to questions about it. Then she pretends to be a first-grader and role plays, asking her students to watch to see if she does things right. She designates one of them to take her role as the teacher. As she role plays, she verbalizes her thinking aloud so that students can see the principles and decision-making routines that guide her behavior. Then the students critique and discuss her actions.

When talking about how her students may interact with one another during and following work on assignments, Barbara uses modeling to help them understand the need to speak quietly during these times, to avoid distracting classmates from assignments. She says, "Listen, this is how our class should sound when we are working," then speaks to them using her "whispering" voice.

After Barbara completes her modeling, but before she has everyone practice the new routine, she has one or more students perform the routine or role play their behavior in a situation that calls for it. This modeling enriches her students' understanding of what to do and how to do it, and by allowing them to see the routine performed effectively by someone similar to themselves, it also has a motivational function (i.e., "If Travis can do it, I can do it too.").

If necessary, the modeling includes inappropriate as well as appropriate behaviors, to help students distinguish between them. When this occurs, she asks her students to tell her to stop when she is behaving inappropriately, then explain what she is doing wrong and how she can correct it. Franklin the puppet is often used in these situations.

When Barbara thinks that the class understands what to do and is ready to display this knowledge, she says so, but first asks if anyone needs additional information or modeling. Once the class appears ready, she will engage them in role play and other practice of the routine, providing further reinforcement by praising successful implementations (specifying why the child is being praised) or providing constructive feedback (and additional modeling if necessary) when students are confused about what to do or are carrying out the routine inappropriately.

When conveying guidelines for particular situations, Barbara clearly specifies both the situation and the expected behavior. For example:

> "When the secretary gives me direction over the intercom, you need to remain quiet and calm. For example, when she says, 'Mrs. Knighton, you can bring your children to the gym,' you need to stay where you are until I ask you to line up."

To help her students remember these guidelines, she will follow up with cues ("In this situation, what is your job?") or reminders ("If you are doing _____ in this situation, you are doing your job.").

As Barbara installs rules and routines, she regularly explains the rationales for them, so that her students can "see the purpose, not just the demand." She emphasizes cause–effect linkages in explaining the ramifications for others when students do not do their jobs properly, and in the process, reinforces norms of interdependence, responsibility, and related learning community principles. For example, she wants students to place notes from home in a designated spot. She explains, "I ask you to put your notes here in this special place, because if you just hand them to me, I might put them down and then forget where I put them."

Barbara takes pains to explain and model her expectations for how students should react to the comings and goings of her teacher aide and other frequent visitors to the classroom. She recognizes the students' desire to be welcoming to these classroom visitors, but also emphasizes the need to avoid unnecessary interruptions to their own learning, as well as distractions to the learning of their classmates. She asks, "When she comes and goes, what do we do? Do we talk to her, or do we just give her a smile acknowledging that we're happy she's here, or that we realize she has to leave now but she'll come back." Then she models desired and less desired responses, concluding, "When these people come in and out of the classroom, you don't need to carry on and go talk to them. A smile will do. When you see a friend you know, smile but keep working and thinking. That way both of you can feel good and you'll still get your jobs done."

Besides developing students' self-regulation by helping them to see the reasons for desired rules and routines, Barbara believes that her sharing of rationales helps build relationships with students ("You let down the walls, and this brings you closer to them") and supports her year-long agenda of teaching her students how to think and make decisions. Frequently, rather than just explain the rationale herself, she will ask her students why they think she is asking them to follow a particular rule or routine, then lead a discussion clarifying the desired outcomes that the rule or routine supports and the problems it prevents.

Making It Memorable

Barbara makes a point of presenting rules and routines in expressive ways that make the learning memorable. She advises other teachers to "Consider being expressive: It matters so much!" She also believes that voice inflection is a powerful tool ("Think about yourself as being on a stage. Make sure that everyone in the room is connecting to your emotions"). She has conversations about this with her students, helping them to understand, for example, that "My voice is loud, but not angry."

Although Barbara is careful to explain the rationales underlying her rules and routines at whatever length is necessary, she also provides *memory supports* that make it easier for her students to remember and access the rule or routine when needed. For example, she often hangs posters, pictures, or other visual illustrations to serve as cues or reference resources. She uses songs, raps, rhythmic language, or humor to provide students with memorable and easily accessible representations of rules and routines.

She also frequently uses short, memorable *catch phrases* that connect to her behavioral expectations ("Remember, gentle voices, quiet working," "Do the best you can, then move on") or describe what needs to happen in the immediate situation ("We will be ready to leave when everyone is peaceful and calm," "Zippy zoom—move quickly so we will have more learning time," "Zip, zip, zip, so I don't have to fuss at you."). These phrases also signal to students what to do. For example, when she gives directions, students listen until they hear the phrase, "Off you go." Then they get to work. Another phrase is "Check yourself," which tells students that they should self-evaluate to see if they need to fix their behavior, because "fussing" comes next. Making her rules and expectations memorable helps her students to become more self-regulated and thus less dependent on her to tell them what to do in any given situation. Barbara hopes that students will repeat the words used in class as they make decisions. "I want to be inside their heads even when I'm not around," she says.

Personal Responsibilities

In the early weeks, Barbara pays special attention to making sure that her students learn to care for their belongings and fulfill other personal responsibilities. She begins the first writing assignment by telling students to write their names and magic numbers at the top of their papers, showing an example that she has written with her own name and number. As the students begin to do so, she circulates to make sure that they do it correctly and help any who need help.

Concerning the work itself, she maintains a delicate balance between instilling self-confidence and dispositions toward self-regulation when working on assignments, yet making it clear that students are expected to get help from her or from some of the classroom resources she has put in place whenever they need such help. For example, she builds trust by assuring her students that she will not ask them to do something that they cannot do, yet also helps them to understand that learning frequently involves making mistakes or polishing initially crude efforts.

At the beginning of the year, she has her students use pencils without erasers, to underscore her expectation that, "when they make a mistake, they will cross it out and move on," rather than take time to erase. During practice activities, she wants them to concentrate on developing understandings of big ideas and mastery of basic skills, without obsessing about creating a perfect paper. They can worry about fine details later, when they create "published" versions to place in their folders.

Similarly, Barbara often invites her students to express their thinking about a topic through drawing instead of or in addition to writing about it. In these situations, she emphasizes that the expected drawings will be relatively crude or simple sketches that convey the students' ideas about the topic, not finished, detailed artwork. She teaches them to distinguish between quick sketches meant to illustrate thinking and detailed artwork meant for publishing, and she incorporates these distinctions into her activity instructions. To help students avoid obsessing or getting frustrated when they cannot spell a word or draw something just right, she frequently tells them to "do your best and move on," and even has them practice saying this to themselves.

Barbara provides detailed explanation and modeling of how to do each new kind of activity that she introduces. For example, to introduce the first mathematics worksheet, she models by filling out the worksheet herself, talking out loud describing what is going on in her head, and taking care to complete each problem in the first row, then each problem in the second row, and so on, until the paper is completed. Once the students begin working on their own papers, she circulates to monitor their progress and intervene where needed.

Much of her scaffolding takes the form of questions rather than statements, as part of her efforts to socialize self-regulation. If a student has skipped a problem, for example, she might ask, "Did you do all of the problems in the first row?" When a problem has been answered incorrectly, she will try to determine whether the mistake is rooted in a lack of understanding of the mathematics involved or in simple carelessness in applying mathematics that the student appears to understand. In the former case, she will provide instruction designed to clear up mathematical gaps or misunderstandings. In the latter case, she is likely to ask, "Did you think first or answer first?" or "Is this your best work?"

Barbara also makes sure that her students know what options are available to them when they complete an assignment. Standard options include coloring the picture on the assignment sheet (if relevant), doing a sketch or drawing on the back of the sheet, or finding a book to read. In addition, she often distributes or calls attention to additional options, such as playing a game (usually a game related to the content of the assignment).

Barbara's students quickly learn to keep track of and care for their belongings. This responsibility has special importance in her class because her students are expected to gather whatever they need and work at tables (not always the same tables); they do not sit in desks that include storage space for personal materials. There is a basket for them to use for submitting their completed work, and another basket where they can temporarily store assignments that are not yet completed. Materials ready to take home are placed in their individual mailboxes. Contributions to class books are kept in book boxes containing color-coded folders (green for writing, red for word work, yellow for reading time notes, and so on).

In the first few days, Barbara conducts relatively formal checks on students' fulfillment of personal responsibilities. For example, she may ask students to stand behind their chairs while she does a homework envelope check, telling those who have fulfilled their responsibilities to sit down when she calls their names. She then praises these students for their "good remembering," and reminds any students who remain standing to remember to bring their envelopes with them to school every morning. If students have not returned their home assignments, she tells them that "We're counting on you to bring us this information," and adds that they will have to generate responses in their heads when the home assignment responses are reviewed that day.

She also encourages students to take responsibility for handling their own personal problems. When a student complained that she had not brought a snack, Barbara first helped to solve the problem by providing a snack. Then she suggested that the student write her mother a note about it. Frequently she observes students doing what she has suggested.

Lesson Participation Expectations

As part of teaching her students about learning with their heads and their hearts, Barbara places special emphasis on her expectations for participation in lessons. She emphasizes that *students are expected to pay careful attention and be prepared to respond thoughtfully*, both when it is "her turn" (she is providing basic instruction) and when it is "their turn" (one of their classmates is speaking). As she begins lessons, she reminds them about getting physically and mentally prepared to learn, especially if they are making a transition from lunch, recess, or some high-intensity activity. At these times, she will make references to sitting flat, sitting calmly, doing your job, and getting ready to learn with your head and your heart. During "my turn" segments, if students begin to ask questions or make comments that would shift the flow away from her intended agenda, she will remind them that it is her turn and they need to pay close attention to what she is saying.

During "your turn" segments, she encourages her students to listen carefully and respond thoughtfully to her questions and to the contributions of their classmates. She makes it clear that when she's interacting with an individual, that student "has the floor." Other students are expected to listen carefully to the exchange between Barbara and the student who has the floor, even if that student is having trouble generating a response or if the exchange extends over several question/answer/feedback sequences. Onlookers who blurt out answers are encouraged to "keep your answers in your head" until called on, and admonished that "You're keeping him from getting his own ideas."

Barbara's students learn that they will need to listen to her questions, think about them, and generate responses, because if she calls on them and they remain silent or just take a wild guess, she is not going to accept this and give the answer or move on to get it from someone else. Instead, she is going to stay with them and extend the response opportunity, typically by first providing some feedback or explanation but then posing at least one additional question. These lesson participation expectations place strong accountability pressures on all of her students, but within a learning community that features mutual support and collaborative learning, and Barbara tries to support the student to conclude the response opportunity on a positive note. Consequently, the emotional tone of these interactions is supportive, not threatening.

Early in the school year, Barbara frequently can be heard socializing her students concerning lesson participation expectations. For example, she may tell individual students that she is disappointed that they have not yet participated today and she expects them to do so. During ticket-out activities, she reminds students that they are expected to say something that has not already been said by a classmate, so it is important for them to listen to their classmates' answers. If necessary, she will caution students about laughing at or putting down classmates' responses (e.g., "Kids won't feel safe to give answers if I let children laugh at them."). She frequently gives cues and reminders such as, "Look my way," "You are ready when your card is on the table and your body is calm," "Think first and then answer," or "When you are calm and you listen, great things happen." If a child has no response, he/she is expected to provide one later, such as after lunch if it's a "ticket out" activity. Barbara is vigilant about following up and checking in with the child as promised.

Social Stories

Barbara sometimes uses a method known as social stories as a way to introduce her students to social cues and expectations regarding appropriate behavior. Social stories provide teachers with opportunities to give information to their students in non-threatening, meaningful, and memorable ways. They provide specific information about how to be successful both socially and academically, including reasons why the desired behavior is important.

Social stories are written from the perspectives of children facing situations they find confusing. They include descriptive sentences about what happens in the situation, perspective statements describing the thoughts and feelings of the focal child and perhaps others in the situation, directive sentences that signal appropriate responses, and affirmative statements that praise desired actions. Research suggests that social stories facilitate young children's transition to school (Ali & Frederickson, 2006; Briody & McGarry, 2005; Toplis & Hadwin, 2006).

Social stories often are used with autistic children, and information about them can be found on these web pages: www.thegraycenter.org (accessed December 29, 2009); www.polyxo.com/socialstories (accessed December 3, 2009).

Guided by examples shown on these websites, *Barbara has developed her own social stories, adapted to the needs of her students.* Each social story begins with an explanation of how and why the topic is important to the class. It then explains, step by step, what students should do, why they should do that, and what will happen if they do not. It finishes with a summary of what students need to do to be successful. Much of this information is conveyed using memorable language that will be repeated frequently in class as reminders ("No one likes to be fussed at," "Pick a spot away from your recess friends.").

Barbara finds social stories helpful not only for her autistic students but for the class as a whole, especially when introducing expectations that may be difficult for her students to meet initially. She says, "I choose social story topics by thinking about areas where students have struggled in the past. I also think about what is not going well so far or where children need more information. I try to be proactive rather than just react to problems." Topics include quiet reading, assemblies, walking in line, and the ones illustrated in Figure 2.1.

Figure 2.1 Three of Barbara's Social Stories

Guest Teacher

When Mrs. Knighton is not at school, we will have a guest teacher. It is important to do a great job when we have a guest teacher. We want the guest teacher to think that The Fabulous Frozen Family is great!

When we have a guest teacher we will follow the same routines and have the same rules as always. Students should pretend that Mrs. Knighton is in the room. You should ask yourself, "What would I do if Mrs. Knighton were here?"

You must do your work and get your job done. If students don't do their job when the guest teacher is here they get fussed at by Miss Jones, Mrs. Smith, Mrs. Romano and even the guest teacher. They will be sad, angry and disappointed. When she comes back, Mrs. Knighton will fuss too. No one likes to be fussed at.

When we have a guest teacher we need to listen to what the guest teacher says. If we listen, the guest teacher will know that we are a great class. If we don't listen, the guest teacher will be sad, angry and disappointed. If we don't listen, we will have an awful day. No one wants to have an awful day at school.

To have a great day with the guest teacher we need to listen, get our jobs done, follow the rules, remember the routines and work quietly. We want our guest teacher to think great things about us and say, "The Fabulous Frozen Family is a great class!"

Using the Bathroom

Everyone needs to use the bathroom. We must use the bathroom carefully so that it will be neat and clean for the next person to use.

There are good times to use the bathroom and bad times to use the bathroom. When Mrs. Knighton is teaching, it is not a good time to use the bathroom. When kids are working at the tables, it is a great time to use the bathroom.

When you need the bathroom, knock on the door loudly and say, "Is anybody in there?" Then knock again and say, "Is anybody in there?" If no one answers you can open the door and go inside.

After you go into the bathroom, use the toilet quickly. If you are a boy, be sure to put the seat up. No one likes to use a messy bathroom. When you are finished with the toilet, flush it. No one likes to use a messy bathroom. Check the toilet. If it is wet, clean it up. No one likes to use a messy bathroom!

Next you need to wash your hands. Be sure to get soap on your hands. Then rub them together under the running water. Count to 20. Make sure all the soap is gone. Turn off the water and get a paper towel. When your hands are dry, put the paper towel in the garbage basket. No one likes a messy bathroom!

When you are finished in the bathroom, check it one more time. Look at everything. Make sure that everything is clean. No one likes a messy bathroom! Turn off the light and go back to work.

Carpet Time

When Mrs. Knighton says, "Meet me on the carpet by the calendar!" it is time to clean up quickly and meet her there.

When we get to the carpet, we need to sit down carefully. We always pick a spot away from friends so that we will remember to be quiet. When we sit at the carpet, we stay in our own space and keep hands to ourselves.

At Carpet Time it is important to listen to Mrs. Knighton. She will tell us important information and help us learn. If we don't listen to Mrs. Knighton, we won't hear the messages and we won't learn. If we don't learn, we aren't getting our job done at school. Mrs. Knighton fusses at children who don't listen at Carpet Time.

At Carpet Time we also need to think about the learning and be ready to share our ideas. Mrs. Knighton knows that we are listening, thinking and getting ready to share our ideas when we sit flat and look in the right direction. Students who play with clothes, shoes or the carpet are not learning and helping our class. It's important to pay attention and learn at Carpet Time.

Students should never interrupt Carpet Time. When you talk, make noises, play or touch other children, you are interrupting Carpet Time and making our learning hard. When children interrupt Carpet Time, Mrs. Knighton will fuss at them. No one likes to be fussed at. Children who keep interrupting Carpet Time will have to leave the group. They will sit at a table or leave the classroom. When you leave the group, you will miss learning and fun. No one likes to miss learning and fun.

At Carpet Time, children should sit with a calm body, listen, think and be ready to share their ideas when Mrs. Knighton calls their name. That is how to do a great job and help our class at Carpet Time!

To supplement the verbal content of her social stories, Barbara illustrates them with photos of her students displaying (or in some cases, failing to display) the desired behaviors. Initially these illustrations are photos of her students from her class the previous year, but as soon as possible she shifts to photos of students in the current class, taken in the first few weeks of school. The photos provide valuable visual images to supplement the verbal descriptions of desired behavior, and they add a compelling immediacy because they depict the students themselves or their classmates. Barbara is strategic in selecting photos to include, illustrating only the behaviors that need illustration and confining depictions of inappropriate behaviors to students who can handle being shown behaving inappropriately.

Social stories are reviewed a few times after they are introduced, then kept in an accessible folder for subsequent reference. Barbara sometimes uses them as tools to scaffold students' evaluation of their own behavior (by telling them to reread a relevant social story and compare their recent behavior to the ideal depicted in the story). Occasionally she will send social stories home as a way to invite families to help in a manageable way.

Follow-up Cues and Reminders

During most of the first few days and a significant portion of the first few weeks, Barbara focuses on initial socialization to school rules and routines, explaining and modeling what she expects, and if necessary, providing opportunities to practice. Once she has made sure that her students are able to do what she wants them to do, she shifts from teaching rules and routines to providing cues and reminders in application situations. Throughout the year, but especially in the early weeks, she communicates messages such as the following:

> Thanks for tucking in the chair. That helps us to get around safely.
>
> I like the way that Laurel found a seat and is doing her math work. She's being a great learner.
>
> Tim and A.J. remembered to put their names on their math papers.
>
> When you bump someone, say "Excuse me."
>
> (When two students seated at a table group are talking and off task) "This doesn't seem to be working. You will need to move to the gray or red table where there's an available seat."
>
> You need to make sure to return your homework sheet, so you can have a page in our class book.
>
> I only call on children who are sitting flat and calm (i.e., not waving their hands or engaging in attention-getting behavior).
>
> If you are looking at me, you are doing your job.
>
> Are you helping our class right now?

Occasionally, she will stage more elaborate reminders. For example, one student had turned in a book page on which he had used only one color, when multiple colors were expected. Barbara showed him several of the books turned in by his classmates, in each case asking if the pages had one color or lots of colors. He responded, "Lots" each time, and then Barbara encouraged him to add more colors to his pictures.

On another day, she celebrated those who had remembered to complete and return their homework assignments. Each child who had done so was sung to by the class (individually) and allowed to use the chimes to make music.

If students come to her with questions that they are supposed to get answered on their own, she refers them to the resources she has established around the room (posters, books, word walls, etc.). If students ask about the day's agenda, she will remind them that it is posted for their reference. If necessary, she occasionally will structure a discussion to review a rule or routine, emphasizing its rationale ("Why we do what we do.").

Typically Barbara spends at least three weeks setting the stage for a thoughtful, collaborative and responsive learning community. She is convinced that her investment in these activities yields dividends throughout the school year by improving students' behavior in addition to their understanding of community. The classroom community provides a forum for living informal social studies in a safe, orderly, and enjoyable environment. It serves as a natural way to connect cognitive, socioemotional, and moral development. It also facilitates Dorsett's (1993) concept of a good curriculum as one that respects and balances the need to educate three people in each individual: the worker (in this case, the student whose work is to attend school), the citizen, and the private person.

Barbara finds a unit on childhood to be a natural segue for launching formal social studies after the class community has been firmly established. The topic of childhood fits nicely with the development of the classroom community because it focuses on the idea that all people share some common experiences as they grow from a child to an adult (Alleman & Brophy, 2003, 2004). It is particularly useful in promoting ideas of diversity and tolerance. As the class learns and talks about children growing, it is easy to see that everyone is unique. It personalizes learning for both the teacher and the students in multiple ways; it provides an array of learning opportunities for all students to experience, value, and apply; it introduces students to geographic, historical, economic, cultural, and other aspects of their lives that will be revisited throughout the year and lead to more sophisticated understanding; it affords opportunities to make the familiar strange and the strange familiar; and it appeals to students because they are at the center of the content.

Here in Chapter 2, we have described how Barbara launches each year's learning community through the modeling and socialization that she provides as she interacts with her students during the early weeks of the school year. In Chapter 3 we will shift focus to her interactions with her students' family members, as she enlists their support for her agenda.

Chapter 3

Communicating with Families

Much of what Barbara does to establish and maintain her classroom as a learning community is done within the classroom, but she is very aware that her classroom community is nested within a larger school community, which in turn is nested within a larger school district and residence area. Consequently, she takes pains to communicate and collaborate with significant others within these larger communities. Most directly, these significant others include her students' family members. Barbara understands the impact that her students' families can have on learning in her classroom. She values those family members and seeks to develop working relationships with them. She establishes and maintains contact with families both to keep them informed about what is going on in her classroom and to identify ways in which they can collaborate to support her students' learning and general well-being.

Communicating with Families

Barbara's communication with family members often begins the year before they enroll in her class, because she takes advantage of opportunities to meet the students in the previous grade and establish initial positive relationships with them. Many of these occasions include meeting their parents as well. Also, some of the students in each new class are younger siblings of students that Barbara has taught previously, so she already has established good relationships with their families.

For other families, the first communication from her arrives in the form of a letter that she sends each year before school starts. It begins with a warm welcome, communicating that she is delighted to have their child in her class, she is eager to meet them and work together to support their child's development, she will be needing their help in certain areas, and they are encouraged to contact her by phone or e-mail or arrange to meet her at the school if they have anything they want to discuss. The tone communicates that, "We are a team; let's work together to support your child's learning and general well-being as best we can."

After establishing this initial positive tone, the letter goes on to outline Barbara's hopes and expectations for the year (both academic and behavioral/communal), identifies some of the specific forms of help she will need from the families, and provides them with basic information about what she will be doing with their children and how they can be supportive of her efforts. This information is spelled out in more detail in a handbook that she sends home on the first day of school. The nature and tone of the information she provides are exemplified in the following excerpts from one of her handbooks.

General Information
Welcome to room 106! I am delighted to be your child's teacher this year! I am excited about our time together and look forward to working with you. I have put together some information that will help answer your questions and let you know what is ahead.

Family Name. A fun way to create a community feel to the classroom is by having a class name. I've selected a name and theme that will help identify our class and connect to our learning. We will be **THE FABULOUS FROZEN FAMILY**. We will begin with some fun snowy stories and continue with this name and "chill out" throughout the year.

Choice Theory. During my years here at Winans Elementary School, some of us have been trained in William Glasser's Choice Theory. Basically, the theory states that all behavior is chosen and that everyone is responsible for his or her own choices. Part of my job as a teacher is to help your child learn to make more efficient choices and see how the behavior he/she chooses affects others. Also, relationship building is the focal point of a Quality Classroom. Therefore, we will work in many ways to create a caring, friendly, family-like atmosphere. [An accompanying poster identifies four conditions of a quality school or classroom: safe environment with non-coercion, self-evaluation, meaningful learning, and relationship building.]

Magic Numbers. I will be using magic numbers to help identify your child's things in our room. Please feel free to use the magic number to identify your child's things from home such as backpacks, snow pants, coats, etc. Many unlabeled items end up in the lost and found every year.

Team T-Shirts. To help create a fun learning community and build ties with each other, I have decided to make tie-dye T-shirts this year. I already purchased the supplies and created the shirts. The shirts will stay here at school for special events, regular learning celebrations and field trips. The shirts cost about $5.00 each and students who pay for the shirt may keep it at the end of the year. I will personalize the shirt they will wear on our field trips and celebration days.

White Envelopes. Papers and information will be coming home **every day** in a large white envelope. Be sure to check the envelope daily and return it to school the next day. **Use the envelope to send notes, lunch money, book orders, etc. to school.** In addition, you will be getting a school folder to help organize school notes. Please be sure to save all newsletters and notes for future use.

Parent Volunteers. I will be sending home a calendar at the beginning of each month. Please mark on the calendar, what day or days that you would like to come to school and help out, AM or PM. I have a variety of jobs, ranging from working or reading with students to clerical tasks to art projects. I will also add on the calendar any special projects, field trips or parties where I will need more than one parent to help. After I receive your calendar with the dates marked, I will let you know if the times will work out. Also, I occasionally have jobs for families that work during the day. These jobs can be done at home in the evening and returned to school the next day. If you could help out with typing stories, washing tie-dye shirts, cutting out materials, etc., please let me know. I *love* to have parents help out and so do the kids!!

Student of the Week. Each student will get the opportunity to have a turn to be our Student of the Week. Before your child's week, I will send a poster and an instruction sheet home to help you know what to do. Be sure to take a look at my board. It will be up for the first two weeks of school. I will also provide a schedule showing when your child will have a turn.

Our Students. At the end of the first week of school, I will send a list of the students in our class. It's so much easier to have great conversations about school if you know who is in our class!

Pledge. Winans continues to use a school-wide pledge to remind students about the correct behavior to use at school. Our pledge is: "Today I am respectful, responsible, ready to learn and safe." As a class we will discuss what the pledge means and follow it.

Curriculum Information
Most of our time each day is devoted to literacy and math skills. I have included a possible average day in this handbook to give you an idea of what we will be doing. We will rotate through Science, Social Studies and Health as our afternoon lesson and theme.

Literacy—Reading & Writing. A large part of our daily schedule involves different reading and writing activities. We will work to improve and connect skills related to reading, writing, thinking and speaking. The children will be involved in observing, trying and practicing those skills in many ways throughout the day. Any opportunities to practice at home help your child become a better learner!

Reading Groups. This year I will be meeting with children in small groups for reading. I will pull the small groups while the rest of the children are participating in Literacy Choice Time. The groups are made of 2–5 children and change frequently, even weekly. At the end of each reading group, students receive a copy of the new book to keep in the classroom to practice reading.

Literacy Choice Time. Literacy Choice Time provides students with an opportunity to practice using the reading and writing skills that they have been learning. It also provides the chance to learn independent and responsible working skills. Students pick their own jobs for the day from the following list: reading, writing, poem books, ABC projects and listening center. Students keep all their work in a folder. They are expected to work independently while I meet with reading groups.

Book Bags. Some of the children will bring home a clear plastic folder called a Book Bag. It will contain the book that we've read for the day. Have your child read the book several times and be sure to return it to school the next day. That way we can send home a new book. Any families that choose to participate in the book bag program will need to sign a contract to cover the $10 replacement of any lost books.

Literacy Bags. This year I will be trying a new program called Literacy Bags. A Literacy Bag contains 2–5 books on a topic. It also contains activities related to the topic or story. Each child will get to keep the literacy bag at home for 1 or 2 nights, but then it must be returned for the next family to enjoy. Please find a safe place to keep the bag at your house and check the content list carefully before returning the bag.

Poem Books. Each week your child will be learning to read a new poem. There will be a special binder to hold all of the poems. These binders will come home each week. Please take time to read it together over the weekend and then **return the binder every Monday.** ***Be sure to return it so that your child will be able to receive all the new poems!***

Sight Words & Spelling. We will begin the year by focusing on a few words for your child to work on learning to read automatically and easily each week. I will send home a new list each week with the words to learn. Each third week is a review week when we will work with all the words we've had so far. Please take a few minutes to practice these words daily. They are the words that your child will see often as we work on learning to read. Later in the year, we will be learning to spell the words that we had earlier in the year. By the end of the year, I hope that your child will have a large group of words that can easily be read and spelled.

Writer's Workshop. Your child will be participating in a daily writing program that will encourage planning, writing and sharing stories about themselves. At the end of this handbook, you will find a letter from the author of our writing program. It will share the goals of our program as well as give you information about how you can help.

Handwriting. Our school district has adopted D'Nealian handwriting for our students. D'Nealian was created to make learning to write in print and cursive easier and faster for children. I will be working with your child to learn to correctly use this type of writing. At the end of this handbook you will find a sample of the letters that we will be learning to write!

Trailblazers Math. The district has adopted Trailblazers as our math curriculum for grades K-4. This program has students working with objects called manipulatives to solve math problems. We will work to build counting and addition skills while we solve those problems.

Homework. Our math program, Trailblazers, will occasionally have a homework page. Please try to complete the activities and return it the next day. Often, today's homework is used in tomorrow's math lesson and needs to be back. Once in a while, I will be sending a special assignment or project that matches our classroom work.

Social Studies. Our Social Studies will include units covering Childhood & Thanksgiving this fall and Food & Families this winter. The Childhood, Food and Families units are part of *Social Studies Excursions*, a series I co-authored with two professors from Michigan State. We will also include some team-building and character education lessons early in the year.

Behavior Bees. Our district-required character education lessons will be The Behavior Bees. Bee and Franklin the Turtle share stories to help kids learn how to "bee." I've included a poster at the end of this handbook. [The poster reminds students to "bee" friendly, honest, cooperative, kind, fair, patient, responsible, polite, and a good listener.]

Science. Our science units for the year include Balance and Motion in the fall, then Solids and Liquids and Pebbles, Sand and Stones this winter. In the spring we will learn about Critters and Life Cycles. During our science units, students will be doing lots of hands-on exploring and then journal writing about what they see. Throughout the year we will be working on observing and describing using science words.

An Average Day:
- Math skill-building & catch-up time
- Morning meeting & Calendar
- Sight Words or Spelling
- Writer's Workshop
- Poem Books
- Recess & Snack
- Literacy Choice Time & Reading
- Lunch
- Quiet Reading Practice
- Math
- Student of the Week or Story & Surprise Box
- Social Studies/Science/Health
- Specials (Art, music, gym, library)
- Home

Family Orientation Meeting

Barbara's school schedules an orientation meeting for family members (especially families new to the school) right at the beginning of each new school year. She tries to take advantage of these meetings as opportunities to "open the door—let the parents know that they are part of the community that I am building. That I want help and input from them. That there are lots of ways they can communicate with me easily. That I really want it to be a partnership—we are working together."

During the meeting, she communicates enthusiasm and high expectations and helps the parents begin to know her and one another. She also emphasizes that she assumes responsibility for their children's security, so she needs to know which bus they should board, how they will be getting home if they are not riding a bus, and the specifics of any changes in plan on a given day. She also informs them that they can find her (and their children, if they need to pick them up) at the flagpole in front of the school at the end of each school day ("Remember, I'm always at the flagpole at the end of the day, so if you need something or you need to pick up your child, that's where you will find me.").

Other Communication Methods

Barbara also communicates with parents through home/school journals, which her students take back and forth between the home and the school each day. These are pieces of paper on which the upper half is reserved for students to write about what they learned in school that day. Next is a space for Barbara to comment on what the student has written or to write some other communication to the student or the parents. At the bottom is a space for the parents to write something in response to the student or perhaps a note to Barbara (continuing on the back of the page if they wish).

Besides their son or daughter's own work, the parents frequently get to see "class books" containing each class member's response to a question relating to a topic addressed in one of the school subjects. For example, during a social studies unit on families, a class book assignment called for writing about family members who resembled each other, especially any that resembled the child. These entries can be eye openers for parents, who see quite a variety in the quality and content of the students' writing, which gives them some context for interpreting their own child's responses. As a side benefit, reading these responses enables families to learn about one another.

In the early weeks of the school year, Barbara makes it a point to follow up by initiating communications with each family. She has found that many families do not initiate communications with her, even though there may be something they would like to talk about, until she first contacts them. So, in addition to sending home newsletters and other communications meant for all of the parents, she makes a point of contacting each family individually to communicate things of interest about their child and find out if the family members have any particular questions or concerns.

Recently, her family communication goal has been "eight by November," meaning that she will have at least eight interactions with each family before the first family conferences scheduled in early November. Her goal is to build collaborative relationships with each family prior to that conference, so the conference can take place within an already established positive relationship and include discussion of a range of issues and events—mostly positive things to celebrate rather than problems and concerns. These communications may take the form of notes brought home by the student, phone calls, e-mail messages, or contacts with family members at the school, during either scheduled meetings or informal chats when parents come to drop off or pick up their child. Barbara keeps track of these contacts, to make sure that they reach or at least approach her target goal of eight per family, because she has found that if she does not, she ends up neglecting a few families without realizing that she is doing so. This is especially likely with families of average students who do not "stick out" in any way and thus are easy to overlook.

Barbara has found that this policy has paid off well for her, because all or almost all of her families typically come to scheduled conferences. During the conferences, she builds on her prior communications to initiate easy and natural conversations that begin with, "Remember when we talked about . . .?" or "I've already mentioned to you that this is how she's doing in reading." In rare cases where family members do not show up for conferences, she connects with them to schedule a conference on another day, and in the process, reinforces the ideas that she wants to work collaboratively with them and considers it important to stay in close contact as part of doing so.

Weekly Newsletter

Once the school year begins, Barbara's primary form of communication with families is the weekly newsletter that goes home every Friday. She sends it on Friday because this is convenient for both summarizing events of the current week and looking ahead to the next week.

The first part of the newsletter provides the families with updates on what is going on in each of the subject areas, especially if the class has just completed a unit or is about to begin a new one. This section also includes information about recently completed or upcoming special projects or home assignments.

The next section focuses on things that are happening school-wide, particularly announcements or reminders about special events in which families might want to participate (family council meetings, fundraisers, etc.) or events that might require the parents to make special arrangements or preparations (half-days, construction of a class float for a parade, special assemblies or programs). There is also a section about individual students and their families, noting when new students move in or current students move out, information about birthdays or the student of the week, elections to the student council, and so on.

A "Send to School" section alerts or reminds families about things that they will need to send to the school during the next week. Perhaps a book order is due, some paperwork from the office needs to be filled out and returned, or empty cereal boxes are needed for a construction project.

Finally, a closing section alerts parents to specific upcoming events ("Look for our latest writing project that will come home this week. Be sure to read it with your child."), along with significant calendar dates coming up in the next month (beyond the next week).

Besides sending these newsletters home with her students, Barbara distributes copies to the principal and to other teachers who interact with her students, to keep them updated on what is going on in her classroom.

She also saves copies in her computer, to provide reminders and to save her time when she prepares newsletters at parallel points in the next school year.

Daily Exchanges via "The White Envelopes"

Barbara prefers to send home student work samples and any necessary individual communications with family members every day rather than include these in a larger packet to be sent home with the newsletter on Fridays. She believes that family members are more likely to pay attention to each component in a small number of documents included in a daily package, but might ignore or pass quickly over much of the contents of larger packages delivered on Fridays. Consequently, at the beginning of each school year, she socializes her students to be sure to pick up their "white envelopes" as they leave the classroom each day, take them home to show to parents or other caretakers, and bring them back the next morning. She also socializes the family members to expect to receive the white envelopes each day, inspect their contents, and then follow up by interacting with the child about them and (if relevant) sending replies or other communications back to Barbara.

The white envelopes are large (11 × 14 inches) envelope-shaped containers that Barbara purchases (special ordering if necessary) from OfficeMax or Staples. They are made of a whitish substance called Tyvek that is durable enough to last throughout the school year without tearing or falling apart. If something spills on them, they can be cleaned and dried easily. They are large enough to include almost anything that Barbara might want to send home (including artwork or other content that appears on pages larger than the standard 8 ½ × 11-inch size), yet still convenient enough for her young students to take back and forth each day.

Besides work samples, the white envelopes may contain notes from the principal, updating of lunch accounts or other requirements of money from the families, bus slips or updated transportation information, reminders of upcoming special events, or individualized notes from Barbara to the parents or caretakers. The envelopes keep all of these materials in one place and make it much more likely that they will get back and forth between home and school than if they are tucked into backpacks or coat pockets. The outside of the envelope includes Barbara's name and room number and the student's name, so if the envelope gets left on a school bus or lost somewhere, there is a good chance that it will be returned to her.

Many of Barbara's students are being raised in non-traditional family structures. Besides biological and adoptive parents, Barbara frequently deals with caretakers who are foster parents, grandparents, or unmarried partners of the child's mother or father. Consequently, her newsletters are addressed "Dear Families," and notes to the home are labeled, for example, "To Joey's Family." In situations involving shared custody or a non-custodial parent who wants to be kept informed, she tries to find out what each parent wants and respond accordingly. In some cases, this has meant creating duplicate white envelopes, one for the children to take to their mothers when staying with their mothers, and the other to take to their other parent.

In a few cases, one or two per year, parents or caretakers make it clear that they want daily communication with Barbara beyond the level of exchanging notes through the white envelopes. Many of these have been parents of autistic children or other children who do not communicate very well. Some have asked Barbara to use a notebook or steno pad to write down anything noteworthy that occurs each day, particularly anything involving their child. Barbara accommodates their wishes up to a point, but she also helps them to understand that the best way for them to learn about their child's day at school is to establish a pattern of reviewing the day with their child each afternoon or evening. She has worked with such parents to develop these patterns, beginning with simple questions that the child can answer easily (what did you have for lunch, what special class did you have today?) but working up to a longer set of questions. Barbara, a paraprofessional, or the speech and language teacher would work on these questions with the student during the day, so the student could "rehearse" what he or she would say to the parents or caretakers when they asked the same questions at home.

With all of her students, Barbara tries to make sure that a note is sent home about anything traumatic or upsetting that happened to the student during the day and is likely to be reported at home (an accident at recess, a time-out, etc.). She writes these notes on pressure copy paper so that she can send an original home and keep a copy for herself.

At times when she is placing short-term priority on working intensively to address a particular academic or behavioral issue with a student, she may send home daily updates for a few weeks until significant progress has been made. These notes include information about how frequently and in what way the child became upset, disrupted her teaching, etc., but also indicate "particularly successful chunks of the day" where good things happened. She does not suggest attaching particular rewards or punishments to the contents of these notes; she makes it clear to family members that they are intended only to keep them abreast of the situation.

Due to parental requests or Individual Education Plan (IEP) requirements, Barbara has had some experience with daily behavior sheets calling for her to record a happy/sad face, a plus/minus, or some sort of point system that will have consequences when the child gets home. She says:

I find that when you rate the kids' behaviors, they have a tendency to argue with you if it doesn't match what they want. This often creates even more disruptive behavior in the process. Also, the parents often end up being punitive if things do not go well at school, which makes it worse the next day because a kid is mad at you even though the punishment was done for something done at school.

I have tried to stay away from that kind of communication with families. If forced into doing it, I try to structure it so that students are evaluating their own behavior and have more options than just good or bad. I try to make it more descriptive ("Here's the incident and what happened, and what I am going to do differently next time," as opposed to "I was good" or "I was bad."). I want it to be a problem-solving, planning, making-things-better experience rather than "I was good so I am going to get rewarded" or "I was bad so I'm going to get punished."

Home Visits

In previous years, especially when she taught the same group of students for two years in a row as part of a looping arrangement, Barbara visited her students in their homes. She presented these visits to parents as opportunities and asked the families beforehand if they wanted to invite her to come. She made it clear that the visit would be very informal and would last only 15 to 30 minutes. Her rationale was that, "The more I know about the student, the more I can make connections between home and school and therefore personalize instruction for the kids." During these visits, Barbara would meet and chat briefly with whichever family members were present, then ask to see the child's room and any pets, hobbies, collections, or other things that might be of special importance to the child. Where feasible, she would ask the child to read a favorite book to her.

Tie-backs to these visits would appear later in Barbara's teaching. During a social studies unit on food, for example, she might be heard saying, "Laura, remember when you showed me the garden at your house?" or if the class was reading a story that included a pet bird, she might say, "Ruben, remember when I came to your house and got to meet your parakeet?" Barbara found these home visits to be very helpful in deepening her connections to her students and their families and providing her with opportunities to further personalize her curriculum, but setting up and carrying out the visits did impose significant costs in time and effort.

Family Involvement in Homework

In addition to newsletters, home visits, and face-to-face communication, Barbara uses homework assignments to communicate with families.

Throughout the year, she assigns two types of homework: activities designed to increase basic skills, and more authentic assignments that support and advance curriculum goals.

Skill building is important as early learners gain the skills they will need to be successful students. Parents of these students often ask for ways to help their child. Barbara finds that skills-building homework is most successful when you help families set a predictable routine for practice.

Take-home book bags, as described in the handbook excerpt, are one way to establish a nightly reading routine. Another system is sending home a blank calendar for families to record the names of books read on each box/day of the calendar.

Memorizing sight or spelling words and math facts is another form of skill-building homework for Barbara's students. She begins by prioritizing and organizing the information she wants students to learn. Then she breaks up the task into weekly lists and sends the lists home with suggestions on ways to study or practice.

Barbara treats homework as a basic part of her curriculum, even when teaching first-graders. She is noticeably planful and reflective about it, with respect to both its nature and purposes and how it will be presented to and used with her students.

She tries to make sure that each homework assignment meets two key criteria. First, it is based on and serves to develop one of the big ideas being emphasized in her current unit. Second, it is something that must be done at home (not at school), or at least has some connection with the home. This is because she views homework in part as a way to keep family members abreast of what is happening at school. She explains:

> I create homework assignments with the big goals from the lessons in mind, so the majority of the students' effort and thinking and time on the assignment is spent on information that connects directly to the big idea. For example, if the idea is counting by twos, I want the kids to spend most of their time thinking about groups of two, counting up groups of two, rather than agonizing over drawing pictures just right or collecting objects and presenting them just right or writing answers in some particular way. If the idea is for them to get practice counting by twos, that's what I want them to be doing lots of during the assignment. So, I structure the assignment so that the biggest amount of effort is for the student to focus on gaining skills, gaining practice with whatever the big idea is.

The teachers' editions of her textbooks include assignment suggestions, and Barbara sometimes uses these as homework assignments (if she views them as sufficiently well connected to big ideas and otherwise cost effective). She often adapts or supplements them, however:

I do use the homework from our math program. It usually has an activity that goes home maybe once or twice a week. Often the activity is very similar to whatever we have done in class. For example, when we counted by twos, one of the activities was to go home and draw pictures of things we talked about in class. Like, eyes come in pairs of two and feet come in pairs of two and hands come in pairs of two. Their job was to go home and draw like pairs of eyes and then count them by twos. I supplemented that by going a step further and creating another homework job that involved searching their house for things that came in pairs and then reporting back, so we could add to a list of things that come in pairs, practice counting by twos, and talk about why it is important to learn to count by twos.

Most of Barbara's homework assignments are in literacy or math, which she teaches every day. Most are related to big ideas such as counting by twos, but:

> Then there's homework related to skill building. In first grade, for example, addition facts or memorizing sight words or (in the second half of the year) working on their spelling list. The folders they take home every day include books or other materials to be read with family members. Daily reading is considered a homework job.
>
> In general, the policy I share with families is that I expect the kids to do some homework jobs every day. One of those is reading. Another is either practicing sight words in the fall or spelling words in the winter. Other homework jobs will come home occasionally, connected to other parts of the curriculum—math, science, social studies, and health. The assignments come with a due date, and I urge families to try to return them by their due dates, but if that is not possible, to make the effort to return the homework as soon as possible thereafter.

Much of her homework is designed to provide extra practice on things already done in class and provide information to family members about what their child is learning. Many assignments involve information gathering, either before or after a lesson. An example of gathering information in response to a lesson occurred when her students took home a word web identifying different uses for shelter.

> Their assignment was to add to the web other ideas that their family members had about ways we use shelter. An example of gathering information beforehand was when the kids took home a questionnaire about where their ancestors had come from. This information was used in class during the introduction to the next lesson, when we

marked on a map of the world where each of their different ancestors had come from and then talked about how people still come to the United States from countries all over the world.

When we started our weather unit, the assignment was to make a list of ten weather-related words and bring them to school. We used these words to create a running list and later a poster. Also, we used the list to sort the words, such as putting all of the words relating to precipitation together, all the words related to wind, all the words related to temperature, and so on. So that was another case of gathering information ahead of time to use later in the class. It was how we started talking about the different components of weather and the different kinds of precipitation.

One of the goals I have for homework is to make it as meaningful as possible: we always use or acknowledge the homework, or it becomes part of what happens in class. It is used somehow as part of our lesson, even if it is just simply shared with one another. And I participate myself. I had my list of ten weather words. When we searched our closets looking for things made of silk, I brought in one of my husband's silk ties. When students see me participating, these homework jobs become more valuable in their eyes.

In addition to completing homework assignments herself and contributing the resulting product to the information sharing or data analysis that occurs in a subsequent class, Barbara takes several other steps to insure that her students and their families take the homework assignments seriously and get the intended benefits from them. She says:

To begin with, I make sure that I plan for the homework. If I'm giving a homework assignment today, it is part of my instruction today. It's not just, "Oh, by the way kids, here's a homework page" or "You'll find a homework page in your folders." We use part of our learning time for the day to discuss the homework assignment—it's never just an afterthought. I plan my instruction to make sure that I have time to connect whatever they're taking home with what we have done at school.

I also make sure to model for them what they will be doing at home. Using an extra copy of the actual page, I help them to envision what will happen when they get it out at home. My modeling might even include deciding which person at home would be the best person to work with on the assignment. For example, if they're going to be creating a list of words that describe solids, I might ask, "Who at your house do you think is really good at thinking of ideas? Who has some extra time tonight? Who can help you come up with a great list? ... OK, now, how might you ask that person to help you? ... 'You know, Mom, we're making a list of describing words in science. Will you help me write them down?' "

I have them plan for when they think they will get it done: "Think about what your family has said you are doing tonight. Do you think you'll be able to get this job done tonight? Will you do it in the morning instead, or right away when you get home?" I want them to know exactly what they will be doing and to make plans for when and how they will get it done. Sometimes I even have them get started in class by asking questions like, "What is the first weather word you can think of?" or "Are you already picturing something in your head that comes in twos at your house?"

In addition to this preparation work, Barbara includes two forms of follow-up that help emphasize the importance of homework and encourage her students to value it. First, she uses a variety of methods to celebrate and reinforce returning homework to school. For example, she may simply read out the list of names of students who have returned the homework assignment and ask them to stand up, then compliment them or say, "Wow. Doesn't it feel great to have your homework done?" She may elaborate this approach with one or two individuals, questioning them for details about who they did the homework assignment with or commenting about how great it is to finish an assignment and how enjoyable it is to work with their family members when doing so. Besides verbal compliments, other forms of celebration include ringing chimes, doing cheers, or singing.

To connect with students who have yet to return the assignment, she will question them as to why they have not, whether they know where the assignment is, whether they need a new sheet, and so on. She also will ask how she can help them to get started or address any reported barriers. For example, if they report that the family was busy last night or they did not have enough time, she may say, "Well, think about tonight. When do you think you can get it done tonight? . . . Do you think it was a good idea to wait until it's too late and then you didn't have enough time, or should you do it right away? What did you do right after school yesterday?" So, Barbara both acknowledges the students who have completed the assignment and helps the remaining students to make specific plans for doing so.

The second thing that she does (among other reasons) to enhance the perceived importance of homework is use the homework in subsequent activities at school. For example:

When we brainstormed all the different kinds of weather words, we then sorted those weather words into different categories. These became posters that went up on the wall and were used for the rest of the science unit. And the kids knew exactly whose words were whose. They would say, "Oh, that one was my idea," or "That was my dad's idea," or "This is part of the list of words that I brought from home."

Or, we might collect information, such as having the kids identify a box of cereal at home and talk with the family shopper about why that particular box was purchased (we like this brand, we had a coupon, we wanted to try something new, we like the illustration on the box, etc.). Then we use that data to make a graph so we can look at purchasing trends and talk about how families decide what to buy.

So we try to use the information that comes from homework assignments. We go over them, and the kids get a chance to share their answers out loud or respond to questions like, "It says your family bought Frosted Flakes. Why did you guys buy those Frosted Flakes?" Often there is a story or explanation behind the short answer on the homework assignment, and I can invite students to explain these and get opportunities to give extended presentations to the class. In any case, the majority of the homework is used in some way, so kids see that if they do not bring theirs in, they miss out on getting to share their information.

Also, we need it. When we developed an graph of cereal purchases, for example, we entered the kids' names in each box in the display that represented one of the cereals that their family buys. Kids who did not yet return this assignment could look at that illustration and think, "Oh, gosh. My name's not on there. I need to go home, get this homework done, and bring it back tomorrow so my name will be on the graph, too, and my data will be added to the collection."

Sometimes we do family project assignments. For example, during our weather unit, we talked about different kinds of clothing worn for different kinds of weather. Each of the kids got a little outline of a person and was asked to place that person in a picture that would include indication of the weather, then talk about the clothing they would add to the person and why that would be appropriate for that kind of weather. This was going to end up being a display in the hallway, so the kids wanted to make sure that they got theirs back to school. As the first few came in, those kids got to stand up, share their picture, and read the paragraph they had written about it, and then it was displayed in the hallway. The kids who had not yet done the assignment were motivated to get it done so they also could read their paragraphs to the class and have their pictures displayed in the hall-way. As we would walk by the display each day, I would call attention to how we had more pictures up and remind the class that a spot was reserved for everyone.

In an assignment like that, I not only explain and model what to do as usual, but I post my contribution to the display immediately. This way, if there are kids who haven't started theirs yet and still are not sure what it is supposed to look like, they can see the posted example. Also, if family members come to pick them up and also are not sure about how the pictures should look, they can look at mine, and shortly thereafter, those done by classmates.

Despite these efforts, Barbara occasionally encounters students who consistently fail to complete and return home assignments. When this occurs, she closely questions the student (and typically the parents or caretakers as well) to determine the problem. In cases where no one at home is available to help, she negotiates with the students to agree to do at least part of the work on their own:

> If he says that he has not turned it in yet because there's nobody at home to help him, my conversation will be, "Well, what part of it can you do by yourself? Can you draw the picture of the weather? Do you think you can start drawing and coloring some clothes on there? . . . Because if you can do that part and bring it in, I'll help you do the writing part that goes with it." So I try to get the kid to do at least part of it at home and have the experience of whatever the activity is. I could simply say to him, "Let's just do it here at school—at recess or when other kids are reading." But this gives him the message that I don't have faith in him to be able to do some of it on his own.
>
> What I find most often is that they've lost track of the assignment—they can't find it. So I always make extra copies to give to kids in this situation—definitely if they say that they do not know where it is, and sometimes if they claim to know where it is, but not very convincingly. If I haven't seen anything within two or three days past the due date, I usually send a second copy home.

In the rare situation where none of Barbara's efforts produce consistent return of completed home assignments, she will require the student to work on the home assignment during literacy choice time. This reduces the students' opportunities to engage in self-chosen activities, but Barbara does not present it as a punishment. Instead, she will say something like, "You know, you need to get this done. We've all been waiting for you to get it finished."

Authentic homework assignments are activities that connect to what is learned in class. They are designed to help students make real-life connections to what they are learning at school, support the goals of the unit, and provide additional information for class discussions. These assignments also help Barbara communicate to families what their children are learning in class.

For example, at the beginning of the weather unit in science, Barbara has students look for sources of information and forecasts. Families receive a note explaining what the class has learned so far and how to record the sources and weather words on the worksheet to return to class. Families are involved early on in each unit of study and frequently are updated throughout with additional assignments.

Through these many forms of communication and collaboration with family members, Barbara embeds her classroom learning community within larger social contexts and arranges for family support of her in-class socialization and teaching priorities. So far, we have described how she socializes both her students and their families to learning community norms and expectations. In Chapter 4, we analyze how she manages her classroom throughout the year in ways that reinforce these norms and expectations consistently.

Chapter 4

Managing the Learning Community's Everyday Activities

Barbara's class displays seemingly automatic, smooth functioning in which her students spend most of their time productively involved in lessons and learning activities. We have described how she sets the stage for this development by taking a lot of time during the first few weeks to socialize her students to learning community norms and make sure that they learn and follow basic rules and routines. Her heavy focus on socialization at this time might strike some observers as unnecessarily rigid or directive, but it reflects the respect she has for her young students' potential for regulating their own learning and social behavior productively.

Barbara puts it as follows: "Make sure that you have routines in place, because they foster independence." Her routines are designed to match the learning and socialization goals that she sets for the class. Teaching these routines (and the rationales for them) supports students' sense of efficacy because it gives them information they need to act independently and responsibly. "Students want information! They want to know what is going on." Barbara's routines and accompanying rationales establish the idea that she is supporting her students and empowering them by enabling them to know what to do. "It takes the mystery out of school—that's what kids worry about the most. It gives them tools to figure out whether they are doing what they are supposed to be doing. They don't have to wait for the big voice. My goal is to provide a framework that guides students as they have the opportunity and freedom to make many decisions throughout the school day."

This early socialization is designed to build students' capacities for and dispositions toward self-regulation. It reflects four major sets of goals and big ideas: 1) shape the class into a learning community in which all members understand and fulfill their roles, rights, and responsibilities; 2) post resources for easy reference and model use of thinking and decision making to guide behavior; 3) maximize the time that students spend engaged in productive lessons and learning activities; and 4) teach them to engage "with their heads and their hearts."

During these early weeks, Barbara's students learn when, where, and how to store their belongings, get out and put back supplies and work materials, check the daily schedule and other posted resources to help them orient themselves and regulate their own behavior, and so on. Barbara gradually shifts from explaining and demonstrating these routines to merely cueing them as the need arises, and as students begin doing them automatically, she can even fade out most of the cueing. At this point, the basic learning community structure is in place, and she can work within it, using *situational management strategies* to keep her students productively engaged in learning activities.

In this chapter, we describe these situational management strategies, especially as they apply to locating learning activities physically and managing transitions between them, maintaining awareness of who has the floor during lessons and what this implies about participation expectations, supporting understanding of the nature of the activity and what this implies about the kinds of questions or comments that are appropriate, maintaining or recapturing thoughtful attention to lessons, and structuring students' group and individual work on independent learning activities.

Managing Transitions between Activities

After the early weeks, Barbara's classroom is remarkable for the very high percentages of time that her students spend engaged in curriculum-related activities. One major reason for this is the way that she handles transitions between activities. Typically, her students not only make these transitions quickly and smoothly but keep their minds on curriculum-related issues as they do so.

Different lessons and learning activities are located at different places in her classroom, so transitions occur frequently. If she is going to be teaching from the whiteboard at the front of the room, she will have her students sit in the closest seats, facing the board. If students are going to be working in pairs or small groups, she will have them distribute themselves around the room. When she is reading a book from which she wants to show illustrations, she sits in a low chair and her students sit in front of her on a rug, gathered close to her and one another. This allows each of them to get a good look at the book illustrations or other instructional resources she wants to display (if necessary, she will lean forward and hold out the resource so that it is no more than a few feet from even the students seated at the back of the group).

As everyday transitions become routine, Barbara does not need to say anything more than, "It's time for reading. Please meet me on the carpet by the calendar." If her students would not be expected to know what to do on their own, she gives more complete, yet brief and efficient, instructions. For example, one day, as her students were completing work in small groups and she wanted them to gather at the front of the class for a lesson to be taught from the whiteboard, she said, "If you are not at the brown table or the blue table or the red table, you need to move to one of those places now, so that you will be able to see and learn." She then named nine students and said, "Please stand up and go to the red table, the blue table, or the brown table."

When working at her carpet time area, Barbara wants to create an intimate setting in which her students are seated very close to her and to one another. Yet, she also wants to maintain each student's individual space and avoid situations in which some of them become distracted from the lesson because of physical contact with classmates. Consequently, she teaches her students to sit "pretzel style" during these lessons (upright with their legs crossed—the basic position for yoga exercises). This minimizes the rug space they require, yet enables them to sit in a comfortable position that makes it easy for them to maintain attention to the lesson and see the illustrations she displays. She uses carpet time across all curriculum areas, especially when introducing new content.

To help her students retain a learning set as they carry out transitions, Barbara's instructions often include content designed to keep the students' minds focused on the curriculum. For example, one day, after reviewing the food pyramid during health class (focusing on its implications for balanced meals), she wanted her students to move from the front of the class to the carpet, where the lesson would continue into social studies with an examination of the foods included in typical meals that might be eaten in the United States, Mexico, and China. Upon completing the review, she initiated the transition by saying, "I'm going to have you come over and sit on the carpet by the calendar, and I'm going to show you what somebody might have for lunch or dinner from three different places in the world. Sit quickly, and I will show you what the meals might look like." At this point, Barbara moved to her low chair and her students quickly assembled close together on the rug. She did not have to say anything more to the group as a whole or to any individual. Everyone knew what to do without further direction, and her advance organizer had them thinking about the next segment of the lesson as they made the transition. The lesson resumed less than a minute later, as Barbara held up an illustration and said, "For people living in the United States, this is a meal that you might have for lunch or dinner . . ."

One day Barbara had just finished modeling and demonstrating patterns in math and needed a moment to retrieve and set up some manipulatives to be used in the next lesson segment. To keep her students focused on the lesson while she did so, she told them to turn to a partner and create patterns together.

On another day, after reviewing responses to a home assignment, she said, "We are going to move to the tables to discuss a problem that I think will surprise you. Here is my problem. My niece, Jessica, needs a new coat for winter because her coat is too small. We are going to write Jessica and her mom a letter, telling them what we think she should do to buy or to get a new coat. So, as you walk to a table, your job is to think about all the places and all the things that Jessica and her mom could do to get her a new coat." After her students quickly made this transition, Barbara followed up by engaging them in brainstorming possible options (buy a new coat from a store, make the coat themselves, get a hand-me-down from a relative, buy a used coat at a garage sale, etc.), then discussing the pros and cons of these options, then composing the letter.

Sustaining Curricular Focus during Lesson Interruptions

Barbara finds that providing students with something to occupy their minds during transitions minimizes disruptions or other behavior problems, so she usually provides such a focus. As a change of pace from thinking directly about curriculum-related issues, she sometimes suggests other activities that allow students to communicate with one another about other aspects of the topic. For example, during a brief pause between the end of a lesson on mass communication modes and the beginning of a follow-up application activity, she told her students to, "Talk to the person next to you and tell him or her one thing that you like to watch on television—a program that's not a cartoon. What's on there that is not just entertaining and fun?" For a minute or two, her students talked about the news, the weather, and other informative television content.

On another day, Barbara needed to go to the closet to get some game materials as she was concluding a discussion about whether (and why) her students would have preferred to live in the cave days, in the Pilgrim or pioneer days, or in modern times. Most of the students had opted for modern times, so Barbara signaled the transition as follows: "Alright, folks, I'm going to walk over to the closet to get a game for us to play. While I'm gone, talk to the kids at your table, and listen closely: this is a new question. Here's the question: what would have been good, or what do you think would have been interesting, about living either as a cave person or as a pioneer or a Pilgrim? Talk about what would have been cool or interesting."

During literacy time one day, there was a short break after Barbara finished reading a Tomie dePaola book. As she prepared materials for the upcoming quiet reading time block, she asked students to mentally create a list of Tomie dePaolo books. As they listed the books, students put up a finger for each book they named. This engaged students as well as building in an expectation for each child to participate.

Occasionally, especially when the interruption to her teaching is expected to be very brief, she fills the gap with a "just for fun" activity. For example, if she needs to leave her seat to get a book and then come right back to resume teaching, she might tell her students what she is going to do and then ask them to hold their breath while she does it. Besides providing an enjoyable diversion, this activity keeps her students focused on her and avoids dissipation of their readiness to learn.

In general, whenever Barbara has to leave the group momentarily, write something on a co-constructed learning resource, or do anything else that might interrupt the continuity and flow of a lesson, she either does something herself or engages her students in doing something to help maintain their learning set. For example, if she needs to interrupt the forward momentum of the lesson in order to write on a graph or timeline or to show an illustration to each individual student, she will continue with her narrative or maintain a patter of conversation the whole time. One day she needed to assemble some drawing materials and set up the beginning of what would become a timeline across the front of the classroom. While she did so, she followed up the previous activity (review of home assignment responses to questions about healthy snacks) by asking strategically selected students what they had had for their snack that day and whether or not the snack was nutritious.

Barbara also is adept at doing more than one thing at a time, and in particular, handling behavior management or personal communication issues that arise during lessons while still continuing to sustain the momentum of the lesson. Kounin (1970) called this "overlapping" and identified it as an important skill common to good classroom managers. Barbara calls it "jogging in place." For example, one day a child carrying a note from the kindergarten teacher arrived while Barbara was in the middle of a lesson. She beckoned the child to approach her and deliver the note, read the note, and wrote a response, all the while carrying on a conversation with her about birthdays and other celebrations that occurred in her family (the topic of the lesson).

Traffic Control during Lessons

Barbara has developed several "traffic control mechanisms" for regulating who has the floor during whole-class activities, and for what purpose. At the beginning of the year, she socializes her students to listen carefully and respect the "turn" of whoever has the floor. She establishes that lessons include *"my turn"* segments (in which all students are expected to listen to her as she teaches) and *"your turn"* segments (in which students are invited to ask questions or make comments). She sometimes uses these terms as a way to signal transitions and cue expected behavior, as well as to remind students about expected behavior when necessary ("It's my turn now, so I want you to put your hands down and listen carefully while I teach.").

Barbara is especially likely to emphasize that it is her turn to speak (so students need to hold their questions or comments and listen carefully) when she is introducing a new network of information. At these times, it is important to get a shared knowledge base into place during an initial lesson segment in which Barbara tells the story the way she wants to tell it (emphasizing big ideas and using selected vocabulary). Consequently, she asks few questions and minimizes student contributions during these times, especially contributions that might divert her from her intended lesson flow or inject misconceptions or other complications that she does not want to address until after a coherent knowledge base has been established.

Because she teaches young students whose prior knowledge of the topic may be quite limited, Barbara often finds herself in situations where, instead of being able to build on an already existing knowledge base that is reasonably coherent and shared by everyone in the class, she has to establish this knowledge base in the first place. Consequently, although references to "my turn" or "your turn" are control mechanisms, they are used in ways that are consistent with her learning goals and her emphasis on student self-regulation.

Waiting until the basic network of big ideas is in place allows her to respond more coherently to unanticipated questions and comments by fitting them into the developed network (e.g., in response to a student's comment about President Lincoln, who is depicted in an illustration shown during a clothing unit lesson, she focused attention on Lincoln's clothing and connected it to points made earlier in the lesson). If Barbara finds it necessary to cut off a student's comment or question that threatens to disrupt the intended flow during a "my turn" segment, she will return to the student later during a "your turn" segment and invite the student to raise the issue at that time.

She recognizes that students often want to tell her or their classmates about some personal connection to the topic, so she provides opportunities for them to do so. If they ask a question or make a comment that cannot be responded to adequately within the lesson framework, she will get back to them later to discuss the matter further in private interaction. Some teachers, including Barbara, use a question box or question book as a placeholder for questions—and as a way to show students that curiosity is valued. Periodically the class revisits these questions and either Barbara or a volunteer student finds an answer.

Reminding students when it is her turn serves as a form of advance organizer that alerts students about what is to come and cues expected behavior. It also minimizes situations in which students find themselves being criticized for interruptions (unpredictably, from their point of view). Enforcing the my turn/your turn rule sometimes means cutting students off when they begin to ask a question or make a comment that threatens to disrupt the intended lesson flow, but it protects coherent discourse and avoids the rambling without apparent purpose seen in many primary classrooms. Her students learn that even when it is their turn, they are expected to be on topic with their comments and questions. As a result, their comments and questions tend to be relevant, substantive, and supportive of (or at least, convertible to) Barbara's efforts to elaborate on the big ideas she is introducing. She frequently incorporates or refers back to student contributions as a way to incorporate them into the lesson and provide recognition for them.

In situations when she thinks that most if not all of her students need an opportunity to communicate, she will temporarily shift from the whole-class lesson format into a pair-share format, in which she invites students to turn to the person next to them and interact in some topic-relevant way. Typically, she will give brief instructions about what the students are to do during these pair-share interactions, then say, "Ready to start? . . . OK, go." As the students interact in pairs, she will listen for questions or comments that she wants to follow up on once the whole-class lesson resumes. When she is ready to resume, she says, "Five, four, three, two, one, stop." Early in the year, Barbara establishes this brief signal as shorthand for, "This 'your turn' segment is ending now; I want you to stop talking to each other and pay attention to me, because it is my turn now." These mechanisms make for almost instantaneous transitions from my turn to your turn to my turn again, so Barbara can easily incorporate several such transitions within a 30–45 minute lesson period.

In combination, Barbara's traffic control mechanisms make her unusually successful in simultaneously addressing the conflicting agendas that teachers face during lessons: maintaining the lesson's continuity and coherence, yet also being responsive to the needs and interests of individual students (Kennedy, 2005). Also, her interactions with students that occur during these lessons not only enforce accountability demands but also project respect for their potential as learners and support for their efforts to regulate their own learning (Beck, 1998). For more information (including lesson excerpts) about how Barbara establishes initial knowledge bases during lessons, develops them through questioning and providing feedback to students, and incorporates student comments and questions, see Brophy, Alleman, & Knighton (2008).

Calling for Choral Responses

Another way that Barbara allows for active but even briefer responses is to invite her students to respond as a group rather than waiting to be called on as individuals. She is especially likely to use this method during reviews or other occasions where she expects most of them to know the answer. She wants them to listen to the questions and respond thoughtfully, however, so she uses verbal directions ("Get ready . . . tell me . . . now!") or hand signals to ensure that students withhold their response until she has concluded her question and allowed time for all of them to think about it.

She often uses playful variations on the technique, such as extending the pause longer than usual, asking for a response from just one student instead of the whole class, or asking for responses from just the boys, just the even-numbered students, etc. These are positive ways to preserve time for slower students to process and respond to her questions. If choral responses yield more incorrect answers than she was expecting, she will follow up with feedback and explanations that are directed to the whole class but meant in particular for the individual students who responded incorrectly.

Barbara also uses other mechanisms that allow all of her students to respond to a question simultaneously. For choice questions, she may ask them to respond nonverbally, such as by tugging on their left ear if they prefer one alternative but tugging on their right ear if they prefer the other. Or, before directing a question to an individual student, she may tell the rest of the group to listen to their classmate's response and show thumbs up if they agree with it, thumbs down if they do not, or thumbs to the side if they are not sure (she teaches this three-choice version of thumb signals at the beginning of the year).

Cues and Reminders

As the school year progresses, Barbara's students become more and more self-regulated, so there is less and less need for her to say very much about where they are supposed to be, how they are supposed to get there, or what they are supposed to do when they arrive. Occasionally, however, she does need to review expectations with them. The following excerpt occurred during a lesson in which Barbara was eliciting contributions to a list of modes of transportation. Things were proceeding smoothly until a student responded, "A motorcycle." During that year, the term motorcycle functioned as what Barbara calls a magic word: as soon as it is mentioned, the students become excited and immediately want to tell stories or react to it in some way. In this case, as Barbara went to write the word on the list, one student began making motorcycle sounds, another said that his father had a motorcycle and he let the boy sit on it, and a third said that his father had a motorcycle and he let the boy ride on it. These responses led Barbara to temporarily suspend the lesson, scan the group with a serious facial expression indicating displeasure, and direct a question to the student making motorcycle sounds:

T: What will help us get through this lesson?
S: Calm.
T: What does that mean, Renee?
S: Be quiet and listen.
T: What about sharing your ideas? When will it be your turn to share your ideas?
S: With my homework.
T: Your homework. Whose turn is it right now?
S: Derek's.
T: So, if you have a really cool thought about something that Derek says, what can you do?
S: Say it in my head.
T: Say it in your head. You can nod your head if you're thinking that you've heard of that one too. [At this point, turns to Derek and asks for his suggested addition to the list.]

After the first few weeks, such extensive reviews and reminders occur infrequently. Instead, Barbara relies primarily on brief cues and reminders such as the following:

> Remember, we're thinking of ones not already on the list. Stop and think first. Raise your hand only if you think of one that is not on the list.

> If you have an answer, just keep it right in your head. I'm going to pick somebody to see if they can figure this out.

> I'm going to tell you the story, but if you're not looking, listening, and thinking, you'll miss it.

> If you have an answer but I haven't called on you, say the answer in your head. If you agree with someone else's answer, nod your head but don't call out.

> When several students start talking excitedly about a book Barbara has brought to read, she both quiets them and builds anticipation by saying, "Shhh. A.J. wants to know the next part of the story."

> When students begin to get restless near the end of a long lesson, she says, "Look me in the eyes. I have one more message to tell you about solids and liquids, then you are going to tell me what you learned before you leave."

> I know Cole is going to do great on his homework because he is looking at me and he is going to know what to do.

> When only three students respond to a choral question, she says,

"Only three kids answered that one." This elicits a much broader participation when she repeats the question.

Before showing an illustration about toddlers learning to use the bathroom (a topic that sometimes elicits giggling or other immature responses), Barbara says, "I need to know that you are calm when I show you this picture."

Scootch forward. I want to make sure that you are hearing this. This is pretty important.

When Barbara inserts such brief cues and reminders about behavior during lessons, it is usually because just one or two students are not behaving appropriately. However, she usually addresses these messages to the class as a whole. This is much less disruptive to lesson momentum than messages directed to individuals, and it avoids putting these students on the spot or calling group attention to their misbehavior. Where she does feel it necessary to single out a specific individual, she tries to do so in brief and non-disruptive ways.

The simplest way is to drop an inattentive student's name into the midst of an explanation, as a way to refocus his or her attention (e.g., "Another kind of mass transportation, Linda, is trains . . ."). She also might direct a question to a student who has not been paying attention, although usually only after forewarning the student that he or she will be called on next. The warning gives the student time to refocus and begin processing in preparation for the question. This reduces the likelihood that the question will produce no response or an off-the-wall response that will lead to a greater interruption of lesson flow than the brief forewarning does.

Even when she does decide that she needs to address insufficient or inappropriate lesson participation by a particular individual, Barbara focuses her message on reminders about what the student is supposed to be doing, not dwelling on the student's inappropriate behavior. Consequently, many of these messages directed at individuals are very similar to the ones that she addresses to the group as a whole:

If you sit flat and look here, you'll find out what I have to say next.

Come up and join us. I haven't heard any answers from you. I'm ready for you to be learning with us (directed to a student who had been sitting at the back of the group and not paying close attention).

Your job right now is learning.

Do you have a wonder or a story? (In response to a student who began to tell a story instead of contributing a wonder at a time when Barbara was eliciting wonders.)

Sometimes Barbara needs to take special measures to make sure that everyone is fully attentive to messages that are especially important. For example, if a lesson has concluded with a "your turn" segment in which the students are interacting in pairs or small groups, she will need to settle the class down and gain the students' full attention before concluding with instructions for the home assignment. It is at times like these that she is likely to combine her "5, 4, 3, 2, 1, stop" signal with a "Look me in the eyes, folks!" directive. If the students have been particularly active or noisy, she may focus first on getting their physical bodies under control before moving on to address mental concentration. She has developed several alternatives to shushing students in these situations, including many that her students find easy and enjoyable to respond to. For example, she might say, "If you can hear my voice, clap once . . . clap twice." Frequently she will say, "Touch your nose . . . Touch your ears . . . Touch your hair . . . Touch your tummy . . . Touch your lips . . . Here's your job. Your job is to go home and . . ."

Barbara may call on all or at least most students in some situations, but just a few students in other situations. If she is developing a list, for example, she will continue until she gets a good range of responses, including any that she wants to be sure to elicit before shifting to the next phase of the lesson. When questions are likely to elicit quick and easy answers, she is likely to let most or even all of her students respond, if time allows. She also is likely to call on everyone, or if necessary, a strategically selected subset of the group, if she has been developing a knowledge base and now wants to check for understanding.

Sometimes she will use the students' magic numbers as a way to identify respondents quickly and make sure that everyone is included. If she only has time to call on a subset of students, she will draw number sticks randomly (which has the effect of holding all of the students accountable for the information).

When she shifts into "your turn" segments that allow for student questions and comments, she typically calls first on the students whom she perceives to be in most need of an opportunity to communicate. These include students who are generally hyperactive or prone to blurting out questions or comments, students who "know everything" and want to show it, and students who are intrigued with everything and have lots of questions. She makes sure that the calmer and more self-regulated students are accommodated as well, however, and she goes out of her way to solicit and reinforce participation by students who seldom contribute. Finally, she often allows extensive "your turn" time to students whose questions and comments are on topic and of interest to classmates, but cuts off or redirects those who drift off topic, keep adding new questions that seem designed more to hold the floor than to satisfy genuine curiosity, or in other ways channel the discourse down unproductive paths.

If she is concerned about running out of time, Barbara adjusts her traffic control strategies accordingly. For example, one day she was going over a home assignment in which students had been asked to write sentences about each of three communication modes. There was not enough time for her to read and react to all of these responses, so she asked her students to indicate which of their three responses they would like her to read to the class. She still was able to include a broad range of communication modes, because most of her students intuitively picked responses concerning communication modes that had not yet been discussed. If they did not, Barbara would steer them toward a new one or ask permission to read a second answer.

Enforcing the Rules

Given her goals of socializing her students toward self-regulation, Barbara emphasizes articulating and following through on positive expectations, not threats of punishment for failure to follow the rules. However, she consistently holds students responsible for fulfilling their responsibilities, and those who have not responded to her more generic reminders will find themselves confronted about their behavior during private interactions. These interactions are mostly confined to applications of Glasser's techniques (questioning students to elicit recognition of the ways that they have been behaving inappropriately and what they should be doing instead). They typically do not involve punishment in the usual sense of the word, although they may conclude with Barbara imposing a requirement. A student who did sloppy work on an assignment might be required to redo the assignment, for example, or a student who struggled to behave might conference with Barbara at recess.

Barbara's disciplinary interventions confront students about their misbehavior directly, call attention to ways in which it is hurting themselves or others, and place direct and indirect pressure (via references to the pledge, etc.) on them to accept responsibility and specify needed improvements. These interventions place strong accountability pressures and self-regulation demands on students who present chronic behavior problems, so they are more likely to elicit improvements than interventions that merely require them to endure a scolding or punishment.

Barbara's students quickly learn to be honest during these exchanges, because she will not accept lies or evasions. If she has reason to believe that students are not being honest with her, she will confront them about it. For example, one home assignment called for talking with whoever does the shopping at home about reasons for purchasing a cereal. Home assignments usually call for discussing some question and then entering information on a response sheet that is returned the next morning, but this assignment did not include a response sheet. As Barbara was leading the class in discussion of responses to the home assignment question the next day, she noted that a couple of students apparently had not done the assignment but were pretending that they had (by generating answers based on cues from what had transpired so far during the lesson). She has found that in these situations, most students will admit that they have not done the home assignment if she conveys her suspicions and the reasons for them. Furthermore, most of the rest (who lie initially) will admit the truth if she first asks who they talked to at home and then follows up by asking, "So, if I see your mom later today or tomorrow and ask her if you two talked about cereal, what would she say?"

In view of Barbara's persistence, most of her students quickly conclude that it is better to answer her initial inquiries honestly. Noting that it provides opportunities for students to come clean and accept responsibility for their behavior, Barbara calls this approach "narc yourself out" (a major theme in her mentoring of novice teachers is that it is important to find ways to amuse or entertain yourself as you discharge your daily responsibilities, including—and perhaps especially—those that are unpleasant or stressful).

Time-Outs

Barbara's preferred method of dealing with repeatedly disruptive behavior is to speak to the student privately, as described previously. She cannot do this during lessons, however, and especially not during initial "my turn" segments in which she is establishing and developing a new knowledge base. In these situations, with students who continue to be disruptive despite repeated cues and reminders, she will use temporary exclusion (time out) from the lesson. She views time-outs not as punishments but as opportunities for these students to "get it together" or recover. Consequently, she makes it clear that, rather than being excluded for a fixed amount of time, they are welcome to return as soon as they can "do their jobs."

She handles these time-outs quickly, so as to make them minimally disruptive and place emphasis on the learning occurring in the group, not the behavior of the excluded student. Most of the time, the excluded students remain in the room (e.g., if the lesson is taking place on the rug, the excluded student is required to sit at a table 10 or 15 feet away—close enough to follow the lesson yet no longer a part of the group physically or psychologically). In these situations, Barbara is likely to simply tell the student to take a seat at the table and add, "You're welcome to come back anytime you can be here and not take other folks' turns."

More serious exclusions might involve sending the student to the project area outside of the classroom ("Pop right on out to the project area and then come back in when you think you would like to be a learner.").

When excluded students do return, Barbara simply motions them to take a seat and continues with the lesson, without breaking its flow to comment on or quiz them about their behavior. She attempts to make every lesson so inviting that students want to hurry back to learn.

Barbara's use of time-outs is infrequent and concentrated at the beginning of the year when she is focusing on establishing and following through on rules and routines. Throughout the year, she continues to focus on learning community norms and learning goals, not threats or punishments. Her approach is consistent with both parenting practices in the home and classroom management practices at school that produce well-socialized, self-regulated, personally and socially responsible children (Evertson & Weinstein, 2006; Good & Brophy, 2008).

Independent Work and Learning Centers

Independent learning, especially if it occurs within specially established learning centers, is an appealing but challenging curriculum component for primary teachers whose students still have limited literacy skills and self-regulation capabilities. Learning centers provide opportunities for students to get needed skills practice within the context of authentic activities, exercise some choice of learning activities, and begin to function independently as autonomous learners. They also provide a way to keep the majority of students engaged in independent activities while the teacher works intensively with a minority of the students, as when teaching small-group reading lessons. To enjoy the potential benefits of learning centers, however, teachers need to establish the centers, stock them with worthwhile learning activities, and socialize and scaffold for their students sufficiently to enable them to carry out center activities independently. Barbara struggled with these challenges early in her career, but she eventually developed an approach to learning centers that she believes to be effective with her students.

She wants her center activities to support progress toward two primary learning goals, so she has designed these activities accordingly. First, she wants her students to practice the literacy skills they are developing, so center activities focus them on reading, writing, and structuring their thoughts "around words and how words work." Second, she wants her students to be able to carry out these activities as independently as possible, to free her to conduct guided reading lessons with small groups (targeted to their current literacy progress and particular learning needs).

Ad Hoc Groupings. Some of Barbara's independent work activities call for students to collaborate in groups of three or four. She uses *ad hoc* groupings in these situations, having determined that it is not worth the trouble to form groups that will stay together for weeks or months, because of absences, student turnover, and behavior problems that sometimes develop when group members have been together too long. When groups are needed, she forms them quickly, but tries to make sure that each group includes an academic leader and no more than one student who may have difficulty understanding or may present a behavior problem. Also, if she knows that two students do not work well together (even though they may be friends socially), she assigns them to separate groups.

The Culmination of the Learning Community at the End of the School Year

After heavy socialization during the first few weeks, Barbara's basic classroom management system is in place. Her students become increasingly self-regulated and mostly follow learning community rules and routines on their own, needing only occasional cues and reminders. A major exception to this is the first week of school in January, following the long holiday break. At this time, student role expectations need to be refreshed for many students, so Barbara reviews the pledge with them (including having them point to where they signed it) and temporarily increases the frequency and specificity of her cues and reminders. These preventive steps set the stage for smooth sailing throughout the rest of the school year.

In the last few days of the school year, when many teachers are just playing out the string, Barbara leads her students through a series of *culmination activities* designed to revisit their hopes and dreams for the year and begin looking ahead to next year, "when you will be part of another learning family." These activities include *revisiting of learning highlights* and *distribution of learning resources and products to keep as mementos.*

One *reminiscence activity* involved listing the people and events that the students would "keep in their hearts" when they thought about the Fabulous Frozen Family in the future: Barbara herself, the reading teacher, the librarian, fun on the playground, making friends in the class, learning to write and doing a lot of writing of their ideas to share with family and friends, making fairy bread, exercising with the coach in the gym, drawing pictures to illustrate their learning, calendar time, playing soccer, singing, etc.

Prior to the class's last visit to the library, Barbara suggested that her students express their appreciation to the librarian for all the help that she had given them during the year. Then she followed up by suggesting that they give the librarian a hug and think of a personal message to convey to her as they did so.

On one of the last days of the year, she gathered the group on the carpet and displayed all of the *class books* that had been constructed during the year and taken home to share with families. She revisited some of the highlights of these books and the comments that family members had written in response to them. She then announced that each student could have one of the books to keep, and began randomly selecting individuals to claim their choices ("It's an easy, sneezy job if you know what book you want.").

After all 22 students had claimed a book, there were seven books left over. Barbara led a discussion of what to do with these leftover books, culminating in a decision to vote on two alternatives: there is no fair way to decide, so leave all seven books here, or use the number sticks again to randomly select seven recipients. About two thirds of the students favored the latter alternative, so Barbara carried through with the plan. Still socializing to the end, she observed to some students who did not get one of the seven extras, "Isn't it nice that some of your friends got two?"

On the last day of school, Barbara continued to distribute mementos (pieces of the number line, mathematics books compiled by the class, posters, timelines, etc.). Often there were not enough items in a given category for every student to get one, so she attempted to make sure that things balanced out. In the process, she scaffolded decision making, problem solving, and issues of coping with disappointment. If a set of items contained almost but not quite enough for everyone, she suggested that some students might be willing to decline the item in order to allow it to go to a classmate who wanted it more. When there was only one or just a few of a particular item, she combined items to create sets that would contain something for everyone. As these distributions proceeded, she frequently made comments such as the following:

> If you don't get one, will you fuss at me?
> In your head, think about how you will get something else.
> What will you be thinking as I pick the sticks?
> Fussing makes no one happy.
> Thank you if you get one and are willing to give it to someone else.

As Barbara showed the mementos that would be claimed, she often reviewed the ideas connected with them, especially posters or graphics. Topics reviewed in this way included living things, counting by fives, key ideas learned in health class, food careers, types of potatoes, being patient, helping versus hurting, drugs and alcohol abuse, making leads in writing, the quality teacher poster, and rules for measuring. She also led the students in a review of the wish list that they had constructed on the first day of class, talking about things they had done to make these wishes come true.

Observing these final days spent revisiting and distributing materials produced during from the year, including both student products and

co-constructed learning resources, Jan found it to be a powerful culmination and fitting end to the learning community. She was impressed with
both the students' eagerness to claim these mementos and with Barbara's
use of the decision-making model and related scaffolding to engage the
students as decision makers in the distribution process. She observed
that it was a rich and rewarding experience for the students to revisit
their individual and group progress across the school year. Barbara
emphasized celebration of learning all year long, but this grand finale was
special and encouraged her students to treasure all they learned during
their year with her.

Having described in Chapters 2 to 4 how Barbara sets up and maintains each class as a learning community, we now turn to an examination
of the substance of her teaching. We begin in Chapter 5 with her use of
narratives to establish initial content bases as she introduces her young
learners to new topics.

Chapter 5

Using Narrative to Build a Content Base

The Special Challenges of Teaching Young Children

Teaching content-rich subjects (primarily science and social studies) is especially challenging in the early grades. Young students almost always have at least some experiential base to bring to bear, but their prior knowledge about topics addressed in these subjects is usually very limited. Furthermore, this limited knowledge base is mostly tacit (not organized or even verbally articulated, and perhaps never consciously considered), and it often includes many misconceptions. Consequently, unlike teachers in later grades who usually can begin stimulating new knowledge construction by making connections to an already-established knowledge base, *primary teachers often are faced with the task of helping their students to develop and begin to integrate an initial knowledge base in the domain.* This requires taking little or nothing for granted, teaching (in some respects) as if the students know nothing at all about the topic.

In addition, primary teachers usually have to assume most of the burden of conveying new information to their students. They cannot rely on texts for this purpose, because kindergarten and first-grade students cannot yet read informational texts fluently, and even second- and third-grade students usually have not yet acquired a critical mass of reading fluency and study skills that would allow them to learn efficiently from reading. Thus, most of the content that primary teachers believe is important for their students to learn must to be conveyed by themselves personally during lessons. They may use books, photos, physical artifacts, or other instructional resources in the process, but their students' initial exposures to new information mostly involve listening to what the teacher says during teacher-led classroom discourse.

Primary teachers need to work within certain constraints as they construct and manage this discourse. Their students' attention spans are limited, and they are not yet able to retain lengthy and complicated explanations, so extended lecturing is not a feasible teaching method.

Also, their students do not yet possess a critical mass of cognitive development and domain-specific knowledge that would enable them to comprehend and use the disciplinary content structures and associated discourse genres that are used in teaching subjects at relatively abstract and advanced levels. For example, children have experiences with money and personal economic exchanges, but know nothing of macroeconomics; they can comprehend basic ideas about rules, laws, and authority, but not about comparative governmental structures or other advanced aspects of political science; and they can understand stories about everyday life and key events in the past, but not abstract analyses of macrolevel historical trends.

Consequently, although it is just as important for young students as for older ones to offer curricula featuring networks of knowledge structured around big ideas, teachers cannot do this through lengthy explication of concepts, principles, logical arguments, or other advanced disciplinary structures that young students are not yet prepared to understand and use. Instead, they must stick to aspects of a domain that can be made meaningful to students because they can be connected to the students' existing knowledge, and especially to their personal experiences. In addition, it helps to convey this content using text structures and discourse genres with which the students already have some familiarity (and preferably, some fluency).

Narrative Structures as Teaching Tools

One particularly useful tool that meets these criteria is the narrative structure, because even the youngest students are already familiar with it through exposure to stories. Bruner (1990), Downey and Levstik (1991), Egan (1988, 1990), and others have noted that *even very young children are familiar with and adept at using narrative modes of thinking for describing and remembering things that are important to them. That is, they formulate and remember in story form.* The stories are built around one or a small group of central figures and include attention to their goals, the strategies they use to accomplish those goals (often involving solving problems or overcoming obstacles in the process), and the outcomes of their actions for both the central figures and others in the story. The narrative format provides a natural way to remember a great many of the details that fill out the story, organized within the goal-strategy-outcome "story grammar."

This makes the narrative format a powerful vehicle for teachers to use in helping young students bridge from the familiar to the less familiar. Children can understand information about the long ago and far away when the information is represented as stories of people pursuing goals that the students can understand, using strategies that involve doing things that the students have done themselves, can be shown, or can be helped to imagine. Just as children can understand fictional creatures (e.g., hobbits) and worlds (e.g., Harry Potter's) conveyed through narrative formats, they can understand stories about life in the past or in other cultures, so long as the depicted events lie within their own experiences or can be understood and imagined based on those experiences.

Many aspects of social studies are amenable to representation within narrative structures, especially those that involve human actions that occur in steps, stages, or series of events unfolding over time. History is the most obvious example. Although it has its abstract and analytic aspects, much of history involves reconstructing stories of specific events (e.g., the American Revolution) or changes over time (e.g., in modes of transportation). Studies of children's historical learning indicate that much of what they retain about history is organized within narrative structures, usually compressions of larger trends into stories that focus around goal-oriented activities or conflicts involving a few key figures (Barton & Levstik, 2004; Brophy & VanSledright, 1997). They tend to think of the American Revolution, for example, as a fight between King George of England and George Washington and other Americans who resented his taxes and unfair treatment, not as a protracted and multi-faceted conflict between a sovereign nation and a federation of colonies about to become a nation.

Primary-grade children may be limited in their ability to understand the geopolitical aspects of the past, but they can understand stories about wars as attempts to gain control over land or other resources, voyages of discovery as attempts to satisfy curiosity and acquire riches, immigration as attempts to escape oppression or exploit economic opportunities, and so on. Most historical events and trends involved people engaged in goal-oriented behavior, and thus can be conveyed using narrative formats.

Although it is less commonly recognized, narrative formats also are well suited to conveying information about many of the physical and social science aspects of primary curricula, especially those involving human actions related to cultural universals. To teach about societies and cultures, whether past or present, teachers can construct narratives explaining how the people meet their basic needs for food, clothing, and shelter within the affordances and constraints of local climate and natural resources, how they communicate and travel locally and across longer distances, and how they act both individually (or as families) and collectively (through their governments) to meet needs and pursue agendas.

These stories provide frequent opportunities to introduce basic concepts and principles, as well as to explore causal relationships and make explicit the human intentions and processes that underlie and explain human behavior but often go unrecognized and thus unappreciated by children. Stories about how key inventions made qualitative changes in people's lives, about why Americans eat relatively more wheat and beef but the Chinese eat relatively more rice and chicken, or about the land-to-hand processes and occupations involved in producing common foods and fabrics and bringing them to our stores all incorporate process explanations (of how and why things are done as they are and how products are developed) and cause–effect linkages (explaining why things are done the way they are and why they change in response to inventions).

Barbara's Use of Narrative

Barbara uses narrative structures to introduce new topics. She typically begins with stories drawn from her own life, selected not just because they relate to the topic but because they offer opportunities to highlight big ideas or life applications. Next, she typically draws connections to her students' lives (e.g., family origins in or vacations taken to countries that will be featured in the lesson; jobs held by family members that connect to products or services to be discussed) or to local examples (farm products, stores, government offices, etc.). Then she begins developing a knowledge base structured around big ideas, typically rendered in an informal, story-telling style, and often making additional personal or local connections in the process. Narrative structures are especially frequent in two situations: when she is building timelines or in other ways talking about the past, and when she is describing land-to-hand relationships or other processes that occur in steps or sequences.

Barbara's narratives are highly personalized. She frequently uses "I" and "you" language rather than impersonal third-person language. This gives her narrations a more authentic feel than traditional lecture/explanations, and her frequent references to what "you" might do help make students aware of potential life applications. They also subtly reinforce her efforts to develop her students' perceptions of efficacy when she talks about things that they could do right now or when she talks about things they might do in the future.

Barbara's personalizations extend to family members. Her students learn the names and many of the significant events in the lives of her husband, parents, sister, and other relatives through their appearances in her stories. The same is true of the families of her students and of other teachers at the school, including adopted children, foster children, and others. Along with personalizing and localizing the curriculum, these references and connections lend intimacy to the learning communities she creates.

She often uses objects or photos as props, especially if introducing something that she expects to be unfamiliar to many of her students. She routinely uses rich imagery and examples to build "word pictures" of what she is describing. For processes, she often adds hand choreography to supplement the verbal explanation. She also frequently inserts invented dialogue or mini-dramatizations. These are fictional but realistic conversations that might have taken place between people living at the time and place under study, or even thinking (self-talk) carried out by a single individual (such as an inventor).

These devices not only advance the storyline but provide opportunities to model (and thus make visible to students) the thinking and decision making that mediate people's problem-solving efforts and goal oriented behaviors. She routinely depicts inventions, for example, as occurring because people became aware of a problem, brainstormed possible solutions, devised and tested prototypes until they found one that worked effectively, and added improvements later.

Although her narratives are engaging as well as informative, Barbara is careful to keep them focused around big ideas. She does not carry dramatization farther than it needs to go (she might don a hat to signify that she is temporarily personifying a character, but she does not use elaborate costumes); she does not use unnecessary props (ordinarily, there is no need to show apples, cars, or other familiar objects, unless she wants to stimulate her students to think about the objects in unusual ways); and she uses instructional resources only for as long as they are needed and for the purposes for which they were included (e.g., if she wants to show an illustration from a book, she shows and discusses the illustration with reference to the ongoing lesson, but then puts the book aside rather than interrupt the lesson to read the book at this time or look at other illustrations that are not as relevant). "Don't get lost in the props" is one or her rules of thumb for planning informational segments of lessons. This helps her to keep these segments brief and focused.

Barbara typically tries to get through her initial narratives without significant interruption, both to sustain their coherence and flow and to minimize students' exposure to misconceptions. However, she sometimes opens slots for student participation by asking questions or by making partial statements and then pausing to allow students to complete them (typically by supplying a key idea that she already has expressed or modeled two or three times previously). She concludes the initial presentation with a review/summary, highlighting big ideas and explicitly noting connections between successive steps in a process or linkages between causes and effects.

Then she goes back through the content again, but this time shifting from a narrative to a questioning mode. Gradually, as students become more familiar with the content, and to the extent that their responses to simpler questions are encouraging, she progresses from short-answer questions to questions that require extended explanations, and from questions that only require retrieval from memory to questions that require higher-order thinking. When students answer correctly, she often elaborates on their answers to reinforce big ideas or add information not brought out earlier. When they are unable to respond or respond incorrectly, she ordinarily stays with them to try to elicit an improved response, using the techniques described in Brophy, Alleman, and Knighton (2008).

Barbara's narrative presentations can be described as teacher-centered, but they contrast with more typical modes of teacher-centered instruction, such as lectures, word webbing to develop concepts, rule/example methods of teaching principles, or drill-and-practice methods of teaching skills. Less obviously, they also differ in important ways from typical historical or literary storytelling.

Although they have an informal, spontaneous feel, her narratives are carefully planned to develop big ideas using purposefully chosen examples and illustrations. They offer simplified explanations that her students can follow and relate to their prior knowledge and experience. Her initial pass through the storyline sticks closely to the flow of main ideas, being careful not to insert unnecessary information, teach unnecessary vocabulary, or in other ways make it difficult for students to follow the flow. She will add more details later when she goes through the material again, especially when she frames questions and elaborates on students' responses.

We will illustrate Barbara's narratives with two examples. The first, on clothing in the past, is representative of the majority of these narratives. The second, on the land-to-hand story of bananas, illustrates how she sometimes assigns roles to her students as a way to personalize the information and add cues that will help them to recall it in the future.

Clothing in the Past

This example is taken from Barbara's fifth day of teaching our clothing unit (from Alleman & Brophy, 2001). The unit begins with lessons on clothing in the contemporary United States, focusing on its functions and on different kinds of clothes worn for different purposes or occasions. The next lesson looks at changes in clothing over time. Barbara decided to spread this lesson over two days because it includes several big ideas and a lot of information that would be new to most of her students. On the first day, she taught about clothing Long, Long Ago (in the cave days). On the second day, she taught about clothing Long Ago (in the Pilgrim and pioneer days) and in Modern Times. The excerpted material is from the first half of the second day, when Barbara reviewed material on Long, Long Ago from the previous day and introduced new material on clothing Long Ago.

The lesson is designed to develop four main ideas:

- Long Ago, clothing was used for protection, decoration, communication, and later modesty as well.

- Clothing has undergone a variety of changes over time. These changes have produced clothes that are more durable, water-repellant, light-weight, and convenient to use.
- Thread/yarn is spun from wool (or cotton, etc.).
- Cloth is woven from thread/yarn. It is a fabric, not a solid.

The first of these big ideas focused on the four functions of clothing that had been introduced in previous lessons. It would be reinforced in this lesson rather than introduced for the first time. The other three big ideas would be introduced and developed in this lesson. They focus on progress made over time in improving clothing and on helping children to under-stand the fundamental nature of cloth (i.e., it is a fabric woven from thread or yarn which in turn has been spun from raw material). Our interview studies had shown that most K-3 students either could not explain what cloth is or mistakenly viewed it as a solid akin to leather or plastic (Brophy & Alleman, 2006).

Barbara begins with a more extensive review than usual. Students' answers to her questions during the second part of the previous day's lesson were not as solid as she had hoped, and she wants to make sure that certain key information is in place. This involves "cementing" accur-ate information for students who need it, while at the same time adding a few new details to keep other students interested. It also involves repeat-edly using key words (e.g., fiber) and describing or demonstrating key processes (e.g., stretching and spinning fibers, weaving them into fabrics).

As she speaks, she refers and sometimes points to objects and events depicted on the Long, Long Ago portion of a timeline that she began during the previous lesson and will complete today. Note that even though she is talking about prehistoric people, she sometimes refers to them as "we" (i.e., human beings), as a way to promote empathy.

T: Now, let me go ahead and remind you of some things that we said about Long, Long Ago. People were living in caves Long, Long Ago. When they first started living, they didn't need clothes because they lived in warmer places and they had more hair on their bodies. But as people started to move to places that were colder and we started to get shorter hair on our bodies, we needed ways to protect ourselves. One of the things that we were already doing for food was hunting—animals like buffalo and deer. So we took what we knew about those animals and we started using their skin to make clothing. One of the things that we were good at gathering was plants. Then people started noticing that they could use the plants that they had gathered to make parts of their clothing and to keep their bodies covered and protected. You can see: these fibers came from a plant. They

picked the plant and they took it apart to get these long . . . they
look like strings or fibers, and then somebody came up with the
idea to weave those fibers together.

This review continues for a few more minutes until Barbara concludes it
and makes the transition from Long, Long Ago to Long Ago as follows.

T: But the big idea was cloth, and people first started making cloth
      out of things—plant pieces or plant parts. One of the plants that
      they used was a plant that had little puffs on it. Those puffs
      turned out to be puffs of cotton. Have you ever had cotton
      balls? [Barbara "drops in" a mention of cotton puffs here, not
      only because it is an example that her students should be famil-
      iar with, but because later in the unit she will be teaching the
      land-to-hand story of cotton, and she knows that cotton plants
      are unfamiliar to her students.]
Ss: Yeah.
T: OK. What they would do with the cotton balls is they would
      take the cotton and they would stretch it and pull it and clean all
      the dirt out of it, and they would stretch it and make it long and
      they would twist it and pretty soon it would be a long fiber and
      then they would take the fibers and . . . [pauses to invite students
      to finish the sentence.]
Ss: Sew it.
T: Weave them together. They would use that to make . . .
Ss: Cloth. [As she talks about cotton puffs and cotton fibers, she
      shows examples to the students, and she stretches and twists the
      fibers to demonstrate what she means as she describes these
      processes. Then she attaches the cotton puffs and fibers to the
      timeline for future reference.]
T: Cloth. But then they came up with another thing that they could
      weave or that they could pull into fibers and make into cloth.
      And this is going to surprise you. Are you ready? What did they
      start doing between Long, Long Ago and Long Ago to make
      having food easier? What did they do so they didn't have to go
      out and hunt and they didn't have to go looking for berries, they
      didn't have to go kill an animal? They started thinking, "I know
      what we'll do. We'll do. . . . What? [In making this transition to
      the next point, she does not just stick to clothing but also ties
      back to the food unit, as part of her attempt to impart a general
      sense of the contrasts between life Long, Long Ago and life Long
      Ago. Then she models inventive thinking but leaves the sentence
      unfinished, hoping that one or more of the students would finish
      it for her. When no one does, she indicates more directly that she

would like them to respond, and one of them supplies the answer she hoped to hear.]

S: They had a farm.

T: They had a farm, and what did they do on the farm?

S: They grew plants.

T: And?

S: Vegetables.

T: What else did they do other than grow things on the farm?

S: Um . . .

T: What do you have on a farm other than plants? . . . Baaaaa. [Less direct efforts to elicit "animals" were not successful, so Barbara uses a "give away" clue here.]

S: Animals.

T: Animals on the farm. They figured out that if they cut the hair off of the sheep, they could . . .

S: Have wool.

T: They could (students repeat after teacher) pull it . . . and stretch it . . . and twist it into long fibers, so they could take the fibers and . . .

Ss: Weave them together.

T: Weave them together. [Barbara does not directly tell the students to repeat after her here, but the combination of her voice tone and modulation (accompanied by physical demonstrations) emphasizing each of these key steps, followed by a brief pause with an expectant look toward the students, communicates this invitation to them, and they respond accordingly. She then shifts to an informational book on the pioneer days, not to read it but to use some of its photos and provide her own commentary focusing on the big ideas she wants to develop. She first clarifies that although these are photos rather than drawings, they were not taken during the pioneer days. Instead, they depict modern people reenacting pioneer activities.] Let me show you some pictures I have.

S: Cool!

T: These folks are people who are pretending to be pioneers— people who lived Long Ago—one of the groups were pioneers. They are cutting the wool off of the sheep and they are going to make it into fabric. Sometimes they tied them to a tree or a post and then they would use scissors, because by Long Ago people had come up with ideas like making knives and scissors . . . and metal—they were using metal to make tools, so they would take the sheep and cut the wool off. They also did the same thing to goats and rabbits, and they would cut all of the fur off of them. Then they would take it and they had these great big combs.

This was called combing because you had two combs and you would do like this with your combs. (Teacher illustrates.) I don't know if you've ever seen somebody's hair get combed, how it gets all straight and all going in the same direction. That's what they would do with these fibers from the sheep or the goat or the llama or the rabbit, and they would do like this with two brushes, and they would get all those fibers going . . .

Ss: Straight.

T: . . . nice and straight and in the same direction. [Here again, Barbara uses hand choreography along with the photos to help students visualize the processes described. She uncharacteristically includes unusual examples (goats, llamas, rabbits) along with sheep. After reading and reflecting on this transcript, she noted that she would not do this in the future. Except for those that students are likely to bring up themselves at this point, anomalies should be avoided in favor of focusing on prototypes (in this case, sheep) when introducing basic information.] They would make nice loooonnng fibers and they would spin them with a spinning wheel . . . there's a picture of a spinning wheel. See, it's got the wool right here, and it's spinning it around and around and getting it tight. If you take some yarn and you twist it and kind of pull, do you see how it twists up, and it gets longer and you can kind of stretch it out, and that's what they did. They would twist it and it would get tighter and tighter and longer and longer and it would twist up, and then what do they have to do with these big long fibers when they're done twisting them nice and firm and tight?

S: Make them into fabric.

T: Right, and how would they do that, Tim?

S: Weaving it.

T: That's right, they would weave it and they would do that with fibers.

S: I think I saw one of those kind of wheels before. [Barbara does not pursue this comment because doing so would not advance the lesson. In these situations, she shows acceptance of the comment with a brief nod or smile, but then resumes the intended flow. As this segment develops, she addresses several agendas simultaneously: repeatedly describing and illustrating processes involved in spinning and weaving; personalizing using the students' shirts; stimulating awe and wonder by emphasizing the large number of fibers needed to make a shirt and the fact that the pioneers had to do most of this work themselves and mostly by hand; reassuring the students that the shearing process did not harm the animals; and helping the students to understand the operations of the machines that were available during the pioneer days, appreciating them as advances even though they were not as advanced as today's machines.]

T: So they started to use wool and cotton . . .

S: And fibers.

T: And they would spin it to make a fiber and then they would weave the fiber into cloth. Then they could take the cloth and cut it out in shapes. People would sew things by hand. They would cut out the pieces and they would sew the pieces together until they had a whole piece of clothing. Imagine if everything you were wearing, somebody had to cut the hair off the sheep . . .

S: And weave it.

T: That's not even all of it. They had to cut the hair off the sheep; they had to comb it into long pieces; then they had to spin it into long fibers; then they had to weave it into cloth; then they had to cut it out with scissors; then they had to sew it with their hands; and I mean, if you look really closely at your clothes, one single string in Curtis's shirt is one fiber. Can you imagine how many fibers they had to have to make this shirt? I mean you can see all the fibers in it. Goodness gracious, can you imagine how long it must have taken just to make the cloth, let alone cut it out and sew it by hand?

S: And the buttons.

Cole: I wonder how long it was before they had machines?

T: They didn't have machines. They did all of this with their hands. Let me show you. She's sewing it by hand. This one's working to spin it, this one's sewing it, this one little girl is using yarn and she's knitting it into a sock. Everything they made was by hand.

Cole: Today we have machines. [Cole has now twice indicated that he wants to talk about machines. This is not exactly a "teachable moment," because the lesson plan already calls for teaching about machines involved in manufacturing clothing. In fact, Cole's second comment is something of an unwanted intrusion because responding to it directly would require Barbara to make the transition from Long Ago to modern times before she is ready to do so. So, she compromises by shifting to talk about machines, and in the process, drops in Cole's name to signal to him that she is responding to his question. However, rather than jump prematurely to modern machines, she talks about the machines of the time such as looms and spinning jennies.]

T: Here's the good news, Cole. Somebody came up with the idea to have a machine. Now the very first machine they had to help them—they still had to use their own arms and legs to make the machines go. Even the spinning wheel is a kind of machine to help them spin those fibers, but she's using the machine . . .

S: That they had to use their hands and feet.

T: Yeah, and she's weaving this by hand and then using the machine to make it nice and tight and strong. So the first machines were helpful, but they still had to do a lot of it with their hands, and it still did take them some time to get it made. Joellen?

S: How did they get it off the animal? Would they like put them to sleep or something?

T: It was just like a haircut. They didn't take the skin like they did when they got fur. They just cut all his hair off and used his hair. So that would be like if we were to take Laurel and we were to cut all her hair off. We would spin all of her hairs together into really long fibers, and we could weave. I mean, we wouldn't do that with a person. But that's what they did with the sheep and the goats and the animals. . . . Soon somebody even came up with a machine that would do the sewing job with the needle, only look: She's pushing with her foot to make the machine go along. So she's like pushing with her foot and it's making the machine go around. It's not plugged into the wall. There was still no electricity here. So she's making it go by pushing it with her foot, and that's the first sewing machine that they had to use. So instead of sewing it up with their hand, they got to use a machine to sew the clothes together.

S: That would make some exercise.

T: It probably took a lot of strength. She probably got a lot of exercise by doing that.

At this point, Barbara diverges from the lesson flow for a couple of minutes in order to allow students to make comments and ask questions about the illustrations she has been showing. Then she makes a transition into the next part of the lesson dealing with clothing in modern times.

The Story of Bananas

The story of bananas is the seventh lesson in the food unit (Alleman & Brophy, 2001), following lessons on the functions of food, food choices and snacks, changes in food over time, changes in farming over time, development of the food industry, and types of farming. It is one of four lessons on land-to-hand steps involved in bringing common foods to our tables (bananas, peanut butter, pasta, and apple pie). It is placed first in this sequence because it is the simplest story: Bananas are grown, shipped, and eaten as is, whereas other foods undergo transformations before they reach the final form in which they are consumed (e.g., milling of wheat into flour, combining with other ingredients, etc.). The lesson is developed around two main ideas:

- Bananas are an example of a food that is grown only in certain parts of the world due to climatic conditions but can be transported to other parts of the world. Bananas must be carefully preserved from the time they are picked until they reach the supermarket.
- We depend on many workers to bring this food to us.

As a series of successive steps, the land-to-hand story of bananas is well suited to the narrative format. In this case, Barbara incorporated student role assignments into the narrative, for both motivational reasons (engage them in the story more directly and help them identify with key characters) and learning reasons (provide supplementary cues—associations between particular students in the class and particular processes/jobs in bringing bananas to our tables—that help the students follow the story on this day and remember it in the future).

For the role assignments, one student was identified as the plantation owner, another as the operations manager, another as a worker who cut the banana stalks from the plants, etc. Although Barbara occasionally asked some of these students to briefly pantomime or act out a minor aspect of their role, this was not a full-scale dramatization requiring costumes, rehearsals, etc. Role assignments are relatively minor elaborations on her typical narrative approach, but she has found them worthwhile, especially when the story to be developed involves a relatively large cast of characters each playing a unique role (e.g., assembly lines, land-to-hand stories).

Prior to the lesson, Barbara read aloud and discussed with students their responses to the previous night's home assignment, which asked them to think about and discuss with their parents what kind of farm they might like to own. The students recorded their answers and brief explanations on provided forms. During this activity, Barbara noted that Tim had expressed interest in owning a fruit farm. When she asked him what kind of fruit he had in mind, he mentioned bananas. She replied that in that case, he was going to love today's lesson.

She then continued reading and discussing other homework responses. When she was ready to begin the story of bananas, she tied back to Tim's response as one basis for the transition. She also tied back to material in previous lessons on farms, which included the ideas that different kinds of soil and climate are suited to different crops. In addition, because the story would include a banana plantation in Honduras, she showed

Honduras on the globe and referenced it both to the equator and to Michigan. She does this routinely when her instruction mentions other nations.

T: Tim, it's going to be a great day for you because indeed we are going to talk about a particular kind of farm, a farm where they grow bananas. Isn't that the one that you thought you would like? Today the farm that we are going to talk about needs special weather and it needs special land, just like the farms we talked about yesterday. We're going to talk about a banana farm. They have a special name for it. It's called a plantation. They don't call it a banana farm. You'll hear them say it's a plantation. That's just a fancy name for farm. You need to have nice warm weather for a banana farm or a banana plantation. See this line right in the middle of the earth? (points on globe) That's where it's warmest on the whole earth. So when you look at this globe, if you get closer to this line, you get . . .

Ss: Hotter.

T: Or warmer. If you go farther away, it gets . . .

Ss: Cooler.

T: Right. So look at Michigan. Here we are up here. Are we close to the line or far away from the line?

Ss: Far away.

T: So do you think this is a place where it's going to get hot enough for bananas to grow?

Ss: No.

T: So, Tim, the sad news for you is that if you really want to have a banana farm, a banana plantation, you can't live up here in Michigan. What are you going to have to do?

S: Move down to the line.

T: You'd move down closer to the line. You know what? He could decide that. That's what the people who wanted banana plantations did. They either lived there to begin with or they moved down there to be where it's warmer. Some of the countries that we have near us that grow bananas—they grow bananas in Honduras. They probably grow bananas . . .

S: In Mexico?

T: I don't know that they don't grow bananas in Mexico. They might. The place I was thinking of was Honduras and it's kind of next door to Mexico. So it makes sense that they might grow bananas there. [The idea that the climate is warmer near the equator is not stressed in the lesson plans and could have been omitted here, but Barbara includes it because she views it as a "building block idea" needed to make sense of some of the lesson's new information. She has found that each unit includes several of these building block ideas, especially in the early lessons. Working from analogies to a tower or pyramid of knowledge that has certain significant chunks missing, she uses the term as shorthand for her analysis of why students sometimes struggle with certain big ideas. The fact that climate tends to be warmer near the equator but cooler near the poles is fundamental and often assumed as background knowledge to much of what is taught in science and social studies, so Barbara takes pains to teach it explicitly when it first comes up and to reinforce it frequently when it appears subsequently (as here). In this situation, insertion of the building block idea also allows her to elaborate her personalization of the story around Tim as the plantation owner (explaining that he will need to move to a warmer climate).

Note also that when a student suggests that bananas are grown in Mexico, Barbara is unable to respond definitively because she is unsure. Rather than pretend otherwise, she says that she is unsure but thinks that they probably do grow bananas in Mexico, and explains her reasoning. She values such opportunities because they allow her to demonstrate authentic applications of social studies knowledge and model the reasoning processes involved in bringing it to bear on questions of interest.

Issues of whether and when to introduce formal vocabulary can be problematic, especially in the early grades. In this case, Barbara does introduce the term plantation, but uses the more familiar term weather instead of the less familiar term climate, and does not use the term equator even though she teaches that the weather gets warmer as you move closer to "the line around the middle of the earth." Among both social studies educators and elementary teachers, some would agree and some would disagree with these decisions.]

S: Tim could grow bananas right there.
T: Right, he could move. He'd have to move when he was a grown-up. He'd have to take his family and move to Honduras if he wanted to have a banana farm.
S: He could fly there.
T: Look, he's way up here. That would take you lots of hours on an airplane to get there. Now, the reason Honduras works for bananas is because bananas need for it to be very warm . . .
S: Really hot.
T: Yup, really hot. They also need lots and lots of sunlight. As you

get closer to that line, the sun shines more and more and more. So the banana plants, that's where they first started growing. That's where they grow the best, and so he would need a farm where it's very sunny, lots of warm weather, and the banana plants would grow there. Now, we're going to take you through what happens to the banana. What did you have for a snack, James? You've taken a banana from Tim's farm or the farm where it really came from all the way . . . Where's the banana now? It's in his belly. So, we're going to go from the land all the way to James's hand so he could eat it and get it into his body. The reason he ate that banana was because . . .

Ss: It's healthy.

T: It's healthy. It comes from the fruit group. It's got vitamins and minerals. It's going to help him grow. [Barbara now has connected to a second student, James, whom she observed eating a banana during snack time. So, the stage is set for a story of a banana grown on Tim's plantation in Honduras ending up in James's lunch box in Michigan. While she is at it, Barbara takes a brief excursion from today's lesson flow to reinforce ideas about healthy snacks taught earlier in the unit.] The banana is going to start at the plantation. It's going to be on a plant. I actually have pictures that I want to show you. This is an encyclopedia. It has all kinds of facts in it. [Barbara shows and labels an encyclopedia here, and then proceeds to model its use as a learning tool. However, she uses just a few pictures that illustrate aspects of the story with which students are unfamiliar (banana flower, giant bunches on the plant), omitting pictures that do not seem necessary (bugs, crates, cutting down stalks with a machete). As she works through the story/role play, she consciously ties each step to the next to bring out the overall sequence and underscore cause–effect linkages.] This picture right here—can you see stuff that's kind of fluffy at the end of it?

Ss: Yeah.

T: Does it really look like the banana that you ate, James?

S: No.

T: It doesn't look very much like it—a little bit, the shape. It's long and skinny. Let me read to you what it says. "Each banana has a large bud at the end of a stem." So a stem is like a stick and a large bud is like a flower that's getting ready to bloom. OK? And as the stem grows, the leaves covering that part peel back and that's when that flower shows up. Then each of the flowers grows into a little tiny banana. Look at this picture. Those are little baby bananas. Look at how they're up in the plant. There are a whole bunch of them together. Look how many of them there are.

S: (Students are excited).

T: You know what the workers on Tim's farm—on his plantation—will call those bananas? Fingers! Can you look at them
and see why they're called fingers?

S: Cause they're so small.

T: They're small and do they look kind of like your fingers?

Ss: Yeah.

T: It kind of looks like a whole bunch of fingers stuck right there
together, doesn't it?

S: Yeah.

S: There's a whole bunch of them.

S: I can see the bananas.

T: This is the first step. You have to grow the bananas. So we're
going to make a card that says "grow bananas." [Barbara often
writes key words on cards that will be posted and used in subsequent review and application activities. In this case, the cards
will depict each of the major steps in the banana story.]

T: We'll write on them as we go. So the first thing you're going to do,
the first thing that happened was they had to grow the banana!
Grow the banana. Now, we have to take care of those bananas
when they're growing. Somebody needs to make sure that those
bananas grow. Do you know what sometimes happens to fruit
and vegetables when you're growing them? Bugs come along.

Ss: Eeeeooooou!

T: Have you heard about that? Yup, bugs will come along and they
want to eat the bananas or they want to eat the fruit and vegetables, so you either have to spray them or you have to get the
bugs off the plants. So we'll say, "Spray for bugs." Clean off the
bugs. So, the workers that Tim hires will spray on the farm to
keep the bugs off the bananas. Tim, who do you think you want
to hire to spray the plants? Somebody responsible. Arden would
be a good worker for your farm. Pick one other kid that you
think would be a good farm worker.

S: A.J.

T: You know what A.J.'s job is going to be? Arden sprayed the
bugs and he's taking care of them while they're growing. Good
spraying, Arden. But now, the time has come when we're ready
to get those bananas off the plant. Let me show you how they
look now that they've grown bigger and they're ready.

Ss: Ooooo!

T: Can you see the plant? It looks a little palm treeish because it's
got those big leaves. What are those things?

Ss: Fingers.

T: They're bananas. They take great big knives called machetes, so you're going to have to be careful. I'm glad you picked A.J. because he's a careful guy. They come along to the tree and they WHACK!!! [Demonstrates.] Gotta be strong. A nice big whack. And the big, huge knife cuts the whole thing off. Then he's going to carry that great big huge bunch of bananas. Kerchop!!!! The big bundle of bananas comes off. A.J. carries it to a storage house on Tim's farm. Now, while he's cutting the bananas off, Tim or someone that he hires needs to be talking with companies who might want to buy the bananas. Do you suppose that James's mom got the banana at Meijer, Kroger, Farmer Jack?

S: Meijer.

T: Tim's going to hire somebody to fly here to Michigan because Michigan is where the Meijer company is, and that person is going to say great things about Tim's banana plants, and he's going to talk them into buying bananas from Tim. Tim, who do you think would be great to come up to Michigan and talk to the people at Meijer about your bananas?

S: Gretchen.

T: You think Gretchen would? So meanwhile, he's gotta find somebody to buy the bananas. So [writes on card], a buyer. Is he going to send somebody to James's house? [Barbara often uses absurd questions like this one to set up or create salience for the point that she wants to emphasize (in this case, that several middlemen get involved between the growers and the buyers). She believes that this helps students to remember the point better, and in some cases, to get the point in the first place.]

Ss: No.

T: He's going to send Gretchen to the Meijer company. He's going to sell all the bananas. Thousands and thousands and just crates and crates and crates. Remember the crates? We looked at the grapes in the crates. [in a previous lesson]

Ss: Yeah.

T: Same thing. Crates and crates full of bananas. She's going to try and sell them to Meijer. So while she's finding a buyer, A.J. is cutting down the bananas . . . We call that . . .

S: Harvesting.

T: Nice remembering! He's going to harvest the bananas. He's going to cut them down. [Writes on card.] Harvest the bananas. [Barbara was successful here in eliciting a key vocabulary term from one student, but she suspects that others had forgotten the term and some might even have forgotten what it means. Consequently, she repeats the term "harvest" twice here and in between provides its definition in simple words ("Cut them down"). She frequently drops such vocabulary reinforcements into her ongoing narratives.] You know what? They don't have machines that could do that job yet. They have to cut the bananas out of the plant by hand just like people have done since Long, Long Ago. People first found bananas Long, Long Ago when they were foraging for food and they cut them out of the plant. We still do it the same way because bananas could get smushed or broken too easy. A.J.'s job—he took the bananas over to the warehouse and his job is done. You need to find somebody who's going to put them in boxes and big old crates. Who do you think could put them in crates?

S: Alan.

T: Alan, can you put all the bananas in the big, old crates? Are you a strong guy?

S: Yeah.

T: [Writes] Put the bananas in crates. You can't just put them in a bag because they're going to go a long way. Look how far those bananas are going to go! They're down here and they're going to go all the way up to Michigan.

S: On a plane.

T: If they're on a plane . . .

S: Nine hours.

T: Yeah, if they went on a plane. Now, you know what? Flying stuff on a plane is pretty expensive. So after they put the bananas in crates, they might not send them on a plane. They'll probably put them on a boat because it doesn't cost as much for a boat. But you know what? It takes a little bit longer. If we don't do any-thing to those bananas, will they last for months and months?

Ss: No.

T: No.

S: They would get black.

T: Right—they would get really brown and then get really black. So you know what they have to do? They have to pick the bananas while they're still pretty green because if they're going to be on the boat for a little while—a couple of days even—getting to the United States, and if they picked the bananas when they were yellow, by the time they got to us, you're right, Mikey, they would be brown. Yeah, look at the picture that somebody painted—this banana picture. See. These are bananas that are already starting to get . . .

Ss: Brown.

T: Yellow's OK, a little bit of brown is OK. This is the way it looked when you ate it today, right, James?

S: Yeah.

T: Yup. So they have to pick it when it's green, so that by the time

James's mom bought it at the store it was yellow, with maybe just a little teeny bit of green. They put those bananas in crates and they put them on a ship. [Writes on card.] Put the crates on a ship. . . . Tim doesn't own the boat. He pays somebody to let him put his bananas on the boat. So Tim doesn't need to hire anybody to go on the boat. But the people that own the boat do. As a matter of fact, Mariah is the captain of the boat, and Tim's going to pay her money to move the bananas to Michigan. Mariah, you probably need to hire somebody to help you out on your ship. [The school secretary announces on the P.A. system that Tim has to leave school with his mother for an appointment.] Tim, you know, you've still got those banana plants growing. Who can you hire to come to your farm and manage it while you're gone?

S: I pick Joellen.

T: OK, Joellen, you don't actually own the farm, but he's going to pay you to take care of it. Do you suppose you could do that?

S: Yup.

T: OK, so if you have to have decisions about the banana farm, you'll have to make those decisions, OK?

S: Yeah.

T: You know what? That happens in real life. People that own the farm might go away for a while, so the bananas are on the ship. Who are you going to hire to help take care of the bananas while they're on the ship? It can't be A.J. He's working on Tim's farm. In fact, Joellen's his boss right now.

S: Cole.

T: Cole, your job's going to be loading the bananas on and unloading them off. OK. Look. Here's the boat. It comes all the way around. It can't get to Michigan so it will probably go to New York City or maybe Philadelphia or maybe one of these cities along here. [Shows on globe.]

S: How come Philadelphia?

T: Because they're right there on the water. New York or maybe somewhere in New Jersey or Delaware—one of these cities along here. Then, Cole's going to unload the bananas off the ship, so [writes on card] Off the ship. Then he'll put them into a truck—a semi truck. Laurel, can you drive the semi truck to Michigan with the bananas on it. [Writes on card.] Semi truck takes crates to Michigan. They go right to the Meijer warehouse. Guess who's working at the Meijer warehouse to unload the bananas?

Ss: Who?

T: A.J.'s dad [who actually does work at Meijer]. So he's got a whole bunch of his family working. So let's say it's dad's job.

It's dad's job to unload Laurel's semi truck full of bananas. So they have to unload the crates. After A.J.'s dad unloads the bananas at the Meijer warehouse, then they need to take the bananas to the store. They might do that in one of the Meijer trucks. Mikey, do you have a job yet?

S: No.

T: Your job—you're working right up at Meijer's. You're going to unload the bananas and put them in the banana section at the store. Have you seen the people that are in charge of the fruits and vegetables? Oh yeah, they're unloading boxes of bananas or boxes of lettuce or boxes of potatoes. So [writes on card] they're going to put the bananas on the shelf—bananas out to buy. They're probably still pretty green because they picked them before they turned yellow. It's been about two weeks since A.J. picked it, and now Mikey is putting it on the shelf at Meijer, and sure enough, here comes James's mom, pushing her cart. James says, "Mom, can I have . . .

Ss: A banana!

T: . . . for a snack tomorrow?"

T: His mom says, "Sure," and she picks out a really nice-looking group of bananas and she puts it in her cart, and now she goes to . . . the cashier. [Barbara paused to open a slot for students to supply the term "cashier" here, but none did, so she supplied it herself and moved on.] Haley, do you have a job yet?

S: No.

T: Haley, you are the cashier, and James's mom can buy from the cashier.

S: You have to be a good reader.

T: Yeah, you do have to be a good reader to be a cashier, and you have to know numbers, too. All right. Are you ready to tell the whole story together? Oh, wait. I forgot James's part of the story. What was your job?

S: Eat the banana!

T: Eat it! That was the last job. Now I might have gotten them out of order a little bit so I have to make sure they're in the right order. All right. Here we go! Ready. Sitting up nice and straight and tall. Beginning again. Here we go! This is the story of how James's banana . . . [At this point, Barbara launches a review of the story, using the cards she has written to highlight the major steps in the right order. When she talks about the time elapsing between the harvesting of the bananas in Honduras and their delivery to a supermarket in Michigan, she uses the class calendar to point out the number of days involved (and in the process, model skills that connect to calendar work done in mathematics). Throughout the review, and occasionally in the future when she makes reference back to this story, she includes the names of students assigned to key roles (Tim owns the plantation, A.J. cut down the bananas, etc.).]

Barbara concluded the day with a pair-share activity in which students talked with a partner about foods they liked to eat that included bananas. This was preparation for a homework assignment calling for them to discuss the same thing with their parents and then write their responses. She omitted the manual's suggestion that the students be invited to draw pictures of workers doing different jobs in the story of bananas because she didn't think that her students could make accurate pictures of that kind of activity yet. However, she did have them record in their journals some of the important things that they had learned that day.

Barbara spent a lot of time on and included the role-playing feature in her story of bananas because it was the first of four land-to-hand lessons that all included attention to a common set of basic steps in crop farming (planting, nurturing and protecting the plants as they grow, harvesting, shipping, etc.). With this base firmly in place, she was able to move more quickly through the following three lessons, without including role assignments. However, she sometimes made use of the banana plantation role assignments by referring back to them to cue students to processes that she wanted to include in subsequent stories. For example, she cued the need to spray for bugs by asking about Arden's job on Tim's banana plantation.

During the transportation unit, Barbara included a similar role-assignment feature in her lesson on automobile assembly lines. Rather than attempt to convey the hundreds of highly specific tasks that line workers carry out, however, she developed a simplified version structured around the major parts of cars that she knew would be familiar to her students (so one was assigned to be the person who would put in the seats, another would attach the fenders, another would put on the wheels, etc.).

Narratives in Other Subjects

Science is another subject in which Barbara uses the narrative style to help students understand concepts and retain information. Science lessons that focus on events in the past, on the actions of an individual, or on how or why questions, usually are more successful with this structure. Barbara uses a narrative to help students follow the life of a caterpillar as it grows to a butterfly. First, she tells the story of a caterpillar beginning as an egg and then reviews the information using the caterpillars that the class is raising as part of their life cycles unit. Later, she again uses a narrative with students as they work together to map out the life cycle of humans. Barbara personalizes this part of the lesson by beginning with the birth of her own grandmother.

Barbara also uses the narrative style during language arts instruction to help show the possible thoughts and actions of readers and writers. In one case, she and her students studied the Michigan author Patricia Polacco. This author lives close to their school, so students quickly began to identify with the central character of the narrative. Identifying or connecting emotionally with the characters helps improve the effectiveness of the narrative.

As she began the narrative, Barbara wove together information that students already knew with logical "guesses" about the actions of the real-life person.

> *T:* All these Patricia Polacco books are . . .
>
> *Ss:* Realistic Fiction.
>
> *T:* That's right. They are fiction, made up but also realistic because they could happen. But here's what I'm wondering. Where did Patricia get all her ideas? Well, first, Patricia was born right here in Lansing, Michigan just like most of you. I bet you didn't know that, huh?
>
> *Ss:* Wow.
>
> *S:* Where was she born?
>
> *T:* Do you mean what hospital? That's a great question. I don't know. I know Sparrow Hospital has been here in Lansing for a long time, so that could be it. Anyway, Patricia's mom and dad got divorced when she was around three years old and she moved with her mom into her grandma and grandpa's farm in Union City. That's not too far from here. She and her brother called their grandmother "Babushka."
>
> *S:* Hey, that's the name of one of our books, *Babushka's Doll.*
>
> *T:* You're right. Who do you think the story is about?
>
> *Ss:* Her grandma!
>
> *T:* Wait until you hear more about her life. She moved away from Michigan and lived in Florida and California. Then, as an adult, she moved back to the farm in Michigan. When she did, Patricia started to think back about growing up on the farm. She drew lots of pictures of things that happened to her. Yes, Mike?
>
> *S:* We draw pictures about things that happen to us.
>
> *T:* Absolutely! We do that when we plan our stories. So what do you think Patricia was doing? [Barbara accommodates Mike's desire to inject a comment here, but responds in a way that quickly restores the flow to her intended agenda.]

Ss: Planning stories.

T: You're right. She was. In fact, she looked through those pictures and found just the right one and zoomed in to focus on the details of that watermelon seed story. The seed was a day when a meteor landed in a field by her grandparent's farm.

S: Meteor!

S: We read that book.

Ss: Cool! Wow!

T: That's right. Patricia took a real event from her life, visualized it in her head, drew it as a picture, and then told the story from the beginning to the middle and then the end. Just like we do! [These comments are intended not only to help her students understand Polacco's story-creation process, but also to support their perceptions of self-efficacy as writers.]

Barbara then went on to connect with the children and find out which step of the process they were on, continually tying back to the narrative and the actions of a published author, Patricia Polacco.

Concluding Observations

Jan and Jere consider Barbara's narrative style to be particularly effective because it encourages minds-on learning. This is especially important where hands-on learning is not always possible, and where many forms of hands-on learning are ineffectual because they distract attention from big ideas. In addition, *Barbara offers several reasons why she prefers her narrative style to more traditional lecture/explanations:*

- It allows her to manipulate vocal qualities to hold students' attention and to include emotional components that engage them at deeper levels.
- It improves recall, both by increasing the percentage of information remembered and by focusing on the most meaningful and logically connected material rather than random discrete facts.
- It helps students see logic and connections.
- It creates a greater sense of intimacy between teacher and students and helps build personal relationships within the learning community.
- It removes much of the distance between the teacher as authority figure or expert and the students as learners, changing the tone from formal lecturing to a more intimate sharing of inside information about how the world works (to enhance this aspect of her storytelling, Barbara creates an intimate physical setting by sitting on a low chair and gathering her students close to her and to one another as they sit facing her on a thick rug).

- It makes it easier for Barbara to incorporate her own interests and specialized knowledge.
- It allows Barbara to control the vocabulary used to introduce and develop topics.
- It makes it easier for her to personalize the content to herself and her students.
- It allows her to begin with familiar content and many examples that build toward the big idea rather than stating it initially as an abstraction.
- It allows her to synthesize and make connections as she goes.
- It allows her to frame the current lesson within the larger picture of the unfolding curriculum by connecting it to previous lessons and foreshadowing future lessons.
- One partial drawback is that the conversational style encourages students to want to respond and give input, which sometimes derails the flow temporarily.

In regard to this aspect of her teaching, Barbara has an image of herself as a storyteller reflecting earlier oral traditions, and she describes herself as teaching in a "campfire" storytelling manner. However, she cautions against carrying it too far, drawing contrasts with language experience activities that overemphasize props at the expense of big ideas. She typically first lays a foundation by focusing students on the big picture, then builds part of it in detail, then reverts to the big picture again to help them get their bearings, then returns to building a little more on the foundation, then returns to the big picture again, and so on. The frequent consolidations help young learners keep track of where they are within the larger lesson or unit.

In order to teach effectively in this narrative format, Barbara believes that teachers must: (1) recognize that it often is necessary and appropriate to convey a significant body of mostly new information; (2) understand that students have sufficient capacity to understand the information; (3) possess a good grasp of the basic content; and (4) understand how it connects to content in past and future lessons (curricular articulation). The narrative format allows her to focus on explanations structured around big ideas, so she offers coherent content rather than disconnected lists of seemingly random facts. In the process, she routinely emphasizes the logic of developments, the motivations for people's decisions, and so on. The combination of simplification and coherence makes her explanations more meaningful to her students and easier for them to follow.

Sometimes she will incorporate role assignment (or occasionally, more elaborate role play) into content development when it is suited to the topic, because it engages the students, provides opportunities for them to participate actively, and appeals to multiple intelligences. However, it can become a problem if it gets time consuming, disrupts the idea flow, or elicits too many misconceptions. Whenever she does use this format, she makes sure to conclude the lesson with review or debriefing activities in which she stresses the big ideas, elaborates on important points that were skipped or poorly developed, and corrects any emergent misconceptions, to make sure that her students leave with correct information.

In summary, what appears to be spontaneous and informal storytelling is actually a carefully prepared narrative constructed to enable Barbara to establish a content base that consists of a network of information structured around big ideas. This chapter has zoomed in to provide a close look at Barbara's everyday teaching style in action. In the next chapter, we will describe how she uses cognitive modeling to help her students see what is involved in constructing their own understandings of the big ideas she teaches.

Chapter 6

Modeling of Self-regulated Reasoning and Learning

In describing how Barbara sets up learning communities in her class-rooms (see Chapter 2), we noted her emphasis on practicing what she preaches: she consistently models caring, respect, collegiality, support, and the other attitudes and behaviors that sustain collaborative learning. Clearly, modeling is a powerful socialization tool, and Barbara employs it consistently and deliberately.

Developing Metacognition and Self-Regulation

Modeling also can be a powerful tool for teaching students cognitive and metacognitive strategies for thinking, reasoning, and regulating their own learning. These self-regulation goals are important even in the primary grades. We want students not merely to decode print, but to understand and reflect on what they are reading; not merely to form letters and sentences correctly but to compose coherent communications of their ideas; and not merely to produce correct answers to computation exer-cises but to employ good mathematical reasoning as they attempt to understand and solve problems. Similarly, we want them to learn to use skills for collecting and synthesizing information, drawing inferences, solving problems, and making decisions, not rotely or thoughtlessly but with awareness of their goals and the strategies they are using to pursue them.

Regulating and applying one's learning in such a strategic fashion requires not only *cognition* (processing information and performing intel-lectual skills), but also *metacognition* (keeping track of what you are trying to accomplish, what strategies you are employing to do so, how these strategies are working, and what repair or alternative strategies you might employ if your efforts are not succeeding). Even if they are learning successfully in other respects, young learners usually are not very reflect-ive about their learning, so consistent teacher attention to metacognition and self-regulation is needed to support their development in these areas of learning.

Unfortunately, many teachers have not been prepared to provide such support. One way is to *teach cognitive processes and skills as empowering strategies* for coping with challenges encountered in life outside of school. Teaching about a strategy should include not only propositional knowledge (what it is) and procedural knowledge (how to do it), but also conditional knowledge (when and why it is used). Thus, the teaching would identify the range of situations in which the strategy is applicable and provide opportunities for students to practice and reflect on its use in some of those situations.

The Power of Cognitive Modeling

An especially critical technique for teaching cognition and related metacognition is *cognitive modeling*: thinking out loud to demonstrate the inner subjective experience (self-talk) that occurs when people carry out cognitive processes with strategic awareness and self-regulation. Reasoning, problem solving, decision making, and other cognitive processes are guided by covert self-talk that remains hidden from learners unless teachers model it for them. Students may not learn much from watching a teacher identify the main ideas in a series of paragraphs, solve mathematical problems on the board, or perform experiments in the laboratory if these demonstrations do not include verbalization of the thinking that guides the observable actions. When teachers do share this thinking, students not only can understand what the teachers are doing and why, but can learn the general approach used in solving the problem and apply it later when working on their own.

Besides making transparent what is typically hidden, *cognitive modeling conveys instruction in first-person language* that is easier for students to follow and retain than the third-person language of traditional explanations. Modeling in first-person language provides students with an integrated, within-context demonstration of how to approach and solve the problem, using language that they can internalize and then apply or adapt relatively directly. In contrast, general information presented in third-person language or even coaching presented in second-person language (first you do this, then you do this . . .) must be internalized and then translated into first-person language before learners can use it to guide their own problem solving. Cognitive modeling allows learners to focus directly on the processes to be learned, with minimum strain on their cognitive capacities (Brophy, 2010).

Cognitive Modeling in Barbara's Teaching

Barbara routinely models self-regulated learning and application of big ideas. For a decision-making lesson near the end of her unit on clothing,

Barbara incorporated an event from her own family (her niece needed a winter coat) to set up an authentic decision-making activity (what are her options, and which one is best and why?). Most of her students had never thought much about the logic behind clothing decisions and other personal economic issues, so Barbara provided sustained modeling, questioning, summarizing, and other scaffolding to help them assess the options, make a decision, and communicate it in the form of a letter to her niece.

> T: Here's my problem. My niece, Jessica, needs a new coat for winter because her coat is too small. We're going to write Jessica and her mom a letter telling them what we think she should do to buy or to get a new coat. So, if you were getting a new coat just like Jessica, what are some things that your family could do? Howell, what could mom do to get you a new coat?
>
> S: She'd have to buy it.
>
> T: From where?
>
> S: From a store.
>
> T: From a store. [Barbara writes this on the board to start a list.] Does anybody have a different idea of what Jessica could do to get a new coat? What were you thinking, A.J.?
>
> S: She could sew one.
>
> T: She could sew one [adds to list]. Jessica or her mom could sew one. Do you have a different one, Dabney?
>
> S: She could make one.
>
> T: That's the same as sewing. Sewing and making. Hey, Dabney, have you ever gotten a new coat but mom didn't buy it and she didn't make it?
>
> S: Yeah.
>
> T: Where did it come from?
>
> S: A company.
>
> T: She might have had to pay for it if it came from a company. Are there any clothes at your house that you've gotten that didn't come from a store?
>
> S: Yeah.
>
> T: Where did they come from?
>
> S: From my grandma.
>
> T: Your grandma got it for you as a gift?
>
> S: Yeah [adds get as a gift to list].
>
> T: Derek, have you ever gotten any clothes that mom didn't make or she didn't buy?
>
> S: A hand-me-down [adds to list].
>
> T: Ah ha! What is a hand-me-down, Derek?
>
> S: It's from other people.

T: Who might you have gotten a hand-me-down from?

S: From kids from my church.

T: Are they older kids than you?

S: Yeah.

T: So they're bigger than you, and why are they giving you clothes?

S: Because they're too small for them.

T: It's clothes that are too small for somebody else, and were they nice clothes still?

S: Yeah!

T: Yeah, and you don't want to throw away nice clothes, right?

S: Yeah.

T: So what did they do with them?

S: Gave them away.

T: Gave them away. At Jessica's house, she's got a sister named Karen who's older than she is. Maybe Karen has an old coat that she's not using that she could give away. Anybody else ever gotten clothes from somewhere other than a store, sewing, a gift, or a hand-me-down? A.J., what other place were you thinking?

S: A garage sale [adds to list].

T: A garage sale. What's a garage sale, A.J.?

S: They sell stuff that they don't need or they don't want.

T: They sell stuff that they don't need or they don't want anymore. Do they sometimes sell clothes?

S: Yeah.

T: Why would you go to a garage sale instead of a store, A.J.?

S: Because it's stuff that's cheap.

T: It's cheaper at a garage sale than it is at the store because at the garage sale, the coat is already . . .?

S: Worn.

T: It's already been worn by somebody, hasn't it? So why would you want to go to a store if it costs less at a garage sale? Why would you pick the store instead of the garage sale, Laurel?

S: Because you're wanting it new or you didn't want something that was used.

T: So something that was new, something that hadn't been used.

S: A tailor.

T: A tailor. It could have been made by a tailor [adds to list]. A tailor or a seamstress might make it for you, just like the little girl in the book who went to the tailor that was her grandpa. Mariah, what were you thinking?

S: My mom went to a flea market instead of a store.

T: A flea market is kind of like a whole bunch of garage sales all in one place [adds to list].

S: Yeah, and sometimes it's not in a garage or a building. It's stuff on tables.

T: And people sell stuff on tables and some of it's new stuff and some of it's old stuff. But usually it costs less than a . . .

S: Store.

T: Store, because they don't have to pay for the building. They just go to a place every once in a while and put up their table and sell their stuff right there. So that's another choice. Did you have one more idea, Arden?

S: Knit it.

T: Ah, you could knit it. That's kind of like making it. It's another way of making it or selling it.

S: Sometimes the Salvation Army.

T: That's another choice that hasn't been mentioned. Sometimes a choice is what we call the Salvation Army or something in town called Coats for Kids [adds to list]. That's a place where families that don't have enough money to buy a coat can go and get coats, so the kids have a coat no matter how much money they have for a coat. So here are one, two, three, four, five, six, seven, eight different choices that Jessica and her family have when they're thinking about getting a coat. Did you realize there were so many things to think about when you were getting a coat? Now Jessica and her family have to decide what color, what kind, what size. She lives in North Carolina and it doesn't snow there, so would she want a great big heavy winter coat like yours?

Ss: No.

T: Why not?

Ss: Because it doesn't snow.

T: So one of the things you have to think about is the . . .?

Ss: The climate.

T: The climate. They also have to think about economics, which is how much . . .

Ss: Money.

T: Money you have to spend. She also wants to think about what's OK for her culture. Do you remember when we talked about wedding dresses? I had to decide what color. Here in the United States, our culture says you need to have a white wedding dress for most people, or maybe peach or like pink. In a place like Japan, white wedding dresses are bad luck and you need to wear a red wedding dress for good luck. So different rules for different places—those are called culture. Now, we don't really have any cultural rules for coats around here. There's no rule that tells you what color coat you have to have, right?

Ss: No.

T: Right, we know that just from our graph in the morning: it says blue and red and black and green and purple and pink and gray coats. [Barbara was teaching about graphs in mathematics. This morning she co-constructed a graph of the students' coat colors, intending to use it again later in social studies.] . . . So do Jessica and her family have to worry about what color to make the coat?

Ss: No.

T: Is she going to have to worry about culture very much when she makes this decision?

Ss: No.

T: Does she have to worry about economics?

Ss: Yeah.

T: Yeah, she needs to know how much money they have to spend. If they have only a little bit of money to spend, what do you suppose they could choose? What do you think would be a good idea if they only have a little bit of money to choose? What do you think, Tim?

S: Garage sale.

T: What would be another good idea if they don't have very much money to spend on a coat? What would be another great idea, Laurel?

S: Tell them you want a gift.

T: Tell somebody that you want a gift at Christmas or for your birthday. What would be another good idea, Gretchen?

S: You could sew one.

T: You could sew one because it usually costs less to sew the clothes than it does to buy them at the store. What would be another idea, Mariah, if you didn't have much money to spend?

S: Go to Coats for Kids.

T: Go to Coats for Kids. That would be if you had no money to spend on a coat. What do you think, Krista?

S: A hand-me-down.

T: Maybe hand-me-downs. Maybe she should use her sister's coat. OK, so she does need to think about economics. Does she need to think about climate when she picks out her coat?

Ss: No.

Ss: Yes.

T: What does climate mean, Arden?

S: How hot it is.

T: Do you think that's important when she's thinking about her coat—how hot or how cold?

S: Yeah.

T: Yeah, she's going to need to think about that when she picks out her coat. Well, let me tell you about my sister's family. Jessica has four sisters. There are five girls in my sister's family. Jessica does have an older sister. The dad at their house works full time. The mom at their house works just a little bit. So does that give you an idea of about how much money they have?

Ss: Yeah.

T: Do you think they have lots of money to spend on a coat, maybe medium money to spend on a coat, or just a bit of money to spend on a coat?

S: A lot.

Ss: Medium.

T: Kind of medium? OK. Because she's got an older sister at her house, what is one of the things she could pick? Tell me. Anybody.

Ss: Hand-me-down.

T: She could pick hand-me-downs. Now, because her mom works, do you think her mom will be able to sew or make her a coat?

S: Yeah.

S: She might if she had a lot of time.

T: What do you think? Do you think a coat takes a lot of time to make or a little bit of time to make?

Ss: A lot.

T: Coats have lots of zippers and buttons and heavy fabric. So you've got to be really great at sewing to make a coat. So do you think that one's going to work?

Ss: No.

T: Nope, so we'll cross that one off. What do you think, Renee?

S: You could have a gift from her grandma or an aunt.

T: Maybe from her grandma. Her grandma could give her a coat for her birthday or for Christmas. What do you think about buying one at the store? Could that be a choice?

Ss: Yeah.

T: What do you think about a garage sale? Could that be a choice?

Ss: Yeah.

T: What about having a tailor or a seamstress make her one?

Ss: Yeah.

T: What did we say about tailors and seamstresses? Was it more money than the store or less money than the store?

Ss: More.

T: Having somebody else make a coat just for you or clothes just for you? That would cost more than the clothes at the store because the clothes at the store were made by . . .

S: A factory.

T: A factory and made by a machine. Clothes made by a tailor or a seamstress are usually made by . . .?

S: Hand.

T: So which do you think would cost more money?

S: Seamstress.

T: Did we say they had lots of money for a coat or just medium money?

S: Medium.

T: So what do you think—should we leave tailor up there?

Ss: No.

T: Flea market is an OK idea, but flea markets usually only happen in the summertime because they're outside. So do you think that she'd be able to get a coat from a flea market now?

Ss: No.

T: Probably not. What do you think about Salvation Army or Coats for Kids?

Ss: Yeah.

T: What did we say had to happen for you to be able to get a coat from Salvation Army or Coats for Kids?

S: You had to be poor.

T: So who would get a coat from Salvation Army or Coats for Kids? People that don't . . .?

S: That don't have money.

T: Is that true for Jessica's family?

Ss: No.

T: Not really, so do you think she would go to the Salvation Army or Coats for Kids?

S: No.

T: I bet they would save these coats for the people who really, really don't have the money and really could use a coat. So that means we have Store, Gift, Hand-Me-Down, and Garage Sale. Get ready, because whatever we decide, that's what we'll put in the letter. Which one of those ideas do you think would be the best? Get ready to tell me why. How many people think she should buy a coat at the store? How many people think she should ask her grandma for a gift? How many people think she should get a coat as a hand-me-down? How many people think she should buy it at a garage sale? Which one of those ideas had the most?

Ss: Hand-me-downs.

T: [Starts letter] Dear Jessica. We heard that you need a new coat. Our class thinks that you should get a hand-me-down . . . from where?

Ss: From her sister.

T: . . . from your sister. Why do you think that's a good idea, Dabney? Why should she get a hand-me-down from her sister instead of going to the store or garage sale or getting a gift?

S: You won't have to pay any money.

T: You won't have to pay money. Do you have something to add, Mariah? [continues to elicit rationale to add to the letter]

Sharing Examples from Her Own Life

As part of her teaching about decision making relating to transportation, Barbara shared the logic behind her own transportation decisions. Explaining that she and her husband own both a car and a pickup truck, she began by comparing and contrasting these two vehicles, emphasizing features that made them ideal choices for some transportation purposes but not for others. She then continued as follows:

T: So, we've got a truck at our house and we've got a car. Sometimes I drive the truck. Sometimes I drive the car. We think about what we're going to do and that helps us decide which one to drive. When we're going camping and we need to pull our trailer, do you think we take the truck or the car?

Ss: The truck.

T: If we're going on a long trip and we want to have plenty of room and be comfortable, what do you suppose we drive?

Ss: The car.

T: The car. If we were going to drive someplace and we wanted to take some people with us, do you think we'd take the car or the truck?

Ss: The car.

T: If we were going to go someplace where there might be a lot of snow or where we need to drive off of the road, would we take the car or the truck?

Ss: The truck.

T: The truck.

At this point, Barbara noted that both the car and the truck were forms of personal transportation, then segued into teaching about the distinction between personal and mass transportation. She concluded with another personal example, telling her students about a vacation trip to Nevada in which she and her husband used several forms of personal and mass transportation and explaining the rationales for the decisions involved.

Modeling Decision Making in Real Time

Occasionally a student comment or question causes Barbara to change the way she frames or thinks about a topic. When this occurs, she usually thinks out loud right on the spot, making her reasoning transparent to students as she considers the problem. For example, early in the communication unit she was defining and giving examples of communication as people sending, receiving, and responding to messages. In developing the point, she started into an example that turned out not to work the way she intended but did enable her to model reasoning and decision making. She was elaborating the point that communication is interactive:

> T: So if I were sitting here by myself and none of you were here and I were saying, "Well, today certainly was a nice day. The sky was a little cloudy but the wind was low." Is that interactive?
>
> Ss: No.
>
> T: Why not, Chad?
>
> S: Because there's no one you can talk to.
>
> T: There's nobody to give my message to, is there? But what if I had Callie here or Mickey [her dogs]? Say I was talking to Mickey, "Oh, Mickey, what a nice day it was today. The sun was shining and the sky was blue and it was a nice day."
>
> S: They wouldn't understand what you were talking about.
>
> T: They aren't really getting the message, are they?
>
> S: No.
>
> T: Are they giving a message back to me?
>
> S: No.
>
> S: What if they barked?
>
> T: But would they be giving a message back to me about what I was talking about?
>
> Ss: No.
>
> T: Wait! Let me try this one! What do you think would happen if I were in here by myself with Callie, and I said, "Callie, do you want a treat?" What do you think Callie might do?
>
> S: Bark.
>
> T: She would beg. So I gave her a message. Do you think she got my message?
>
> Ss: Yes.
>
> T: Did she give me a message back?
>
> Ss: Yes.
>
> T: So that was interactive.

Her student's question about barking made Barbara realize that although her dogs could not understand comments about the weather, they could understand and respond to certain other communications, and that these exchanges would qualify as interactive communication. So, she explained this to her students, underscoring the point by indicating that in addition to or instead of barking when offered a treat, her dog would likely beg.

Subsequently, she was careful to avoid giving the impression that communication occurs only between humans.

Reasoning About the Curriculum

When Barbara was teaching about developments in transportation in the distant past, a student asked if people rode woolly mammoths back then. Barbara wasn't sure, and said so. She not only is quick to admit any uncertainty about a question raised by a student, but she welcomes these situations because they provide opportunities for her to model both the attitudes of a curious, lifelong learner and the reasoning processes that might be used to address the question. In this case, she began by noting that she had seen people depicted riding woolly mammoths in cartoons, but her "best guess" was that this did not really occur. She reasoned that woolly mammoths were large, dangerous animals that probably would attack anyone who tried to ride them. So, people probably did not ride woolly mammoths, just as they do not ride tigers or lions today. She concluded, "So, I have to say probably not, but I'll check on it and get back to you."

Barbara often uses the term "best guess" to signal to her students that she is reasoning from what she does know to make a prediction about what she does not know for certain. For example, when developing the story of bananas, she noted that they are grown in Honduras and showed Honduras on the globe. This prompted a student to ask if they also grow bananas in Mexico. She explained that she was not sure but assumed that they did because Mexico is right next to Honduras and has a similar climate. Another example occurred as Barbara was showing illustrations from a book on transportation in India and Nepal:

> T: In the countryside, animals are also used. These oxen pull a cart bringing in food from the fields, and this is an elephant—another animal that they have in India that carries people and goods on their backs . . .
>
> S: Who is she? [Indicating a person shown in the illustration who "doesn't fit" the scene.]
>
> T: It looks like a tourist, because she has a camera and she's wearing clothes that match the United States or some other country—not necessarily clothes that match that country. So my best guess is that she's a tourist. She's taking a picture of something she hasn't seen before. [Goes on to the next illustration.]

On another occasion, she modeled the process of observing details of cover illustrations to draw inferences about the nature of a book. The book was a fanciful children's book about a chicken who traveled the world to assemble the ingredients for an apple pie and then baked the pie. Barbara included it partly because it was an enjoyable story but also because the content dealing with the ingredients of an apple pie and what was involved in baking the pie was accurate. She introduced the book as follows:

> T: I'm going to show you a picture and you tell me if this story is going to be true or if this story might be a little bit made up. Take a look at the picture on the back. I can see a cow with a parachute and I see a chicken with a parachute. Right away, I should be saying to myself, "Is this a true story or is this kind of made up?"
>
> Ss: Made up.
>
> T: Sure, because this wouldn't really happen. I'm going to read this book to you and then I'm going to tell you what I really do to make an apple pie.

Barbara then read through the book with her students, enjoying its fancifully conceived and illustrated story, but also developing a list of the ingredients of an apple pie and exploiting the opportunities that the book afforded for teaching about geography (e.g., using the globe to locate the various places in the world that the chicken traveled to, and explaining about the climate or other local conditions that made this country a good place to find a particular ingredient).

> T: Here is what I hope that you will do. When you're at home and you're making plans for your snack to bring to school, I want you to think for just a minute as you are putting it in your backpack. Say to yourself, "Hmmm, is this really a healthy snack? Is this really going to help me be a better thinker or learner?" Or, if it's something full of sugar and salt and fat, you're going to want to say to yourself, "Don't eat that." But then if your mom says, "Mikey, that's the only thing I have to give you today." Then you'll say, "OK, it's alright once in awhile." But would you want to eat it everyday?
>
> Ss: No.

Many of Barbara's strategies for modeling and scaffolding her students' thinking were on display in a lesson that she taught on transportation around the world. She began by reviewing the previous night's home assignment, which called for composing riddles describing a form of transportation. She announced that she would read some of the riddles and directed her students to listen carefully to the clues and see if they could figure out the answer. She then continued by saying, "Are you thinking? Here we go. If you have an answer, just keep it right in your head. I'm going to pick somebody to see if he/she can figure this one out." She then led her students through the riddles, eliciting and discussing answers until a consensus appeared. At that point, she would lead the class in determining whether the consensus answer fit each of the clues incorporated in the riddle. If it did, she would ask the author of the riddle to verify that this was indeed the expected answer. Throughout the segment, she repeatedly made reference to "figuring it out," "finding the clues," and "seeing if this answer matches the clues."

To introduce the new lesson, Barbara pointed to two large maps that she had put up for use that day and said, "I have two maps up today, so a really smart thinker would be saying in his/her head, 'Hmmm, I bet we will . . .'" This elicited the answer, "Learn about transportation around the world."

Barbara acknowledged that this was correct, but then said:

> T: Before I get started, I'm going to ask you to vote, but I want you to think before you decide. I don't want you to go, "Oh, this is the answer." I want you to think. Use what you know already and decide whether you think that transportation in other places in the world is more like the kind of transportation that we have here, or more different . . . Then when we're done at the end of today, we'll decide if we're right the way we voted or if we want to change our mind." [The majority of the class voted "more different."]

Next, Barbara began eliciting forms of transportation available in the Lansing, Michigan area, and listing them for later reference. After putting the question, she told her students to, "Give me a thumbs-up if you were thinking." Then, as she called on students individually, she asked, "What are you thinking, A.J.?," "What were you thinking of, Krista?," and so on.

Barbara then shifted attention to Alaska, showing it on the map, mentioning some key characteristics (cold, snow), and talking briefly about visiting her sister when she lived in Anchorage. She then elicited her students' ideas about forms of transportation that she used or saw during that trip. Once again, she compiled a list. Eventually, she said, "So, hmmm, what do you notice so far about this list about Alaska and this list about our city? Look at them. What are you noticing? What do you think, Cole?" This elicited the response that the lists were mostly alike.

Next she showed a picture book about Vietnam and noted that "Dr. A." (Jan) would be visiting that country soon, and the book would show some of the forms of transportation she would use or at least see during her visit. Once again, she compiled a list, directed her students to compare the Vietnam list with the Lansing list, and elicited recognition that the lists were more similar than different. Then she showed a book on Kenya, introducing it as follows:

> *T:* Let's take a look . . . Oh, look—right here on the front cover. How is this woman getting from place to place?
> *Ss:* Walking.
> *S:* There's a boat.
> *T:* Walking. Oh, and I do see a boat there, too, Mikey. Boy, you're looking better than I am. You must really be thinking today.

After developing the list for Kenya, she again had the students compare it with the Lansing list and elicited recognition that the lists were more alike than different. Each list contained a few unique items, but a core group of forms of transportation found worldwide dominated all of the lists. To highlight this point, she concluded this segment as follows:

> *T:* So let's go back. Take a look. What do you think? Get ready to vote again: Do you think transportation around the world is more like our city or more different than our city?

Even though most of the students had voted "more different" at the beginning of class, they now were unanimous in voting "more the same." Barbara underscored that what they learned that day had changed their thinking about this question.

Barbara concluded the lesson with an activity that she introduced as follows: "I would like you to tell me one thing that you learned about transportation, either here in our city or somewhere else in the world. Are you thinking already? . . . Give me a nod when you have your answer ready."

Modeling Thoughtfulness and Reflection

Even though her students are young and prone to think in terms of absolutes, Barbara socializes them to cope with complexity, tolerate ambiguity, and be prepared to rethink things that they "learned" in the past. She emphasizes that teachers need to be ready to respond well to challenges in this regard, by taking time to explain to students who raise questions that begin with, "But you said . . ." She tries to model curiosity and openness to revision, along with steps that learners can take in order to find things out, figure out problems, and so on. Many of these elements are evident in the following excerpt, from a day on which she began a lesson by correcting something she had taught the previous school day.

T: I was thinking over the weekend about one of the things I told you on Friday. I got to thinking because sometimes when I'm driving home, I'll be thinking about things that I said when I was teaching, and sometimes I'll say to myself, "You know what? That doesn't really make sense." That's what happened when I was driving home on Friday. One of the things that I said was that the book I was reading didn't say that you had to comb the cotton. I got to thinking about all those seeds in there, and I thought to myself, "Even after they washed it, I think the seeds would still be in there, because they're kind of stuck into the fibers." And then I said to myself, "If they're going to spin them, they need to have all of the fibers going in the same direction. And no clumps."

After further clarifying that combing would in fact be necessary, she led the class in a review of all of the "land-to-hand" steps in developing cotton garments, emphasizing the need to "get it straight in our heads" and "not be confused."

Cueing Students' Thinking and Reasoning

We have shown how Barbara frequently models the self-talk involved in thinking and reasoning, and how she often uses questions to scaffold students' progress toward problem solving and decision making. In addition, she often cues thinking directly, using statements such as the following:

Talk in your head. You can think of lots of ways to move things on land.

Your last job is to tell me something that people have done to make transportation easier. Give me a thumbs-up when you have an idea ready. Be thinking about more than one idea, because someone else might think of the same idea and say it before you do.

We have talked about this before, so think about stuff you remember—it'll pop into your head. Give me a nod if you already have an idea—something about food that we could add [to a timeline].

If a student is unable to respond now, but might be able to develop a response if given extra thinking time, Barbara may say that she is going to move on but come back to the student when he or she has an idea ready. She even socializes her students to ask for extra thinking time in these situations.

Throughout each day, Barbara models the characteristics of a motivated and reflective learner. She often contributes her own answers to questions that she raises in class, and always develops her own set of responses to home assignments. When she conveys these to the class, she includes the reasoning or evidence that underlie the responses. She contributes wonders of her own when eliciting wonders, and she expresses her own curiosity and interest in following up when a book or a student question raises an issue about which she is uninformed or confused. She typically reasons aloud to develop her "best guess" on the spot, but often follows up by consulting dictionaries, encyclopedias, the library, or the internet to get more information.

Barbara's modeling of thinking about the curriculum makes visible to her students the cognitive self-talk and metacognitive self-regulation that characterize reflective learning. Her modeling also indirectly motivates her students to act accordingly. In addition, however, she uses a variety of strategies for motivating her students more directly. These are described in Chapter 7.

Chapter 7

Motivating Students to Engage in Learning Confidently and Thoughtfully

Along with managing the classroom and preparing effective lessons and learning activities, good teachers motivate their students to learn willingly and thoughtfully. Their classrooms feature *minds-on learning*, in which students follow lessons attentively, construct new understandings and connect them to existing knowledge, ask questions to clear up misunderstandings or pursue their own topic-related interests, and think about how what they are learning might be applied in their lives outside of school. How closely students approach this ideal depends on how successfully their teachers motivate them to do so.

Michael Pressley and his colleagues conducted several observational studies of highly effective primary teachers, including some in which they focused on the teachers' motivational strategies. Their studies supported two important conclusions (Bogner, Raphael, & Pressley, 2002; Dolezal, Mohan Welsh, Pressley, & Vincent, 2003; Pressley, et al., 2003).

First, they found that motivational strategies were linked to other components of effective teaching. The best teachers not only were effective motivators; they also were good classroom managers and used balanced curriculum and instructional approaches to accomplish interwoven academic goals (increasing literacy, numeracy, and content knowledge). What they did to motivate their students to learn was consistent with what they did to socialize behavior and teach the curriculum.

Second, the best teachers did not rely on just one or two primary strategies to keep their students engaged in learning. Instead, they saturated their classrooms with features likely to motivate them, while avoiding features likely to demotivate them. For example, the most engaging first-grade teachers used cooperative learning techniques, held individual students accountable for their learning, scaffolded their learning, made connections across the curriculum, encouraged student autonomy and choice, had a gentle and caring manner, interacted positively with students one-to-one, made home–school connections, provided many opportunistic mini-lessons, made deep and personal connections to students, supported appropriate risk-taking by students, made the classroom fun, encouraged student creativity, attempted to make content interesting and appropriately challenging, connected content to students' interests, made abstract content more concrete and personal, encouraged curiosity and suspense, provided clear objectives, gave effective praise and feedback, communicated that academic tasks deserved attention, provided clear directions, made in-school learning relevant to larger life, encouraged persistence, expressed confidence in students, generally set a positive tone in the classroom, and modeled interest, enthusiasm, and reflective thinking.

A similar study of third-grade teachers identified 45 practices that supported motivation, along with 18 that undermined it. The most impressive teachers frequently used the former, and seldom or never used the latter. The researchers' portrayals of their classrooms overlap heavily with what we observed in Barbara's classroom.

The list of 45 teacher behaviors that support student motivation can be organized within categories used by Brophy (2010) in a textbook on motivating students to learn. Brophy depicted motivation in the classroom as expectancy x value reasoning, within the social context of a learning community.

The expectancy x value model of motivation holds that our willingness to engage in and expend effort on an activity depends on how much we a) *expect* to perform successfully if we apply ourselves (and thus get whatever rewards successful performance will bring), and b) *value* those rewards or the opportunity to engage in the activity itself. Effort investment is not likely if either the expectancy factor or the value factor is missing entirely. We do not willingly engage in activities that we do not enjoy and that do not lead to valued outcomes, even if we know that we can perform them successfully. Nor do we willingly invest in even highly valued activities if we believe that we cannot succeed no matter how hard we try. Therefore, teachers can support their students' motivation to learn by helping the students to view learning activities as meaningful and worthwhile, and to believe that they can complete these activities successfully if they invest reasonable effort.

In addition to their own subjective thoughts and feelings, students' motivation is affected by their interactions with teachers and classmates. Some classroom climates support motivation to learn, but others interfere with it by making students fear failure and public humiliation. So, a comprehensive look at student motivation requires attention to expectancy factors, value factors, and social context (learning community) factors.

Expectancy supports enable students to approach learning activities with a sense of efficacy or confidence that enables them to focus their complete attention on the activity and bring all of their resources to bear in responding to it. They are not distracted by anxiety, feelings of helplessness, expectations of failure, or worries about its consequences. They enjoy appropriate challenges, look forward to gaining new knowledge and skills, and persist in seeking to do so. Expectancy supports observed in the studies by Pressley and his colleagues included accountability and high expectations (making students aware that they are expected to learn and will be held accountable for doing so), articulating clear expectations about students' classroom conduct and learning efforts, attributing students' successes to their willingness to put forth their best efforts, encouraging their efforts and praising their progress, encouraging them to take risks by accepting appropriate challenges, encouraging independence (expecting them to do as much as they can before asking for help), teaching them strategies for organizing their efforts and regulating their own learning, and letting them know that they can be successful on challenging tasks if they maintain their persistence. Supporting the expectancy aspects of learning involves combining high expectations with consistent scaffolding of students' efforts to meet those expectations and frequent celebrations of the progress they achieve.

Supporting the value aspects of learning involves helping students to appreciate learning activities as worthwhile opportunities to acquire knowledge or skills that will empower them or enrich their lives. Pressley and his colleagues observed the following teacher behaviors that support students' valuing of learning opportunities: communicating the importance of learning activities (and the connected idea that schoolwork deserves to be done carefully, then checked and corrected), providing engaging content (lessons and activities that arouse curiosity and anticipation, review content in a meaningful way, lead to creation of authentic products, build excitement when introducing new material, and so on), providing extrinsic rewards for desired behaviors and activities (used not as bribes but as tools to extend learning), including games and playful activities during lessons to make material more enjoyable or concrete, providing students with choices concerning certain aspects of their learning, and consistently emphasizing the importance of acquiring and using the knowledge taught in school.

The following teacher strategies observed in the Pressley studies involve *maintaining a supportive social context or learning community*: welcoming parents and adult volunteers to come to the classroom and using them to assist the students, decorating the classroom attractively with posters relating to the current units and displays of student work, emphasizing cooperation and working together, using cooperative learning strategies and activities, encouraging prosocial behavior and providing roles that allow students to help others in need, discussing the rationales underlying rules and procedures, communicating with families and making them integral parts of their children's learning experiences, using constructive and encouraging classroom management techniques, creating a positive atmosphere (modeling warmth, care, concern for students, positive humor, enthusiasm for learning), and communicating to students how much the teacher values them, cares for them, and wants them to succeed.

The remaining teaching practices that Pressley and his colleagues identified as supporting student motivation ordinarily would be considered curriculum and instruction strategies rather than motivation strategies. However, they have important motivational consequences because they make it easier for students in general, and struggling students in particular, to succeed. These *supportive curriculum and instruction strategies* included: assigning appropriate homework (reinforces the day's lessons, takes an acceptable amount of time to complete, and is appropriately challenging), appropriate pacing (neither too fast nor too slow for the majority of students), clear goals and directions for activities and assignments, concrete activities that allow students to apply what they are learning, connections across the curriculum, critical thinking (explains, models, and provides opportunities for students to develop and use higher-order and critical thinking skills), drama (provides opportunities for students to learn about and practice dramatic arts), learning by doing (giving opportunities for hands-on learning), lesson planning (lessons build on students' current knowledge; materials and activities are well prepared and organized), manipulatives/concrete representations, monitoring (continually assessing students' engagement and understanding, making adjustments as needed), multiple representations of tasks (uses a variety of methods to develop concepts), positive feedback (constructive, specific, and timely), scaffolding students' learning, stimulating cognitive thought (promotes deep processing and higher-order thinking skills), stimulating creative thought, teaching strategies for comprehension and problem solving, and encouraging student understanding and reflection (allows sufficient wait time for students to think following questions, probes and follows up on answers).

Barbara's teaching reflects frequent use of all of these major categories of strategies, as well as most of their specific components. Her strategies for molding her classes into coherent learning communities are analyzed in this book, and her curriculum and instruction strategies are analyzed in the companion volume (Brophy, Alleman, & Knighton, 2008). Consequently, this chapter focuses on her strategies for *providing expectancy support* (helping her students to feel comfortable and confident as learners) and *value support* (helping them to appreciate learning activities as opportunities for empowerment and enrichment).

How Barbara Supports Her Students' Confidence as Learners

When the expectancy aspects of motivation to learn are being addressed most successfully, students' attention is fully focused on the learning activity—reflecting on its content and responding to its performance demands. The students are not thinking about themselves or their levels of ability, let alone worrying about failure or embarrassment. This ideal is most likely to be approached when a) students enter the activity with productive attitudes and beliefs about learning (e.g., they know that it will require concentration and effort, and often involve making mistakes, but eventually be rewarded by acquisition of new knowledge and skills), b) the activity itself is optimally challenging (new and demanding enough to extend the existing knowledge base, but not so difficult as to be overly frustrating), and c) the teacher acts as a supportive resource person and coach but not as a judgmental evaluator.

It is difficult for teachers to create and maintain these optimal learning conditions for all of their students, because the students present individual differences that are difficult to address simultaneously. Even when learning activities are optimally challenging for most of the class, some of the higher achievers may find them overly familiar and thus boring, and some of the lower achievers may find them overly difficult and thus frustrating. Also, some students may have acquired attitudes or beliefs that are counterproductive to their own learning (e.g., tendencies to feel helpless as learners and thus give up at the first sign of difficulty) or to the learning of their classmates (e.g., overly competitive students who tend to brag about their accomplishments or ridicule classmates' failures). The latter problems are addressed through Barbara's strategies for molding each new class of students into a cohesive and collaborative learning community (see Chapter 2). This creates a supportive context within which to apply her more specific strategies for building her students' confidence as learners.

Structuring and Scaffolding Learning

Many potential learner confidence problems never develop in her classroom because her approaches to curriculum and instruction enable most of her students to achieve consistent success and make steady progress if they apply themselves. She teaches networks of connected content structured around big ideas that are developed with emphasis on their connections and applications. Such content is much easier for students to learn and remember than the mile-wide but inch-deep parade of facts that unfortunately constitutes the curriculum in many classrooms.

Furthermore, Barbara carefully structures and scaffolds her students' learning of this content, ever mindful that her young learners have only limited experience with learning in school and poorly articulated knowledge of most of the topics she teaches. She uses her narrative approach to introduce new content, infusing planned redundancy and frequent review of main ideas and key vocabulary to establish a shared knowledge base.

Only when she is satisfied that this knowledge base is securely in place does she begin to make significant response demands on her students.

When she does shift from conveying initial information to developing the content through questioning, she leads her students through several rounds of questions that begin with easier ones (calling only for yes/no or single-word responses) but gradually call for extended explanations. These rounds of questioning are fewer and faster paced when most responses are confident and accurate, but more numerous and slower paced when her students initially have difficulty responding correctly. She includes extra scaffolding and elaboration when teaching content that her students will be expected to apply in subsequent activities or home assignments.

Overall, Barbara teaches more advanced content and has higher expectations for her students' learning than most teachers at her grade level, but her consistent structuring and scaffolding of their learning enables them to make steady progress without experiencing undue frustration that might make them lose confidence in their ability to function as successful learners. For details and examples of her general approaches to curriculum and instruction, see Brophy, Alleman, & Knighton (2008).

Protecting Students' Response Opportunities

When Barbara's students do experience difficulties answering her questions, she makes sure that they receive enough time and (if necessary) scaffolding assistance to enable them to think through the problem and generate a more satisfactory answer. She makes it clear from the beginning of the year that when she calls on an individual student, that student "has the floor." The other students are expected to listen carefully to the exchange between Barbara and the student who has the floor, even if this student has trouble generating a response and even if the exchange should extend over several question/answer/feedback sequences. By *consistently protecting individual response opportunities this way*, Barbara simultaneously: a) eliminates most of the hand waving, calling out of answers, and exclamations of "I know!" and "Call on me!" that plague many primary classrooms; b) eliminates most of the peer distractions and felt pressures to respond quickly that often undermine students' ability to concentrate and think in response to her cues and follow-up questions; and c) makes it likely that other students whose knowledge of the point at issue also is limited or confused will benefit from the exchange (more than they would have if she elicited the answer from an eager responder and then quickly moved on).

Barbara has *standard routines that she applies during these individual response opportunity situations.* If the student supplies the desired response, she usually will simply accept it (or perhaps elaborate on it a bit) and then move on. Sometimes, however, she will address one or more follow-up questions to the same student. When students' answers are incomplete, she will ask additional questions or provide cues to help them answer more completely. When students are unable to respond, or offer a guess that is not even in the ballpark, she will attempt to elicit the desired answer by offering cues or breaking the question into two or more simpler ones. If this is not successful, she usually will provide a brief explanation and then ask a final question that she is pretty sure the student will be able to answer correctly, thus concluding the exchange on a positive note.

These routines make it clear to Barbara's students that they will need to listen to questions, think about them, and generate responses. If she calls on them and they remain silent or just take a wild guess, she is not going to accept this (by giving them the answer or moving on to get it from someone else). Instead, she is going to stay with them and extend the response opportunity, typically by first providing some feedback or explanation but then posing at least one additional question. Her approach communicates high learning expectations and accountability pressures. It also includes provision of any needed assistance in constructing understandings and ultimately responding successfully, however, so the emotional tone of these exchanges is supportive, not threatening.

Supporting Students' Confidence as Learners

Barbara routinely projects respect for her students as learners, treating them as both eager to acquire new knowledge and able to do so if they apply themselves. Her interactions with her students are replete with messages indicating that she views them as capable learners and that she will help them cope with any difficulties they encounter. Most of these messages are subtle or indirect, in keeping with the principle that expectancy supports are most effective when they keep students' attention focused on what they are learning rather than concerns about their progress or abilities. Also, most are directed at the class as a whole rather than at specific individuals, in keeping with her emphasis on maintaining a collaborative learning community.

In Barbara's classroom, learning is about acquiring and using important knowledge and skills, not winning rewards or besting peers in competitions. In addition to encouraging or celebratory statements to the class as a whole, she makes all kinds of comments that help individuals to understand and accept themselves and to be better understood and accepted by their peers. However, she does not draw individual comparisons or use labels that would encourage students to pay attention to individual differences in learning abilities. Any comments about the abilities of individual students tend to be positive ones that are similar to the ones she makes about the class as a whole. Furthermore, these comments tend to come in the context of providing support rather than evaluation (e.g., "Think about the question some more—you're smart, you can figure it out."). Importantly, they are just as likely to be addressed to a struggling student as to a high achiever.

As part of communicating her respect for her students as learners, Barbara frequently whets their motivation by revealing that she is about to provide some important information that "they" (adults in general, and writers of textbooks and children's books in particular) "don't think children like you can understand." For example, she taught a lesson on healthful eating habits, using a food pyramid and associated guidelines to talk about balanced meals and healthy snack choices, then following up by inspecting the nutrition information printed on packages containing snacks popular with children. In the process, she observed that, "They think if they write 'corn syrup' that we don't know that it's really a kind of sugar," and "They put the fancy name (dextrose) on it so they think we won't know."

She often uses a version of this ploy when teaching specialized vocabulary. For example, she introduced the term evaporate by stating that it is a "special name" for when water goes into the air. Similarly, when she introduced the term assembly line, she said, "Get ready, because this is going to be a fancy, fussy word. It's called an assembly line." She went on to note that an assembly line does not refer to a school assembly, although the words have in common the idea that you put things/people together when you assemble them.

When she views something as challenging but important for her students to learn because it is part of a set of big ideas being developed, she sometimes will extend this technique to suggest that a word is one that "They don't expect first-graders to know or remember, but I think you can." Or, she might introduce a key idea by saying, "I'm not supposed to teach you this, but . . .," and conclude with, "Next year, pretend you don't know it already."

Barbara also uses several other techniques for supporting students' learning of particularly challenging content. To begin, she may alert her students to pay special attention by saying something like, "Now I've got a tough question for you," or "This is going to trick you!" Later, when she gets to the main idea that she wants them to remember, she alerts them to this fact and stimulates their attention by saying something like, "Now, here's the news" (or the scoop, the big idea, the thing to remember, etc.). She then emphasizes this and other big ideas in subsequent lesson development and review, to insure that her students do remember it.

Sometimes she will revisit these episodes days or even months later. For example, one day, in the process of introducing a new science unit, she wanted to incorporate some information taught months earlier in a previous unit. Rather than just restate the information, she decided to try to elicit it from her students. Although her actual expectation was that at least several of her students would be able to respond successfully, she prefaced her question with, "I will be astonished if anyone remembers this." Then, when her question yielded the desired answer, she exclaimed, "Good remembering!" Such expressions of celebratory delight are frequent in Barbara's classroom, especially when she has challenged students and they have responded successfully. Occasionally, she will even break into a little dance, with or without the student who supplied the answer.

Another way that Barbara supports her students' confidence in learning challenging content or skills is to convey the message that although the learning task may seem difficult at first, she will provide them with the key information or help they need to navigate it successfully. She may even add a statement to the effect that, once you know the trick, "it's easy sneezy."

Barbara describes herself as mentoring or guiding her students in the spirit of, "I'm going to share (let you into my world, etc.), but I want you to participate, too." Her teaching conveys a sense of telling it all, not holding back, letting her students in on key insights that enable them to understand their world. She often concludes teaching segments by asking, "Now doesn't that make sense?" or stating, "Now you know what happened." Her teaching consistently conveys the expectations that her students will make steady progress in learning, the learning will involve constructing understandings that make sense to them, and these understandings will have applications in their lives outside of school.

As a result, *her students approach new learning opportunities with interest and confidence, and Barbara both encourages and takes advantage of this as opportunities arise.* For example, as she teaches a lesson on newspapers (focusing on what is in them, and how and why one might want to use them), she begins by having her students work in pairs or small groups to examine copies of the local paper, explaining that newspapers are "not just for adults, but for kids, too." She invites them to inspect both the illustrations and the text, looking for words that they can read. Then she begins calling on students to read passages to her or at least tell her what they found in the sections of the newspaper they examined. She lists selected key ideas, creating a graphic that will anchor the rest of the lesson. Meanwhile, her students are already actively and enthusiastically engaged because they have found content that interests them and discovered that they can read many of the words and even make sense of many of the articles.

Supporting Current and Future Self-Efficacy Perceptions

Barbara's lessons are structured around big ideas that have applications to life outside of school, and her development of these ideas includes consideration of potential applications in her students' present or future lives. She does not merely make her students aware of potential applications; she includes modeling and instruction that provides relatively direct preparation for these applications and supports related self-efficacy perceptions (leaving her students confident that they know what to do and will be able to do it effectively).

For example, in addition to modeling reading of health and nutrition information from the packages containing snack items, Barbara provided instruction designed to inoculate her students against undue influences from advertising and marketing ploys aimed at children. She led them through a close examination of a Pop-Tarts box, showing among other things that the illustrations make Pop-Tarts look a lot better than they really are. As a conclusion to the lesson, she said, "Now, here's the scoop. You are all smart about this now, so the next time you go to the grocery store and see a sparkly appealing box, or a box with a celebrity on it, or a really cool toy offer, you smart kids will say to yourself, 'I'm not going to be tricked by just those things. I'm going to think about what's inside. If I want what's inside, then that's OK. If it's healthy for me, if I can afford it, if I like the ingredients, then I'll go ahead and get it.' These are more important. Don't let them trick you with these other things."

One of the themes that Barbara emphasizes in teaching across the curriculum is choices and decision making. She approaches this topic most directly in lessons that teach students strategies for making good decisions, such as identifying the most important criteria that should be weighted most heavily and thinking about the costs as well as the benefits offered by alternative choices. Also, throughout the year and across the curriculum, she provides frequent opportunities for students to engage in thoughtful decision making, especially about potential applications of big ideas. Her food unit includes a lesson calling for students to develop and defend decisions about whether a depicted family should eat dinner at home or at a restaurant on a particular night (trading off time and convenience against financial costs and related opportunity costs), and if they do decide to eat out, what type of restaurant they should choose (cheaper and quicker but plainer food at a fast food restaurant or more leisurely but expensive fine dining at a first-class restaurant). Her clothing unit calls for decision making about which local stores one might choose as a venue for buying a shirt, and what criteria to emphasize in deciding which shirt to buy. The weather unit in science asks students to gather a list of weather sources and decide which sources are most reliable.

Usually these choice and decision-making exercises are not designed to lead students toward a preordained correct answer. Instead, the point is to build students' capacities for recognizing and applying relevant criteria and thus rationalizing their decisions. The decision-making situations she poses include not just relatively trivial personal preference decisions, but decisions relating to personal, social, or civic efficacy. For example, she has her students consider how they as individuals or as members of their families might provide assistance to people in need, acting either directly or through volunteer organizations. Another example is when she has her students first list the characteristics of a great student council representative and then discuss voter responsibility before her class nominates and votes for their representatives.

Some of these decision-making situations are realistic but set in the future, when her students will be adolescents or adults. For example, Barbara's teaching about shelter includes information about the trade-offs involved in renting versus purchasing living quarters, securing mortgage loans that enable families to purchase and move into a house now rather than having to wait until they accumulate the full purchase price, and some of the criteria that people consider when deciding on what kind of living quarters to rent or buy (location relative to work sites and schools, size, appearance, the family's income and budget, and so on). As a culmination to these lessons, Barbara asks her students to project ahead to when they are adults (possibly with families of their own) and write about their ideal living quarters, stating and explaining decisions about issues such as renting versus buying, geographical location, and desired features. In addition, one of the home assignments calls for questioning their parents about the reasons why their family lives where it does.

Many of Barbara's references to future decision-making opportunities focus on choice of occupation. Her health, science, and social studies units, for example, usually include lesson segments on occupations relating to the topic (e.g., food, transportation), depicted as, "something you might choose to do when you grow up." She encourages her students to consider a broad range of possibilities. In the process, she tries to inoculate them against traditional constrictions related to social class, race, or gender, sometimes directly but often indirectly (such as when she depicts a farmer, business owner, or police officer as female). If some of her students' parents or other family members work in an area related to a unit topic, she sometimes will arrange for the family member to come and talk to her class about his or her job. On these occasions, she encourages her students to ask questions, noting that the answers "will help you decide if that is a job you want to do someday."

Another frequently developed efficacy-related theme concerns inventors and inventions. Inventions come up frequently during historical strands of Barbara's units, and she regularly takes advantage of these opportunities to talk about the problem-recognition and problem-solving processes that lead to inventions, in ways that depict her students as potential inventors. She talks about inventions as beginning with a perception of a need (e.g., when early humans began expanding from tropical climates to colder climates, they perceived a need for more and warmer clothing). Then, recognizing the need, people begin experimenting with possible ways to address it (e.g., scraping and cleaning animal hides, then fashioning them into garments). She emphasizes that most inventions are not completely new ideas but ideas for improving on existing technology, and that new inventions appear every day.

Many of her examples focus on inventions that are easy for her students to relate to. Rather than talk about improvements in the kinds of machines that are used in factories, for example, her teaching about developments in clothing includes noting progression from buttons and laces to zippers to Velcro. In the process, she tells how the inventor of Velcro developed the basic idea for it when he began thinking about burrs stuck on his socks.

To further demystify inventions, Barbara models "possible conversations" that might take place as people develop awareness of a problem and begin to search for solutions to it. Some of these are conversations that might have taken place among two or more members of a group (e.g., scientists discussing how to create the scale for thermometers, Fahrenheit vs. Celsius), while others model what might have been taking place in the mind of an inventor working alone (e.g., the Velcro inventor thinking about the fastener applications that would result if he could develop a way to make pieces of cloth or leather stick together the way burrs stuck to his socks). These explanations typically conclude with the thought that some of her students might contribute significant inventions in the future, especially if they began asking themselves how existing technologies can be improved or how everyday processes might be done better.

Several of these efficacy themes were evident in a lesson Barbara taught about children's talents and how they can lead to future activities including careers. She emphasized these ideas with examples including Thomas Edison, her own father, and students who enjoy taking things apart and putting them back together:

> T: There was a kid named Tom—I don't know if his family called him Tom or Thomas or Tommy, but he was really great at taking things apart and putting them back together, putting them back together different than what they started out as, and even coming up with some ideas of things of his own that he could try to make. Let me tell you a little more about Tom. He was always, *always* trying to figure out how things worked. He would ask adults all the time, if there was something around the house he could take apart. He also would think of something and he'd say, "You know, there isn't a machine that can do this yet," and he'd draw pictures and he'd get stuff out, and he'd try and he'd work at it until he figured out a way to make it work. Finally,

he'd make something that nobody'd made before and he'd get some money for it. You know what he'd do with his money?

Ss: What?

T: He'd buy tools and stuff and make new things, and then when he was really great at making that, and it was so cool that somebody'd want to buy it because it was something that had never been around before, he'd get money for that. He had a talent. He had something he was great at. He was great at taking things apart and putting them together and making things that had never been made before. Does it sound like anybody you know—do you know anybody who's really good at taking things apart? Mikey, who do you know?

S: My friend Ethan.

T: Your friend Ethan takes things apart and puts them back together. He wants to know how everything works. You never know, Ethan could end up like Tom. Is that kind of like you, Marty, you have a talent for taking things apart? You know who else I know who was great at that? My dad. My dad was really great at that. We lived on a farm and he would take the engines apart on the tractors and put them back together. He had a talent for that. Well, Tom, he has a whole name, and maybe you've heard of his name. His name was actually Thomas Edison. It sounds like some of you have heard of him. Do you know where you've heard of him before? Do you know, Sean?

S: I think he was a president.

T: He wasn't a president, but he was somebody really famous.

S: He made the light bulb.

T: He was the very first guy who came up with the idea for the light bulb. But you know what, that wasn't the first thing he thought of. He also thought of a record player. He thought of a machine that showed pictures that was not like a movie but it was one of the ideas that came along right before movies and TV. He was one of those who came up with the first idea for some of those really cool things that we use all the time and don't even think about . . . Well, strangely enough, my dad who also liked to take things apart and put things back together again, do you know what he does for his job now? He's an engineer, which means he's the guy who comes up with the ideas of how to put the cars together. In fact, there are some cars in the world that he could walk over to and touch a part and say, "I made that up." He's an engineer. He took something that he was great at and now that's what he does for his job. Maybe Mikey's friend Ethan will be so great at putting things together that someday you'll be sitting around talking to kids and you'll say, "I remember before this was invented . . . and Ethan Moore invented it. He was the first guy to think of it and now look! We all have one in our house." [Shifts into follow-up activity.]

Following this segment, Barbara had her students talk with one another and draw illustrations of themselves doing things that they were good at. She then used the illustrations to anchor discussion of how childhood talents can lead to jobs in the future. In the process, she frequently "lifted" her students' ideas to horizons that they had not considered. For example, one student said that her talent was taking care of younger siblings. Barbara redefined this as taking care of people and suggested that it could lead not only to jobs such as running a daycare program, but also becoming a teacher, nurse, or doctor. When another student mentioned running ability, Barbara noted not only athletic possibilities but coaching and even becoming a police officer (because a police officer "has to do a lot of running while chasing folks").

In summary, Barbara supports her students' confidence as learners by structuring and scaffolding their learning, protecting their response opportunities, acting as a model and resource person, and developing her students' sense of efficacy in applying what they learn in their lives outside of school, both now and in the future. Besides providing these expectancy supports within a collaborative learning community, she displays a variety of strategies for helping her students to appreciate the value of what they are learning.

Helping Students to Appreciate the Value of Their Learning

There are three general ways to entice students to engage in learning activities: a) offer them incentives for doing so (provide extrinsic rewards), b) emphasize content that students find interesting or activities they find enjoyable (capitalize on existing intrinsic motivation), and c) motivate them to want to learn what an activity teaches because they view the learning as important or otherwise worth acquiring for good reasons (stimulate appreciation for the value of the learning). Barbara uses all three of these strategies, although she does less of the first and more of the second and especially the third than most other teachers.

Providing Extrinsic Rewards

Barbara occasionally uses stickers or other minor reinforcers when special circumstances call for it, such as during years in which her students are slow to begin turning in their home assignments regularly. However, she minimizes reinforcement approaches, preferring instead to work from

Glasser's ideas about quality (she wants her students to engage in learning activities thoughtfully and produce outputs that are high in quality, not merely good enough to qualify for a reward).

She received considerable training in behavioral theory and use of reinforcements in college, so her attempts to use rewards to reinforce desired behaviors follow the variable-interval, partial reinforcement approach. She communicates this to her students directly, stating that, "You never know when I'm going to do something cool." To reinforce turning in homework, she might award a prize to a student chosen randomly from among those who turned in homework that day. Or, to reinforce attendance by a frequently absent student, she might occasionally award a prize to a randomly selected student, and in the process, pretend that she picked the absent student's name first but then had to go to a second choice because that student was not present to claim the prize. The next time the student came to class, s/he would discover that s/he had missed out on a prize.

Most of the time, however, any rewards that Barbara introduces are psychological or social rather than material, and introduced in ways designed to socialize desired attitudes and behaviors in her students. For example, in the process of giving instructions about a homework assignment calling for students to develop their own personal timelines, Barbara observed that students who were paying attention and learning would be the ones who could "tell things to your parents tonight and add interesting things to your timelines." During a lesson in which she was reviewing the main ideas taught in a unit, she gave directions for a home assignment that called for students to list (and talk with their parents about) the most important things they had learned. She concluded by reminding them to be sure to bring their lists on Monday because, "We're going to make a big list and everybody's ideas will be on it." She knew that her students would be eager to see their ideas included on the list, so reminding them of this opportunity served as an extra incentive for them to complete and return the assignment conscientiously.

Near the completion of another unit, she reminded students that the booklets they had been working on (identifying and illustrating big ideas taught during the lessons) were due the next day. Then she added that she was leaving the day after that for Washington, D.C. (to attend and make a presentation at the meetings of the National Council for the Social Studies), and that she would take some of her students' books with her "to show them to social studies teachers."

Barbara often uses her students' responses to home assignments as bases for developing a list or some other graphic that will be used in the next day's lesson and then displayed in the classroom. The students' desire to be included on these displays can act as a motivator to help them remember to carry out their home assignment ("If you don't talk to your parents tonight and report back to me tomorrow, I won't be able to include you on the graph."). When she makes use of the home assignments the next day, she may reinforce certain students by saying something like, "You're glad you brought your book back, aren't you?"

More generally, Barbara observes that her young students do not need salient material rewards but often respond very well to social rewards such as a big praise, a high-five, or a brief celebratory dance. Sometimes she even uses bonus learning opportunities as rewards. One day, she passed out pictures of objects during a phonics lesson calling for students to identify the beginning sound. She added that those who did a good job would get an extra opportunity with leftover pictures. On another day, she rewarded a student who had been working hard to improve his classroom behavior by allowing him to participate in a second reading group that day.

By far, the most frequent form of extrinsic reinforcement observed in Barbara's class is *praise or celebration of learning*. Most of these messages are addressed to the class as a whole:

> Praising her students for remembering things from previous units and making connections, Barbara noted, "That's what a great mathematician does." She also refers to great readers, great scientists, great social studies thinkers, etc. when conveying parallel messages in other subjects.

> When Barbara was reviewing the land-to-hand story of wool (the steps involved in progressing from shearing the sheep to get raw wool, through processing the wool into thread or yarn and eventually into garments), her students noted that an illustration in the book she was using had skipped the step of carding the wool. Barbara responded, "They skipped carding, too. It's a good thing you guys worked on these steps yesterday. You know them better than this book does."

> After eliciting the things that can be learned from reading weather forecasts, Barbara said, "Well, you certainly have learned how forecasts can give you a lot of information."

> To reinforce home assignment returns, she said, "Thanks for getting your homework done. That will help us with our learning today."

In certain special circumstances, Barbara also delivers praise and celebration messages to individual students. For example, one day while gleaning responses from individual students' home assignments to add to a master list, she came to a student whose responses were good but already included on the list. Not wanting to make this student feel inadequate, she said, "Those are all great ideas. If other kids thought of them, too, they must be just right." On another day, she provided a moment of intimacy, humor, and reinforcement when responding to a student who reported an idea that occurred to him at home when he was thinking about something that Barbara had taught the previous day. Before addressing the substance of his comment, Barbara exclaimed to the class as a whole, "Wow! He thinks about school even at home. No wonder he's brilliant!"

Stimulating Intrinsic Motivation

Teachers can capitalize on their students' existing intrinsic motivation by emphasizing content they find interesting and activities they find enjoyable. However, compared to camp counselors or recreational group leaders, teachers' opportunities to use intrinsic motivation methods are limited: their primary responsibility is to see that their students accomplish the intended learning outcomes specified in the curriculum guidelines, not merely to see that the students enjoy themselves.

Many of teachers' best opportunities for taking advantage of existing intrinsic motivation involve *developing curricular content through activities that students find enjoyable.* For example, most students enjoy collaborating in pairs or small groups, so they prefer cooperative learning activities to tasks that require them to work alone. Students also enjoy activities that provide them with opportunities to use a wide variety of skills (e.g., conducting and reporting research) rather than requiring boring repetition (e.g., filling in blanks on a worksheet), as well as activities that allow them to create a product that they can point to and identify with (e.g., a display or report).

Barbara's students spend a lot of time *communicating and learning with others.* She often includes opportunities for them to exchange ideas with a partner (i.e., pair-share) during lessons. Some of her activities call for partners or small groups to work together to produce a group product. More typically, her students are assigned to produce individual products (e.g., journal entries, pages describing and illustrating big ideas learned), but are encouraged to communicate with peers before beginning the assignment (to develop ideas about what to do) or after they have finished it (to show and talk to one another about what they have produced). Her students tend to enjoy these collaborative interactions with peers, especially because she goes out of her way to socialize them to interact with one another respectfully and helpfully.

Through her years of experience, Barbara has learned how students are likely to respond to particular types of activities, and she draws on this experience when developing her unit plans. When possible, she avoids activities that have not engaged her students and emphasizes activities that tend to draw enthusiastic participation. For example, she finds that her students like assignments calling for them to first check things that they enjoy or have done, then add some elaboration or answer some questions on the topic. Consequently, many of her home assignments take this form. She generally emphasizes "minds on" over "hands on" as a primary criterion for judging the value of learning activities, but her lessons often include segments that allow students to explore artifacts (e.g., taste samples of foods from other cultures, use maps or scales) or to play active roles in developing the content (e.g., reporting their topic-related ideas or experiences, or enacting roles such as those incorporated into an assembly line).

Another way to accommodate students' individual interests and preferences is to allow them choices about what to do or how to do it. Many of Barbara's activities and assignments, especially those calling for writing, embody opportunities for students to select from a range of possibilities, either on their own or in collaboration with peers (or family members, for home assignments). Sometimes the choice feature is made explicit, as when she asks her students to choose which type of _____ they would prefer and explain why (perhaps adding an illustration). Examples of assignments using this format include asking students to decide with their families which birthday celebration custom from another culture they might like to incorporate into their own next birthday celebration; decide how they will format and share their vacation journal; or decide which of several inventions in an area (e.g., communication) was most important and explain why. More typically, choice is implicit, as when a journal writing or home assignment calls for listing the most interesting or important things learned in a lesson or unit.

Although it is relatively easy for Barbara to engage her students in activities that they find enjoyable, it is more difficult for her to structure her teaching around content that they already find interesting. For one thing, certain content in which her students are strongly invested can become counterproductive to her lessons because it leads them away from the topic (e.g., lengthy recountings of personal or family experiences that may be related to the topic but not to the big ideas that Barbara wants to develop). Also, some topics lead to overly enthusiastic but not especially productive comments and questions (especially currently popular toys, movies, or other products marketed to children), and other topics may be threatening to some students or morbidly fascinating to others (death, violence, war, tornadoes, starvation, etc.). Far from embracing these topics or situations, Barbara seeks to avoid or control them (her techniques for doing so are elaborated in Brophy, Alleman, & Knighton, 2008).

Another factor that makes it difficult to structure lessons around content that students already find interesting is that Barbara's young students do not yet possess much curriculum-related knowledge, and what they do possess tends to be tacit rather than well articulated. Consequently, instead of being able to build on existing interests, she usually is faced with the challenge of developing such interests in the first place.

She is more prepared than most teachers to meet this challenge, however, because her content focuses on big ideas, introduced with examples drawn from her own life and the lives of her students and their families, and developed with emphasis on life applications. Furthermore, her overall approach leads her students to expect that interesting and important things will occur in her classroom, including the unveiling of mysteries that will enable them to understand the world more like adults do. Within this continuing context, Barbara frequently punctuates her everyday lessons with techniques designed to whet her students' anticipation for what is to come.

Building Anticipation

Barbara often precedes or intersperses her presentations with comments designed to whet her students' appetites or build their anticipation for what is to come. If she has photos or illustrations that she wants to show, for example, she usually will gather her students close to her (sitting on a rug if she is sitting on a low chair, or moving their chairs close to her if she is standing at the front of the class). In the process, she often says something that communicates, "You're all going to want to sit up close to see this!" For example, during her transportation unit, she showed illustrations from a picture book about transportation in Asian countries. She prefaced this activity with, "Let's get warmed up and start thinking about transportation. If you tuck up, you'll be able to see my pictures. I'm guessing that you'll want to see these. They are very interesting. From camel cart to canoe, this book is about the transportation that they have in the countries of India and Nepal."

Once into a lesson, she uses a variety of strategies to whet anticipation. If she has been building toward a big idea or interesting item of information and is about to communicate it, she might first say, "And guess what?" for rhetorical effect. As alternatives, she sometimes uses longer phrases, often including cues about what to pay attention to. For example, when reviewing responses to a home assignment one day, she noted that one family had conveyed a particularly good idea, saying, "Wait till you hear this one!" During a lesson on plants, she cued the arrival of a big idea by asking, "You know what's cool about seeds?" When reading a book, she signaled a transition by noting, "An interesting thing is happening to Rachel." During a lesson on government services, she injected a reference to current events as follows: "You know what I heard on the news? Look me in the eyes, my friends. Guess what they're trying to decide whether or not they should do . . . they are thinking about changing how much it will cost to send a letter in the mail."

Barbara frequently builds anticipation when reading or telling stories. For example, having just read that a girl in a story had scooped up some salt water, she said, "Watch what she does with it." When she is about to turn a page to reveal an illustration, or unveil an object that previously was covered, she often projects a hint of mystery ("OK, let's take a peek and . . ."). She even includes anticipation strategies in her conclusions to lessons. One day, for example, she concluded by foreshadowing the following day's activities and then noting that she would leave "these cool pictures" out for students to inspect later in the day, because she was sure that her students "were curious about them."

Making It Fun

Barbara never loses sight of the fact that her primary responsibility is to see that her students attain specified curricular outcomes, but she also does many things large and small to make her lessons and activities enjoyable for them. This begins with her storytelling approach to conveying information or interactive narrative, as illustrated in Chapter 5. Relative to more formal lecturing, her storytelling is not only easier for students to follow but more intimate, lively, engaging, and otherwise enjoyable. Furthermore, Barbara not only uses the narrative format, but frequently injects dramatic elements through voice modulations, pregnant pauses, hand choreography, and role play. She frequently "puts on a show."

Also, even when she is not working in a narrative mode, she deliberately reduces the formality of explanations or situations in which she is questioning students by interjecting folksy colloquialisms (e.g., yup, folks, stuff, okie dokey, easy sneezy, wow!). These antics bring smiles to her students' faces and help them to relax and enjoy what otherwise might be stressful situations.

Besides sustaining a relaxed atmosphere, some of Barbara's colloquialisms are used in particular situations for particular purposes. "Easy sneezy," for example, is often interjected as a way to reassure students that something is not as difficult as it may seem (or at least, not after they have learned the "trick" that Barbara is teaching them). Another example is "jeepers," which Barbara uses to cue awe and wonder. For example, upon showing a photo of several hundred silkworms, she noted that the silk from even all of those silkworms would not be enough to make a single blouse. She then punctuated this with, "Jeepers!" She later described this as an "authentic jeepers" designed to help students appreciate why silk is so expensive.

In another example, as a way to personalize and make concrete the abstract notion of government regulations to protect citizen safety, Barbara focused on Cole, a student whose mother drove him to the bus stop where he boarded the school bus. She began with his mother's truck, identifying several of the regulations that the manufacturer had to follow to produce a safe vehicle (headlights, seatbelts, etc.), then considered the training and certification that Cole's mother had to get in order to qualify for a driver's license, then the regulations she had to follow in order to keep and drive the truck (license, registration, insurance, following the rules of the road).

Having established that all of these things had to occur before Cole could be driven in his mother's truck, Barbara then went on to note that another set of things had to be in place before he could board the school bus. To establish some of these things, she had arranged a class visit by the man who drove Cole's school bus. From him, she elicited information about the special training and licenses needed to drive a school bus, as well as some of the special safety features that manufacturers are required to install on these buses. Then, before going on to address the special rules that the driver had to follow when operating the bus, she said, "So there's a whole bunch of equipment that the bus driver needs to learn how to use. Then, I mean, jeepers, folks! All Cole has done is get out of his truck and get into the bus. Whew! Now they're going to start driving down the road, and there are a whole bunch of laws and rules about that, too."

During lesson segments in which she is questioning her students, Barbara uses a variety of techniques to keep them alert and attentive to her questions (see Brophy, Alleman, & Knighton, 2008, for details). One of these techniques is asking absurd questions, which allows her to repique interest and inject a little humor into the process. For example, when teaching about how different kinds of clothing are worn for different purposes or occasions, she showed an illustration of people dressed formally. As a way to cue her students to pay attention to the people's clothing and think about why they were dressed that way, she asked if these people were going out to play baseball. To stimulate interest in what she was about to teach about erosion and soil, she asked her students if they thought that people dug the Grand Canyon. When a question arose about where cinnamon comes from, Barbara took the opportunity to reinforce what she had been teaching about using information sources: Rather than simply answer the question, she said, "How will I know? I can't ask the cinnamon."

Stimulating Surprise, Dissonance, or Wonder

As part of her emphasis on unveiling mysteries for her students, Barbara highlights aspects of the content that she knows will induce surprise, dissonance, or wonder. She often labels something as surprising to pique students' interest, and sometimes even suggests that they convey the surprising information to their families when they get home. For example, one day she prefaced a new idea by saying, "This one's going to surprise you. Are you ready?" The surprising idea was that eating food helps our bodies to stay warm. Although this idea came up in social studies, she wanted to emphasize it because it connected to big ideas taught in science about calories, energy, and fuel. When the surprise is a big idea, she is likely to preface it with statements such as, "Look me in the eyes, because this is going to surprise you," or "Listen carefully, because my message will surprise you."

Barbara also highlights dissonant content that conflicts with her students' expectations based on their prior experiences, as a way to stimulate their curiosity and interest in learning the explanation. To introduce an important point about healthy snacks, for example, she said, "You know what? Here's the deal. One of the things I want you to realize is that you can take any healthy snack and make it unhealthy by adding things to it." As part of her introduction to a lesson in the clothing unit, she pointed to the sweater she was wearing and said, "This sweater used to be a sheep!" While discussing books, she presented the "shocking" fact that, prior to the printing press, only rich people learned to read because they were the only people with enough money to afford books.

After a student had identified movies as a form of verbal communication, Barbara accepted her answer but added, "Do you know what? Can I tell you something kind of funny that you might not know? . . . A long time ago, when they first invented movies, they didn't have sound with them. They were called silent movies [goes on to explain that they involved pictures with subtitles]." As part of helping her students to appreciate how many fibers have to be prepared for use and then woven to create even a single shirt, and how laborious this work was before the invention of modern machines, she explained that long ago, most people only had a few outfits, so they had to wear them all the time and wash them only occasionally.

Barbara also frequently prefaces explanations with comments or questions designed to induce curiosity or wonder. For example, to pique interest in the land-to-hand story of silk, she began by noting that silk is a popular fabric in our country, but "You can't make silk in Michigan or even the United States." She then went on to explain that silk is spun by silkworms, which are found only in places where it is possible to cultivate mulberry plants. To introduce awe and wonder when teaching about the past, she often contrasts conditions of living before and after key inventions (e.g., before the invention of the wheel, everything that needed to be moved had to be carried or dragged, and before the invention of motor vehicles, possibilities for land transportation were limited to what horses could carry or pull in a day).

Emphasizing the Importance, Value, or Life Application of the Learning

Mitchell (1993) distinguished between catching students' interest and holding it. He found that motivational techniques such as presenting students with brainteasers or puzzles, allowing them to work on computers, or allowing them to work in groups were effective for catching initial interest, but not for holding that interest in ways that led to accomplishment of significant learning goals. The latter outcomes were associated with meaningful content (students could appreciate its applications to life outside of school) and instructional methods that fostered involvement (students spent most of their time engaged in active learning and application activities, not just watching and listening). Other research reviewed by Brophy (2010) similarly concluded that sustained student motivation to learn curricular content and skills results from what Mitchell called "hold" factors. More specifically, *the key to motivating students to learn is to structure the curriculum around big ideas and develop them with emphasis on their connections and applications to life outside of school.*

If the content domains and learning activities they encounter at school have been well selected, students can come to appreciate their value. However, exposure alone may not be enough. Just as it is important for the teacher to scaffold the cognitive aspects of students' engagement in learning activities, it is also important to scaffold the motivational aspects, by *conveying reasons why these ideas are worth learning, explaining when and why they might be used, modeling how it looks and feels when we use them, and encouraging students' appreciation for the learning domain and for their own developing knowledge and skills.*

Barbara creates a context for helping her students appreciate the value of what they are learning by focusing on big ideas and their applications. She tries to maintain what she calls a "need-fulfilling" learning environment in her classroom, and frequently conveys the notion that there's always more to learn and that her students may want to follow up (on their own) to learn more about the day's topic. She often reinforces these ideas through statements such as, "That's why we want to learn more about it—because it's part of your life," or "Now you know what they had to do to make that shirt."

She also depicts learning as empowering and encourages her students to take advantage of learning opportunities. For example, after explaining that many people in the past did not have access to literacy and schooling, she noted that even today, not everyone learns to read and write because not everyone has schooling available like we do in our country, and in many places books are too expensive for most people to possess. When teaching about languages, she noted that her students could learn other languages at the community's high school when they got older, depicting this as an enabling opportunity that they probably would want to take advantage of.

Personalizing the Content

In Chapter 3, we described the emphasis that Barbara places on getting to know her students and their families early in the school year. Besides laying important groundwork for her efforts to establish learning communities, these outreach activities provide Barbara with a lot of information that she can incorporate throughout the year as bases for making personal connections between curriculum content and her students' lives. She follows up by making these connections almost continuously.

One of the most salient and quickly observable features of her teaching is the frequency with which *she notes connections between curricular content and the experiences of her students or their family members.* Barbara's version of the story of bananas not only assigned many of her students to occupational roles featured in the story (plantation owner, ship captain, etc.), but included a highly personalized detail: when the bananas were trucked from a regional warehouse to the local supermarket, the crates were unloaded by the father of one of her students (who actually worked at that supermarket). Because Barbara takes time to learn a great deal about her students and their families early in the year, she is able to drop in these kind of personal and family details frequently, even without prior planning.

She has found that when she makes presentations to groups of teachers, her personalizing of content is one of the features of her teaching that draws the strongest and most enthusiastic responses. Apparently, it never occurs to many teachers that they can personalize curricular content to individual students, their families, and other local examples. As soon as Barbara calls it to their attention, however, they immediately see its value.

Barbara acknowledges that her level of personalizing requires commitment and time, but most of this time is spent building the community and getting to know her students early in the year, not time actually spent doing it in class. She doesn't do it as a separate activity, but instead blends it into her regular lessons. She believes that personalizing engages her students' interest and excitement, gives them a personal connection to the information, and increases the value that they place on it. The personal connections that she makes include sharing of information about herself and her family, her students and their families, the school and community, or local connections to current events (e.g., her own brother-in-law and relatives of several students who were serving in the military overseas). Other personal connections include references to the prior history of the class ("Remember when we talked about . . .") or to her students' common experiences as children (references to games, movies, or other cultural products currently popular with primary-grade students).

When planning lessons, Barbara routinely looks for opportunities to connect content to her students' prior knowledge or experience. However, *she gives top priority to connections to the big ideas she wants to develop, not just connections to the larger topic.* If she does include personalizations that are not tied to big ideas, she will only say enough about them to pique interest, then shift to the big ideas themselves.

Barbara's introduction of a new topic typically begins with a story drawn from her own past or present life. For example, her social studies units all include historical strands, and as a way to introduce her students to key historical concepts, she schedules activities that call for students to construct family trees and personal timelines. She begins each of these activities (respectively) by constructing her own family tree (going back several generations) and her own personal timeline (noting and illustrating key events in her life, arranged in order from her birth to her current age). As she led her students through her personal timeline, she showed illustrations (photos from proms, graduations, her wedding, and other major occasions) and artifacts (her birth certificate, marriage license, teacher certification, etc.). In the process, she shared a great deal of information about herself and her family, past and present.

To provide an authentic opportunity for engaging her students in applying what they had been learning about healthy, balanced meals, she enlisted their help in planning what she and her husband would have for dinner that night. This was an authentic activity (i.e., the planning was real), structured by indicating that she and her husband already had decided that they would have cube steak as their entrée, but needed help in deciding what else to include in the meal. The meal that the class eventually decided upon was the meal that Barbara and her husband ate for dinner that evening.

To introduce a lesson on types of families (nuclear, separated/divorced, reconstituted/blended, adoptive, etc.), she began with herself and her husband and the families of several of her relatives as examples (including photos of a female relative with both her first and her second husbands, presented matter-of-factly as a way to help certain students feel more comfortable about discussing separation or divorce in their own families). As an authentic exercise in use of maps for trip planning, she enlisted her students' help in planning an actual trip she would be making the next day, traveling back and forth between her home (not the school) and Western Michigan University. When teaching about the trade-offs involved in using alternative forms of transportation, she drew examples from her own transportation decisions made when planning a vacation in Nevada and a visit to a relative in Alaska.

Other information about Barbara or her family members that emerged during lessons included:

- many people take vitamin supplements because they don't have enough fruit in their diets, which is why she herself takes Vitamin C
- her husband helped a neighbor extricate a car from a snow drift (used as an example of a way that community members can help one another)
- when her parents were growing up there was no TV, and when she was growing up there was no cable TV (adding that she still cannot get cable TV because she lives in a rural area that is not yet hooked up for it), included as part of her teaching about progress and inventions in communication
- a story about her grandfather paying a doctor in potatoes for a birth delivery (as part of a lesson on barter, money, and other forms of economic exchange
- showing the instruments from her home weather station
- bringing in her own store receipts, tax bills, utility bills, and other documents to use as illustrations when teaching about taxes and household expenses.

Besides adapting lessons to incorporate content that connects to the lives of herself and her own family, Barbara incorporates content that connects to the lives of her students and their families. For example, when she was going through a book illustrating six types of families, Barbara dropped in additional details designed to make the depicted people more real to her students and make it easier for the students to identify with them. Many of these details were drawn from her students' own families or experiences. For example, in depicting a boy named José, the book said that he enjoyed collecting things but did not say what. Barbara elaborated to indicate that José had a bottle cap collection, a rock collection, and an insect collection, reflecting collections maintained by three of her students.

One year, one of Barbara's students was obsessed for several weeks about bosses and boss/employee relationships, because a relative had been fired after getting into repeated conflict with his boss. Besides addressing his concerns privately on several occasions, Barbara elaborated on her usual coverage of the factory/manufacturing aspects of one of her land-to-hand stories, in order to say more about the roles and responsibilities of bosses and employees and about steps likely to be taken when these roles are not being fulfilled responsibly. In developing this content, she specifically addressed several questions and comments to the student who had been obsessed about the topic, and encouraged him to ask questions of his own.

Barbara's classroom is replete with displays of artifacts and illustrations created by her students or connected to them or their families. In addition, she incorporates such artifacts or illustrations into her lessons when opportunities arise. For example, as part of her introduction to farming, she showed a picture that one of her students had done depicting a farm. Later, when she got to the topic of restaurants, she displayed a photo of a local restaurant that was owned by relatives of one of her students. When recreating a book read to the class, Barbara provided pictures of local businesses to look into. During lessons, she often incorporates or even builds on her students' individual interests or other personal connections.

Barbara often solicits contributions to lessons from students who have some connection with the topic at hand:

> In a lesson on healthy snacks, she called on Mikey when talking about granola bars because she knew that he had had a granola bar for a snack. Later she called on Laurel to ask about how people sometimes eat their carrots for a snack because she knows that Laurel sometimes brings carrots and dip.

> When assigning students to the roles incorporated into Barbara's version of the story of bananas (see Chapter 5), she identified Tim as the owner of the banana plantation because his homework response had indicated that he might enjoy running a banana farm.

> When teaching about salt, she called on a student who had just been to Florida and asked him to describe the salt water at the beach.

> She directed a question about getting clothes on babies to a student who had two baby nieces.

> She included coverage of annual Pow Wows as part of her teaching about contemporary Native Americans in Michigan. In the process, she called on Renee to talk about what she had seen and experienced recently when attending a Pow Wow.

> When introducing the topic of trains, she elicited information from Mikey, whom she treated as the class "train expert" because he was very interested in trains and had many toy trains at home.

> When teaching about childhood talents and interests that can grow into adult occupations, she deliberately directed a question about talents to a student who she knew would say something about bikes (he loved bike racing). She did this because later in the lesson she was going to show a book about a boy who started repairing bikes and giving them to an orphanage. When she got to the book, she referred back to the boy in her class and his interest in bikes.

Certain students become "go to" persons for Barbara when she wants to elicit a particular response or reference to a particular topic. This is usually because the student has had a longstanding interest in the topic, or has recently begun showing interest in or curiosity about it.

> Seeking to elicit information about how the Pilgrims and pioneers got their food, she called on Joe because she was pretty sure that he would say something about hunting deer (he had been thinking and talking a lot about this topic lately).

> In a review lesson, she called on a student who had talked about oxen in a previous lesson to provide that response in the current review, and she called on her "tractor guy" when she wanted a reference to tractors (successfully in each case).

> Another student who owned several pets, including an iguana, became the specialist in answering questions about reptiles.

Sometimes certain students become so identified with particular topics that they become "answer triggers" to cue the class when Barbara would like a reference to these topics. During the transportation unit, for example, one student was associated with buses generally and the local bus system in particular because his father drove a bus in the system, and Mikey became the trigger for cueing train responses because of his salient interest in trains.

> When teaching about tortillas she called on A.J. a couple of times because he had mentioned tortillas several times in previous lessons.

> Wanting to make reference to the Mackinac Bridge as a local example of a bridge, she called on a student who had crossed the bridge recently during a family vacation.

Because she is so well informed about her students' families, Barbara often is able to incorporate references to their particular circumstances. This is most obvious in her units on childhood and families, where she calls on students to talk about their family compositions (with reference to six family types), vacation experiences, provision of help to neighbors or others in the community, and so on. If one of her students has a relative who works in an industry related to a unit topic, her teaching will incorporate references to that relative, and the student will be invited to show or tell something about the relative's job. For example, one student's grandfather was a chef, so Barbara included a photo of a chef in a lesson. Another student's father was a firefighter, and Barbara asked her to bring a picture of the father in his fireman's uniform to use during a lesson on uniforms in the clothing unit. If a relative's occupation connects very directly to big ideas taught during a unit, Barbara will try to arrange for the relative to come to the class and talk about his or her job.

In general, Barbara finds that personalizing to students or their families boosts topic interest not only for the particular student involved but for the class as a whole. Consequently, she takes every opportunity to make these connections. In addition to examples already cited, we observed her make reference to a student's father who worked as a mechanic during her transportation unit, incorporate a student's description of the way her grandmother baked potatoes into the activity calling for the class to plan what she and her husband would have for dinner that night, and direct a question about cruise ships to a student whose mother was about to go on a cruise.

Finally, in addition to frequently making connections to her own life and the lives of her students and their families, Barbara frequently makes reference to local (i.e., mid-Michigan) examples of topic-related businesses, institutions, and geographical features. Government conversations usually mention the nearby state capitol. Her food unit includes references to local crops and food stores, her communication unit includes references to local newspapers and television stations, and so on. In teaching about infants, she made frequent references to and showed photos of developments in the first few months of the life of a baby recently delivered by another teacher at her school, and in talking about the importance of trains transporting raw materials and finished products (not just people), she noted that many of the freight cars seen in Michigan are transporting autos manufactured at Michigan-based companies.

In summary, Barbara floods her classroom with motivational elements intended to encourage her students to become active and reflective learners. Key features include her personal modeling and learning community socialization, her high expectations coupled with sufficient scaffolding and encouragement to support her students' confidence as learners, and her emphasis on big ideas, authentic activities, personalization, and other approaches to curriculum and instruction that build her students' appreciation of the value of what they are learning.

Chapter 8

Individualizing to Meet Students' Needs

Previous chapters have illustrated how Barbara forges each new class into a cohesive learning community and frequently makes reference to this community when interacting with her students. In this chapter, we examine the ways in which, working within the learning community context, she also identifies and addresses the unique needs of each individual. Her concern about individuals extends to all of her students, not just those with identified special needs. It also includes their personal and social needs, not just their academic needs.

Barbara reaches out to welcome all of her students and support their development of a sense of belongingness and well-being in her classroom. She is especially welcoming toward those first-graders who already carry special education labels. In fact, she has volunteered to teach not only the special needs first-graders who live nearby and would be coming to her school anyway, but also other special-needs first-graders whose parents have decided to take advantage of the district's schools-of-choice program and send their children to her classroom. Consequently, each year her roster includes basic special education first-graders from the entire district, carrying a range of labels including emotionally impaired, autistic, and cognitively impaired (in one recent year, 18 of her 22 students were receiving some form of outside support for their learning). Barbara pays attention to these labels and coordinates with relevant special education personnel, but she also pushes beyond the labels and gets to know the personal qualities, strengths, and needs of each individual.

As she develops each learning community, one of her priorities is to provide special needs students with structure and support to enable them to feel comfortable and be successful in her class. She already has established positive relationships with many of her incoming first-graders because she made it her business to get to know them during the previous year when they were in kindergarten. The letter that she sends to the families before the beginning of the school year also helps establish positive expectations.

For example, the letter includes an explanation of her "magic number" system for identifying individuals' work and belongings, and it reveals the number assigned to the child. Barbara notes that all of the students she has ever taught, including all of those with diagnosed impairments, have been able to tell her their numbers upon walking through the door on the first day of school. They arrive already knowing something specific that pertains to the class and certifies their membership in the classroom community. Furthermore, as they explore the room, they encounter many spaces and things that "belong to them" because they are marked with their numbers: a seat, mailbox, book box, lunch choice tag, name tag, and folders.

Throughout the year, and especially during the first few weeks, Barbara holds "team time" discussions with her students to "create a common vision of how our class will be." She makes sure that all are present (i.e., none have been pulled out for special education at some other location in the school) during these times, as well as any times in which she is giving information that each student needs to know. *Her special education students are included in all activities that affect the class as a whole* (writing the class pledge, listing responsibilities, assigning classroom jobs, participating in team building games, etc.). They also are included in birthday celebrations, field trips, and other special occasions that no child wants to miss.

Special needs students benefit from the information, cues, and reminders that she posts in her classroom, such as the illustrated daily schedule and the charts listing things that will (and will not) work to help them get what they need. They also benefit from Barbara's efforts to construct her curricula around big ideas that are phrased in repeatable, memorable summary sentences, and developed in ways that connect to their prior experiences and their current lives outside of school.

Establishing Individual Goals

When asked how she supports struggling students, the first thing Barbara mentions is her focus on their individuality. *She develops information about each student's unique strengths and needs*: "I go back to last year's teacher and start to find out what things this kid is good at, and what are places where I am going to have to provide support." She informs herself about any special education labels that her students may be carrying, and about any special support services they get. However, "The first few days I watch the kids to see how they function, regardless of whether they carry special education labels such as ADHD, or get special speech services, or whatever. I look at the kids to see them as individuals and begin to determine what special goals I will have for each of them."

After this initial period of information gathering and observation, she develops what she calls *personal education goals* (PEGs) for each student.

These PEGs are broad-ranging, including not only curriculum goals such as increasing the number of words that the student can recognize on sight, but also social or behavioral goals such as improving the student's abilities to build friendships or resolve conflicts.

Before long, in addition to the many goals she holds for the class as a whole, Barbara has formulated at least three PEGs for each individual. For example, one boy lacked self-confidence in approaching his assignments, so one PEG that Barbara set for him was to help him learn to approach tasks by looking for what he could do rather than what he could not. She also noted that he was overly concerned with getting immediate approval of his work, often right from the beginning, rather than waiting until he completed the assignment. So, a second PEG established for this boy was to help him develop criteria that he could use to evaluate for himself how well he was doing. Barbara also noticed that the boy tended to chew on his collar or other parts of his clothing, so a third PEG was to make him more conscious of this habit and wean him away from it.

For each PEG that she establishes with each student, Barbara develops a timeline specifying markers that will provide indications of progress through an expected trajectory of improvement, accompanied by target dates. She also formalizes at least one current PEG for each student, by sending home a letter explaining the goal, describing the strategies that she will be using in the classroom, and suggesting strategies that the parents can use at home. She welcomes input from the children themselves and from their family members about the appropriateness of these goals and the best ways to approach them.

As the target dates arrive, she confers with the children to evaluate progress and plan next steps. These evaluations also may include follow-up contacts with the families. Through a letter or phone call, Barbara will report on the progress that she has seen at school, ascertain what the family members or guardians have seen at home, and negotiate a plan for where to go from here. If the child has progressed to the point that it is no longer necessary to place special emphasis on the trajectory targeted for improvement, she might say something like, "Joey thinks that he is doing much better at this now, and I agree. What do you see at home? Do you think we need to continue to emphasize this goal, or should we move on to another, different goal?"

By the end of the year, at least three or four of her PEGs for each student have been formalized with input from the student and the family. In addition, she has other PEGs for each student that she does not formalize in this way, but stays conscious of during her teaching. Consequently, even though most of her time is spent teaching the class as a whole, she frequently addresses PEGs for individuals. For example, with "failure syndrome" students who are frequently frustrated or even prone to learned helplessness (those whom she is trying to teach to look at what they can do

as opposed to what they cannot do), she will take advantage of opportunities that arise to "do a drive-by" or "slip in a comment sideways," such
as, "Sure you can finish it, look at how much you've done already!"

Primary students typically progress through relatively predictable trajectories of development, both in personal and social capacities and in
curriculum-related knowledge and skills. Barbara has paid close attention
to these trajectories, and she puts this knowledge to good use in assessing
each student's current status and probable next steps in development and
in setting target dates accordingly (taking into account the assistance that
she will provide).

She knows that supporting their development requires accepting them
as they are now and moving forward from there (rather than thinking
about ways in which they may fall short of some model of an ideal first-
grader). So, with students who do not yet know the letters of the alphabet, or do not know sound-letter correspondences, or have few sight
words, she determines what they do know and then develops plans for
supporting their progress through relevant trajectories (i.e., trajectories of
growth in knowledge of the alphabet, letter-sound correspondences, and
sight words). Meanwhile, with other students who are already further
along on these trajectories, she works on more advanced goals.

She says, "One thing I do that really supports struggling learners is
maintain an ongoing assessment of how I think kids are doing in relation
to their own prior progress. I have a picture in my head, for example, of
kids as writers—the different stages they go through and what I should be
expecting. If you're doing this now, here's what I'm going to nudge you
towards next. I'm going to figure out wherever you are on that continuum
of progress in writing, and nudge you a little bit further. And where you
are, I don't necessarily expect somebody else to be."

Barbara frequently verbalizes these ideas to her students: not everybody is the same, needs the same thing, will be working on the same
thing, needs my help in the same way, and so on. Occasionally she will
make a specific point of emphasizing this, as in "Eliza might go to the
doctor and Shavonne might go to the doctor, but even if they go to the
same doctor, they're not going to get the same treatment if Eliza has a
broken arm and Shavonne has a cold. Eliza will not get a shot for a cold;
she will get treatment for her broken arm. My job is the same way. You
are all here at school to learn, but you need to learn different things. You
are all good at different things, but you all need to get better at different
things. I will find whatever it is that you're good at and that you need to
get better at, and I will help you get better at the things you need to get
better at. Sometimes kids need to get better at learning how to treat
people, and that's what I'm here to do. Sometimes kids need to learn to
get better at how to write words. I'm here to do that, too. Whatever you
need to get better at, that's what I'll help you to do."

In summary, as part of establishing her learning community at the beginning of the school year, Barbara emphasizes that we will all be here learning together and helping one another learn, but also notes that individuals differ in what they have learned already and what they need to learn next, and she will take that into account in teaching them. She then follows through by assessing each individual's progress to date across a range of trajectories, develops both formal goals and informal expectations tied to target dates, and works with them accordingly. She follows the same basic procedures with all of her students, including any that carry special education labels or receive special supportive services.

Coordinating with Support Staff and Paraprofessionals

Barbara willingly assumes personal responsibility for supporting all of her students' progress along the trajectories she addresses. Furthermore, she believes that, as the homeroom teacher, she has the best-informed "big picture" of each student as an individual "whole child," and thus is in the best position to coordinate any special services a student might receive within a coherent overall plan. As she explains it:

> I consider myself for every single student to be the "buck stops here lady." I take responsibility for all of my students regardless of their label, their placement, the supports they may have, or the severity of their disabilities. I consider that I need to be part of all of the decisions made for any particular student in my class. There may be many people working with the student, but when it comes down to it, I am ultimately responsible for making sure that we do the best we can for that student. I consider myself to be an advocate for all of my kids, and I know that my struggling learners need me to be an advocate for them the most.

Whenever possible, Barbara prefers to minimize the degree to which her students are pulled out of class for special instruction in other settings. She also works to make sure that the pulled-out students experience a sense of belonging and acceptance in her classroom. She socializes classmates to be accepting and supportive of those who are pulled out, and she develops routines for the pulled-out students that will help them know what to do when they return to her class and how to get caught up on any jobs that they missed.

Particularly when a student faces multiple challenges (physical, emotional, and cognitive), many different people get involved in developing treatment plans and providing services: resource room teachers, special education teachers, speech teachers, occupational therapists, physical therapists, English as a Second Language teachers, Title I staff and para-professionals, counselors, social workers, and so on. Barbara believes that part of her job is to be the "air traffic controller" in these situations— to make sure that whatever pull-outs, tutors, extra supports, or special services that have been put into place are actually meeting the goals that the group has established for the student. For example:

> Say the speech teacher wants to do the very best she can for the student's speech goals. So when she says, "I will meet with him twice a week for half an hour each time. I also will pair him with a speech buddy and they can work together for 15 minutes a day. Also, twice a week I want them to work on an articulation program on the computer, and I will assign daily work on sounds to take home as homework," it's my job to perform a cost/benefit analysis and ask if all of those things will be beneficial for that student. The student may have needs in four other areas besides speech, and perhaps he will miss something important because we are doing so many speech things. Where this appears to be a problem, I am the one who needs to be saying, "You know, maybe too much is going on with speech, and we need to put some of our resources and energy in these other areas." I believe that I need to be the one who manages all these resources, so I am comfortable raising these kind of questions with colleagues.

Besides the air traffic controller analogy, Barbara uses a medical case manager analogy to talk about her role in these situations. She notes that when someone is in a health crisis and is seeing a lot of different specialists, one individual physician will act as the case manager who oversees execution of the overall treatment plan, stays in touch with all of the other professionals who interact with the patient, and makes sure that their efforts are coordinated (so the different treatment providers do not overlap unnecessarily or even negate the benefits of one another's efforts).

In these situations, Barbara both shares and elicits reciprocal sharing of plans and information about the student, making sure that she has all of the information she needs to keep track of events as they unfold. "If the speech teacher wants to talk to the family, that's fine, but then share that information with me. If the resource room teacher wants to send a newsletter home describing the things the kid worked on, that's great, but send me a copy of it. I need to have all of this information so I can make sure that our efforts are cost effective for reaching our goals for the student, so *I stay in very close contact with all of these specialists and work with them to make sure that what they do with my students is supporting what I am doing in the classroom, and vice versa.*" Recognizing the value of this kind of collaboration, most specialists have responded positively to Barbara's coordination efforts, as the following examples illustrate.

Barbara collaborates with teachers of English as a Second Language (ESL) to develop ESL activities that will help her students to be successful when they return to her classroom. For example, the day's writing activity might call for students to create a personal narrative (a written narration of a personal experience). Native English speakers usually find this easy to do and compose stories such as, "I went to Chucky Cheese and we played some games and we ate some pizza and I opened presents and it was a great party." This kind of writing assignment can be difficult for ESL students, however, so Barbara asks the ESL teacher to help them prepare for it, by "getting the story all together in their head so they've gone through what happened first, what happened next, and what happened last, and then help them record it with pictures so that when they come into the room and it's writing time, they're ready to just record the story because they've already had somebody help them organize it."

Barbara finds that these kinds of activities are more helpful to her ESL students than work with flashcards or games that are not coordinated with her curriculum. She will meet with the ESL teacher periodically to update her requests as her students progress through the curriculum. In the writing example, she initially requested the ESL teacher to help the students create a story about themselves, but later she added the specification that the story should include a distinct beginning, middle, and end.

A paraprofessional comes into Barbara's class to work with students who are struggling to learn the alphabet and sound-letter correspondences. To make sure that the paraprofessional's work reinforces her own teaching, Barbara provides her with directions and materials that she can use to recreate lessons that Barbara has already taught to the class as a whole. In this way, struggling students get additional exposure to this material, but in small-group sessions where they get more frequent opportunities to respond and their progress can be monitored more closely. Alternatively, Barbara sometimes asks the paraprofessional to preview a lesson with a small group before Barbara teaches it to the whole class, so that the struggling students enter the whole-class lesson already familiar with the basic concept or skill to be taught and the pictures or other materials used in teaching it.

Barbara also works with other specialists to coordinate activities and help her struggling students succeed in her classroom. She keeps the resource room teacher abreast of what is going on each week (for example, providing lists of words that the students are currently learning), and she provides copies of all the instructional materials and activities currently used in her classroom. The two teachers collaborate to make sure that the resource room students can make connections between what they do in the resource room and what they do in Barbara's classroom.

Similarly, the speech teacher gets copies of the poems that Barbara includes in her teaching each week and uses these poems for the articulation practice done with students who are working on particular sounds and articulation errors. At the end of the week, when all of Barbara's students will be asked to read these poems aloud to a partner or to Barbara herself, the students getting speech therapy will be much better prepared to do so than they would have been otherwise.

For autistic students, the speech teacher adds visual illustrations to help them grasp the meaning of the poem. For students who frequently present behavior problems, the speech teacher sometimes will use "social stories" written to address those problems as the content base for speech therapy activities. In fact, she sometimes collaborates with Barbara in writing social stories.

These kinds of coordinations enable Barbara's students to use materials and experience teaching techniques during pull-out time that go hand-in-hand with what happens in her classroom. Barbara finds that her students make the connections and carry over the information. She does not expect that all of the pull-out time will be used for these activities, however. She recognizes that the speech teacher, for example, has worthwhile goals and activities of her own that she needs to address using her own materials and teaching techniques.

Consequently, *besides arranging for pull-out instruction to support her classroom instruction, Barbara also arranges to do things in her classroom that support the goals and activities of the pull-out teachers.* For example, among the many books that she keeps available in her classroom, she includes copies of books that some of her students are currently using during pull-out instruction with reading teachers. She makes sure that these students spend part of their individual reading time each day reading the books they are currently reading with a reading teacher.

As another example, Barbara has arranged with both the basic special education teacher and her classroom paraprofessional to make sure that all three of them use the same approach in dealing with a student who frequently presents behavior problems. The approach involves helping the student to recognize and assume responsibility for changing inappropriate behavior. It includes routinely used messages or questions such as, "Are you helping our class?" Hearing the same basic messages and questions, phrased in the same way each time, helps this student to recognize that he is behaving inappropriately and needs to focus on what he has been doing, why it is inappropriate, and what he should be doing instead. To remind themselves that this boy needs these consistent questions and messages, and to make it easier to provide them, both Barbara and the special education teacher keep signs containing the key phrases handy for quick reference, and Barbara has provided the paraprofessional with an index card that contains the same material. She also has requested the boy's family to use the same approach when dealing with behavioral issues in the home.

In summary, Barbara stays in close contact with both educational specialists and paraprofessionals to coordinate the efforts of everyone involved with her students. She tries to make sure that at least part of what goes on during pull-out instruction is coordinated with her curriculum and will help the students to succeed in her classroom, and she does what she can to support the specialists' agendas. This complicates the efforts of all concerned, but Barbara usually gets good cooperation from these colleagues because they recognize that she is fully accepting of special needs students, makes sure to include them as full members of her classroom community, and enables them to learn successfully.

Socializing and Teaching Special Needs Students

Barbara holds high expectations for all of her students, including those with special needs. She firmly believes that whatever her students lack when they come to her, she will help them to become more successful— personally and socially as well as academically. She notes that, "It is really difficult to survive in the world if you don't know how to be a great person, how to treat people, how to get along with people, how to learn about yourself, and how to figure out how the world works." Much of her early work with certain students focuses on socialization toward these goals.

She teaches lessons to the whole class, focusing on big ideas and constructing graphics or other learning resources in collaboration with her students as the lesson proceeds. Then she follows up with in-class or home assignments calling for students to write about or apply the big ideas in some way. When necessary, she will arrange to reteach or elaborate on the lesson for struggling students who need extra scaffolding, and she may elaborate or adjust the follow-up assignments as well.

Her willingness to adjust or even substitute for regular lessons, instructional materials, and assignments is part of a pattern of high expectations and self-efficacy perceptions that is commonly observed in teachers who are notably successful in eliciting student achievement gains, especially with at-risk students (Good & Brophy, 2008). These teachers accept responsibility for teaching their students, believing that the students are capable of learning and that they (the teachers) are capable of teaching them successfully. If students do not learn something the first time, they teach it again, and if the regular instructional materials do not do the job, they find or make other ones.

Barbara never loses sight of long-term goals, but she is willing to make short-term accommodations when students appear to need them. For example, if students faced with a page of 20 mathematics problems become frustrated and begin to develop learned helplessness symptoms before finishing (if they finish), she might temporarily require them to finish only the first ten problems. However, she will emphasize that they need to make sure that they "understand how the problems work"—understand the concept or skill being developed.

As another example, Barbara once taught a child who fatigued easily and had very weak fine motor skills, so writing was a very draining task for him. Consequently, she encouraged him to work independently on writing tasks when he seemed able to do so (in his case, not only to improve his writing skills but to strengthen his muscles and fine motor coordination). When he appeared unable to handle a writing task, however, she would focus on just getting his ideas down on paper. To provide support and encouragement, she might say, "You write the first word in the sentence, then I'll write the next word, then you can add a word, then I'll add a word," or "I'll write the first four words, then you can write the last four words," or even "This time I will do all the writing for you—you just tell me what you want it to say." Her goals for this student also varied with the nature of the activity: "During handwriting practice time, I definitely want him writing. If we're creating a book and they're writing a really long sentence, I want his idea there more than I am worried about him printing it out himself. So, the adaptations flow naturally out of what are my goals for the kid, what are the goals for that task, and what do I most want to get out of it."

Barbara will provide students with this kind of assistance when they need it, but she also socializes them to regulate their own learning by figuring out what they need to do and following through accordingly. For example, she teaches them that if they are called on in class and do not have a ready answer to her question, they should try to determine whether they just need more time to think about the question or whether they need some kind of help. If they just need more time, they should ask for it (by saying "I don't have an answer ready. Can I think about it for a minute?"). If they determine that they need some kind of help, they should decide whether they need help from Barbara herself or whether they can get help by referring to some of the resources posted in the room (calendar, number line, word wall, list of books read, historical timeline, etc.). When students believe that they might be able to answer the question after consulting one of these resources, Barbara will give them time to do so and then raise the question again.

Although they are particularly helpful to special needs students, these techniques reflect Barbara's goals and strategies for all of her students. That is, besides teaching specific curricular content, she seeks to increase her students' metacognitive awareness of their learning strategies and develop their capacities for self-regulated learning. One such strategy is getting help from partners or seatmates, which Barbara encourages her students to do. She cautions them, however, that when seeking or providing help, they should focus on learning or explaining the big idea, not just getting or giving answers to particular questions. Special needs students can use this strategy as easily as their peers can, because their seats are dispersed around the classroom rather than clustered in a separate group or placed in isolation from other classmates.

Addressing Special Needs "On the Fly" During Lessons

When teaching lessons, Barbara provides special support to students who need it and takes advantages of emerging opportunities to pursue special goals for individuals. For example, whenever students return from pull-out instruction, they know that they are expected to join the ongoing lesson or activity. As they take their seat, Barbara welcomes them and provides a brief orientation concerning what the class has been doing and where they are in the process. Time and feasibility constraints prohibit her from starting the lesson all over again, but before proceeding she may briefly review the big ideas developed so far. To further involve returning students, she will call on them when opportunities arise (e.g., when she wants to ask a question that they should be able to answer even though they missed the first part of the lesson).

Barbara also reinforces basic learning community norms and expectations when she teaches, especially when interacting with students who do not join her class until after the early heavy socialization weeks have been completed. For example, one day she was constructing lists of characteristics of schooling in the United States, Japan, and Tanzania, to be used in a subsequent comparison and contrast activity. She had taught about schooling in Japan and Tanzania the previous day, and was now asking students to recall things that they had learned that might be added to the lists. Initially calling mostly on volunteers, she had made a good start in developing a list for Japan. Then she decided to involve students who had not yet volunteered. In particular, she wanted to involve Sarah, who had joined the class only recently and was still hesitant to speak up during lessons:

T: . . . I want to see if I can sneak in somebody who hasn't had a turn yet. Hmmm. Sarah, do you remember what was special about the clothes that the kids wore?

S: [No response.]

T: Look right here for a minute [i.e., at Barbara, not the floor]. I'll help you figure this out. Did the kids all wear the same clothes, or did everyone dress different from everyone else?

S: Different.

T: That's what we are. In Japan, the kids all wear the . . .

S: Same.

T: The same clothes, called a uni . . .

> S: Uniform.
>
> T: They do wear uniforms. Let's see. Erin, I haven't heard from you . . .

Without being overly direct about it, Barbara took this occasion to socialize Sarah concerning what to expect and how to behave in situations in which she could not think of an answer. First, she should maintain eye contact and make some substantive statement (including "I don't know" if necessary), not just avert her eyes and remain silent. Second, she should understand that, if she does not know an answer to a question and cannot figure it out on her own, Barbara will help her to do so.

Barbara communicated these two ideas through two brief statements ("Look right here for a minute. I'll help you figure this out."). These commonly made statements were delivered in a matter-of-fact tone. She did not put Sarah on the spot any more than necessary. That is, she avoided stretching out this part of the interaction too long, providing unnecessary reassurance that it was "OK" if the student did not have an answer ready, or saying something overly direct or authoritarian (such as, "Look at me when I ask you a question—not at the floor.").

Both in the tone and manner of what she did say and in what she omitted, Barbara communicated something like, "I see that you do not have an answer to my question. That is not a big deal. It happens all the time, and I know just how to deal with it. Here's what we'll do . . ." Her supportive tone and manner, coupled with specific scaffolding, orient the student toward coping (listening to what Barbara is saying now, then thinking about the subsequent question) rather than becoming anxious or upset. Furthermore, Barbara followed through on her promise of help immediately, by asking a simple choice question to which Sarah could respond by picking one of two alternatives (i.e., by stating either that Japanese schoolchildren dress all the same or dress differently).

As it happened, Sarah picked the wrong alternative. However, Barbara remained unfazed, responding first by giving corrective feedback ("That's what we are."—i.e., we all dress differently in our country), and then immediately following up with an even more structured question (in Japan, the kids all wear the . . .) that allowed Sarah to come up with a correct answer. She then followed up with an additional question that enabled Sarah to come up with the word "uniform." Barbara concluded the sequence by observing that Sarah was correct—Japanese schoolchildren do wear uniforms. Then she moved on, maintaining her matter-of-fact tone.

Whether public (as in the preceding lesson excerpt) or more private, *Barbara's interactions with special needs students routinely combine a matter-of-fact tone and manner with forms of scaffolding that focus the students on what needs to be done and engage them in beginning to do it.*

This minimizes the likelihood that they will feel shamed or singled out, or will become paralyzed with anxiety or inhibition. It also helps both these students and the onlookers to focus on the big ideas that Barbara is developing rather than on individuals' successes or failures. Repeated experiences of this kind make students realize that Barbara means what she says about providing them with whatever help they may need to be successful in her classroom.

Although Sarah was a new student, Barbara could meet most of her needs "on the fly" because she was generally compliant and eager to please. A contrasting situation arose with a highly disruptive student who had been transferred into Barbara's class from another class. While he was still very new to her class and did not yet have an established place in it, he tended to disrupt her lessons. To minimize such problems, Barbara would have private conversations with him prior to lessons, in which she gave him "the inside scoop" about what would happen in the lesson and some of the things he might want to think about in preparing for it. This addressed his needs for power and attention, and reduced the likelihood of disruption. Later, when teaching the lesson, she would refer back to this conversation when she was about to enter a part of the lesson that she had discussed with the student, cueing him to the fact that this was something he already knew about.

Impulsive and Hyperactive Students

Some students need special help in learning to listen to and think about questions before volunteering answers to them. For example, Barbara has found that general tendencies toward compliance lead most young students to answer yes in response to any yes/no question. Many of them do this automatically, without paying much attention to the content of the question. To counteract this disposition, Barbara makes sure that the correct answer to many of her yes/no questions is no. This is sufficient to cause most of her students to begin attending to and thinking about the content of her questions, but a few individuals sometimes need additional scaffolding.

For example, in a lesson on developments in farming, Barbara had emphasized that although the technologies used to accomplish farm jobs had developed remarkably (e.g., from human to animal to engine power), the basic jobs remained the same (e.g., tilling the soil, planting the seeds, etc.). While reviewing the lesson, she asked, "Did the farm jobs change?" All of her students answered no to this question, except Cole, in whom the disposition to answer yes to yes/no questions was so strong that she had begun to think of him as her "yes man." Because the single yes answer came from Cole, Barbara did not merely give the right answer and move on (as she would do more typically in these review situations).

Instead, she asked Cole a series of follow-up questions that made him think about the issue and reassess his answer:

T: What changed, Cole? ... Did they still have to dig up the ground?

S: Yes.

T: Yes. Did they still have to put seeds in the ground?

S: Yes.

T: Did they still have to weed them?

S: Yes.

T: Yes. Did they still have to bring water?

S: Yes.

T: But what is different from here to here? [referring to two illustrations] Who is doing the work over here?

S: The people.

T: And who is doing the work over here?

S: The animals.

T: Ah, so what changed, Cole?

S: The animals didn't do it over here but now they do.

T: Right, so animals were helping with the jobs but the jobs themselves did not change.

Another dispositional problem is "clang associations," in which students hear one key word in the question and respond to it immediately without taking into account the question as a whole. For example, after eliciting several other responses to a question about products that we get from poultry farms, Barbara attempted to elicit "chicken" by asking, "What are lots of you hot-lunch kids having for lunch today?" One student answered "pizza," even though pizza is not the product of a poultry farm and was not being served for lunch that day. Later in the same lesson, she asked, "How are you going to get the milk? What do you need for a tool?" Most students supplied the expected answer (bucket), but one who didn't pay attention to the "tool" part of the question said, "Cow," and another who did pay attention to "tool" but not to the milking context answered "Shovel."

When students make such clang associations frequently, Barbara works with them on listening to and processing the entire question. She typically responds with some kind of acknowledgement or correction of their initial response, then repeats or rephrases the question (sometimes with additional cueing) to try to elicit a better answer. She also sometimes cautions the class as a whole to listen carefully to the entire question before trying to answer it, or forewarns them that the next question is tricky and will require careful thought.

With some students, the problem is not that they fail to process the question but that they blurt out answers at times when she wants them to wait to be called on or when she is protecting another student's extended turn. She works with these impulsive students to make them more aware of their behavior and strengthen their self-regulation capacities. She teaches them to say the answer in their head but not out loud, and also to give themselves messages to inhibit impulsiveness and exert more control over their reactions. Sometimes she will even refer to these discussions during lessons, as when a student who blurts out an answer is reminded to "Listen to the voice in your head that's saying 'stop.' "

With hyperactive students who find it difficult to sit still and sustain attention to lessons, Barbara finds ways to allow them physical movement or otherwise minimize constraints on their behavior. For example, during a unit on clothing, Barbara invited a hyperactive student to get up, circulate the room, and show off his new Harry Potter shirt to his classmates. His shirt provided a good example of the point she was making (that people sometimes communicate their interests and identifications through their clothing), so this tactic fit within and supported the ongoing lesson flow. However, Barbara also welcomed the opportunity to allow an antsy student to stand up and move around, and perhaps to engage more fully with the topic.

Another tactic that she uses with hyperactive students is to make sure that they are among the first ones to be released from lessons that immediately precede recess or lunch. In these situations, she closes the lessons with "ticket out" activities, calling for students to state something they learned during the lesson and then leave for lunch or recess. On days when her more hyperactive students are showing particularly strong needs to get up and move around, she will call on them first during ticket out activities, allowing them to get up and leave the room a little earlier than most of their peers. However, if they do not provide satisfactory responses to her questions, she sustains her interactions with them until they do.

Shy and Hesitant Students

Individualized socialization of other students is directed at their willingness to participate in lessons. Barbara continually seeks to condition shy or struggling students to volunteer to participate, both by calling on them whenever they do volunteer and by directing questions to them at other times (questions that she believes they will be able to answer). She also is more likely to provide praise or some kind of special acknowledgement to these students when they provide an especially good response. She does not overdo this, because she does not want either the students themselves or their classmates to become aware that she is treating them a little differently. However, occasionally she will respond like she did the time a struggling student with multiple special needs provided an especially good response: "Oh yeah! You're there, man! You're having a brilliant day!"

Barbara also will push students who are capable but passive or lazy to become more persistently attentive and responsive. For example, one day she was asking application questions that elicited a great many ideas from everyone in the class except for one boy whom she characterized as bright but lazy and passive. Before concluding the lesson, she called him by name and said, "I have to tell you, I'm pretty disappointed that you didn't come up with any ideas for me. Usually you have lots of really great and interesting ideas to add." When he did not volunteer during the subsequent lesson segment either, she called on him several times as a non-volunteer. At the end of the lesson she again expressed disappointment that he had not "shared any ideas with us" that day, as well as her hope that he would begin to do so soon.

Barbara provides a variety of cues and other scaffolding assistance to shy students and other reluctant verbalizers, especially if she knows that they have difficulty understanding the content. When calling on these students, she often will call their name before asking the question. This enables them to mobilize their resources to respond to the question and eliminates the "shock" problem that sometimes occurs when they are called on unexpectedly. She usually will ask them a question that she believes they will be able to answer, but if they struggle with it, she will break down the question or provide some other kind of help. When she believes that they know the answer, she will coax it out of them if necessary. For example, when asked what we call people who live today, a reticent student began to say "modern" but left it at "m . . ." Barbara first tried simply waiting, but this did not yield the complete word. So, she then said, "You know it—it starts with an m. I heard you start it. Mmmmm . . ." This was sufficient to elicit "modern" from the student.

The use of several of these techniques in combination is illustrated in the following excerpt. Barbara first alerts a notably unresponsive student that he will be called on next, then asks an initial question that yields no response, then simplifies the question, then simplifies again, and then simplifies a third time until she finally gets an answer. In the process, she pauses to wait after each question and protects the student's turn by reminding other students to put down their hands and not call out answers.

> T: Guess what, Adam, you're next. Adam, what if I wanted to get my message out to a lot of people, but I wanted them to be able to read it and save it. What would I do? . . . What do people read, that lots and lots of people get? . . . Put your hands down—it's Adam's turn . . . What's written down on paper that lots of people read? . . . Look at the round table [a table in the room currently used to display newspapers].

S: Newspapers.

T: Newspapers are one way for people to communicate to a whole
     bunch of folks all at once [goes on to the next point].

A similar exchange occurred in the following interaction with a low-
ability, shy student. Barbara began by calling on the student to answer a
question that she thought the student could handle, but got no response.
Consequently, she shifted to an easier question, but the student still could
not respond. Then, she tried to cue a response but still did not get one, so
she provided a more lengthy statement and finished with a new question
that the student could finally provide a response. She concluded by affirm-
ing the correctness of the student's response and praising it briefly.

T: There are four ways that people can communicate nonverbally.
     First, tell me what nonverbal is. Tessa, nonverbal is . . .?

S: [No response.]

T: Do you know what verbal is?

S: No.

T: Verbal has to do with your voice, Tessa. It means that you com-
     municate with your voice. So what do you think nonverbal is,
     Tessa?

S: No voice.

T: No voice. Good job. [Goes on to address a new question to a
     different student.]

Barbara also integrates specially formulated reminders into her whole-
class teaching, especially about behaviors related to personal goals for
individual students. For example, a student who tends to be too soft
spoken when giving answers to questions may be asked to speak up in
a "big voice." Use of this term is not accidental; it is a key phrase
emphasized in private discussions with the student about speaking up
more loudly and clearly. Consequently, when Barbara uses it in passing
during a lesson, she is not merely delivering a situational message but
reminding the student of the larger goal and the series of discussions they
have had about it.

Speech Communication Problems

Many of Barbara's students present speech communication problems, so
her interactions with them often are complicated by a need to figure out
what they are trying to say or to articulate their ideas clearly. When
students have limited vocabulary or tend to garble language when trying
to convey their thoughts, Barbara often must try to determine what they
mean and put the meaning into more understandable language. In the

following example, she asked several clarification questions to help such a student express his idea (rather than jumping to a possibly incorrect conclusion about what he meant):

> T: What are some ways in which things move or get transported in the water?
>
> S: A boat.
>
> T: A boat [simply repeats answer and waits, hoping that student will elaborate].
>
> S: I was thinking of the one that goes under the water.
>
> T: Oh, the one that starts with sub ... A submmmmm. [At this point, Barbara is pretty sure the student means a submarine, so she provides sound cues to help him remember the word.]
>
> S: Oh, a submarine.
>
> T: A submarine. You're doing exactly what you were supposed to. You stayed calm and I was able to help you out.

Barbara had been working with this student about staying calm and allowing her to help in situations when he could not think of a word. He did exactly that in this situation, so she took time to acknowledge this before moving on to a new question with another student. Another child had both cognitive and language issues: difficulty formulating problems, synthesizing two or more things together, and articulating her ideas clearly. Barbara provided various forms of support that allowed her to participate in lessons nevertheless: calling on her late in a sequence, after peers had modeled acceptable answers; providing extra wait time for her if necessary; and providing both meaning-based and sound clues to help her process and respond to questions. Some of these techniques can be seen in the following excerpt:

> T: Yes, clothes protect you from cold and rain, so that is one reason why folks wear clothes. Gretchen, why else?
>
> S: So in the winter they don't get frostbite.
>
> T: So you're talking about protection again, aren't you? I'm thinking about one more reason why folks wear clothes. Pop your hands down. This is Gretchen's turn. There was one more reason, Gretchen. ... Can I give you some cues? This is the reason why the bride in the wedding doesn't just wear blue jeans and a T-shirt.
>
> S: It's special.
>
> T: Right, it's special, so sometimes we wear clothes for dec ...
>
> S: Decoration.
>
> T: Decoration. Can you think of something other than a wedding where someone might wear clothes that are decorated specially?

[Having elicited the desired response to the original question, Barbara now extends the response opportunity by shifting to a new question to the same student.]

S: For a party.

T: For a party. What's coming up at the end of October that people wear specially decorated clothes? . . . There's a holiday coming up. I bet you have something that you've bought at your house already to wear to school on that day. It's a costume. It's your . . .

S: Halloween costume. [At this point, Barbara shifts focus from this student to the class as a whole, summarizing the reasons why people wear clothes.]

The following excerpt is an extended interaction with a student for whom it was often difficult to determine what he meant or was thinking. In this situation, Barbara had to take a lot of time with him, initially to clarify his thinking and then to discuss it. She was willing to do so, however, because the interaction occurred during a warm-up prior to the lesson proper. The interaction was complicated because the student initially used the word tank when he meant a tanker ship. Furthermore, he actually was thinking of a submarine, because he thought that Barbara was asking about transportation that went under the water, when in fact she had asked about transportation that travels in the water.

Untangling all of this took time and was further complicated by the fact that the student decided that submarines were personal transportation because you do not have to pay to ride them, and when probed, claimed that some people do own submarines if they are rich enough. Barbara persisted through all of this because she had discovered that, despite his frequent confusions and language problems, this student could handle being probed at length. The activity was a riddle exercise in which Barbara read clues describing a particular form of transportation and students were asked to guess which form was being described. They could refer to a posted list of transportation forms if they wanted to.

T: Let's try another one. I'm thinking of a kind of transportation that you would find in the water. It would be personal transportation, and it would have no motor. This type of transportation would be for just one or two people. What do you think, Sam?

S: A tank.

T: Are you thinking of a tank like in the army or a tanker ship? Think about the clues: something in the water, it's personal transportation, it has no engine, and it might have one or two people in it. Does your guess match those clues? . . . Are you thinking of a tanker ship or a tank that the army would have?

S: A tanker ship.

T: A tanker ship . . .

S: Well, I don't know if it's a ship or not.

T: If you don't think that answer matches the clues, you can think again. That's what great thinkers do. Do you think your answer matches the clues?

S: I think, a tank that goes underwater.

T: A tank that goes underwater. So are you thinking of an army tank?

S: Does it go in the water?

T: Not that I know of. I'm trying to figure out what kind of tank you're talking about. So what kind of tank are you talking about?

S: It goes underwater.

T: The only thing I can think of that goes underwater that you might think is like a tank is a submarine. Are you thinking of a submarine?

S: Yes.

T: Well, let's check the clues. I said that this went in the water. A submarine goes in water. I said it was personal. What does personal mean, Sam?

S: That you don't have to pay [to ride it].

T: You don't have to pay. You buy it one time and then it's yours and you don't have to pay to ride it each time. Do people own submarines?

S: Yes.

T: Do they?

S: No, only if they're really rich.

T: Submarines are owned by a navy, not a person. So are submarines personal transportation?

S: No.

T: They're not usually owned by a person. So should you and I figure out a different guess? Let's take a look at our list and see if we can think of something that it might be. You tell me if there's something on there that you can own and if there's something that might fit. [Barbara starts reading through the list, two or three items at a time, but in each case Sam indicates that these choices do not fit the clues.] None of those go in the water?

S: A boat doesn't go under the water.

T: I said it goes *in* the water.

S: Oh, a boat.

T: Did you think I said under the water?

S: Yes.

T: Ahh, that makes a big difference on that clue, doesn't it? Can you think of a boat that a person might own that one or two people would go in?

> S: Ummm . . . a kind of race boat or something.
>
> T: Maybe a racing boat that would have just one or two people in it. Do you think that would have an engine in it?
>
> S: No.
>
> T: What would they do to make the boat go?
>
> S: They'd have to have some kind of stick.
>
> T: Yes. [Addresses the next question to the class a whole.] Kids, what kind of stick is that? What do we call that?
>
> Ss: Paddle, oar.
>
> T: [Returns attention to Sam.] So, you're thinking of a boat that you might race in that you paddle. That's called a kayak. Let's check out kayak and see if it fits my clues. Kayak—does it go in the water?
>
> S: Yes.
>
> T: Is it personal—would somebody buy it and use it for themselves?
>
> S: Yes.
>
> T: Would it have an engine?
>
> S: No.
>
> T: Would you have one or two people in it?
>
> S: Yes.
>
> T: They actually do. Some kayaks are for one person and some are for two people. So, it does fit all the clues. [Goes on to next riddle.]

Helping special needs students process and respond to questions usually involves helping them by breaking down the question or providing cues to help them reason about it—sticking with a single question and working towards the desired answer. However, Barbara has found that a very different approach works better with certain students who are struggling with English as a second language. With these students, she finds that it often is better to ask them several questions rather than just one, because this enables them to respond to at least one of the questions.

Autism and Asperger's Syndrome

Among students that Barbara finds most challenging to reach and teach successfully are those diagnosed with or even showing clear symptoms of autism or Asperger's Syndrome. She gets a better response from these students and makes more progress with them than most teachers, but it is slow going and she often has to settle for less than she hoped for. More often than with other special needs students, she finds that her efforts to elicit improved responses are not successful (so she ends up giving the answer) or that she needs to modify or reduce their assignments.

Barbara often develops successful techniques through persistent trial and error. For example, one of her Asperger's Syndrome students was very visual. When asked to write his name on his paper, he drew his face instead; he could remember visual chunks of words or phrases; and he could recreate phrases seen on toy or cereal boxes. To help him learn to monitor his own behavior, she took pictures of him posed doing what he was supposed to be doing at various times and in various settings. When his behavior became a problem, she would lead him through the pictures and sort them into a happy face pile that corresponded to praise for "You're doing well" and a frowning face pile indicating need for improvement.

Barbara always has posted the daily schedule as a resource for referral by both herself and her students. When this student was in her class, however, she added drawings to the schedule to provide visual cues along with textual ones. She also frequently used sign language when speaking to this student, providing cue redundancy and a visual focus for attention and guidance. Most of these were basic signs for common management messages (yes, no, stop, sit, listen, calm down, etc.). Even so, it often was difficult for Barbara to elicit good responses from this student during lessons. For example, the following interaction occurred near the end of a lesson on transportation in the cave days, the pioneer/Pilgrim days, and modern times. The student was interested in transportation and had been unusually verbal earlier in the lesson, and the question she addressed to him was one that most students could answer easily. Yet, the result was disappointing.

> T: What is a form of transportation that we use today?
>
> S: You move things from one place to another. [Provides a definition of transportation instead of an example of modern transportation.]
>
> T: You move things from one place to another, but tell me a way that you move today . . . How did you get to school today? . . . How did you get here? . . . [These cues and simplifications did not yield any response, so Barbara shifted to an absurd question.] Did you come on an airplane?
>
> S: No.
>
> T: Did you get here on a spaceship today?
>
> S: No.
>
> T: Then how did you get to school? . . . How did you get here? . . . [Although her absurd questions yielded correct answers, the student once again was unable to respond when asked how he got to school today, even though this was an even easier question than the original question calling for an example of transportation. Under these circumstances, Barbara shifted to providing even more scaffolding.] Mom or Dad drove the . . .

S: Car.

T: Yes, you got here in a car or a van. [Moves on to another question to another student.]

This was one of many examples of ways that Barbara had to work harder to get less from this student than from most of his peers. Autistic students present similar difficulties, and Barbara has developed a variety of strategies for addressing them. For example, when aides are available to work with these students, she will have the aides preview lessons with the students, so that they will be more able to respond successfully when called on. The aides also review the lessons afterwards to help the students to remember what was taught.

Even with this kind of support, autistic students often are distracted or unresponsive during lessons. For example, one day Barbara was telling the land-to-hand story of peanut butter, and in the process, assigning her students to represent people who performed some of the jobs involved (e.g., peanut farmer, truck driver, factory worker). One of her most autistic students was assigned the role of the store worker who stocks the shelves with the jars of peanut butter delivered to the store. The following interaction occurred at the end of the story, when Barbara was expecting to wrap it up quickly and move into a review.

T: Okay, A.J.'s uncle takes the peanut butter to the store. Then we need to put the jars on the shelf. Who puts the jars on the shelf?

Ss: Curtis.

T: Curtis, you're putting the jars of peanut butter on the shelf. What would people do at the store, Curtis?

S: On the shelf.

T: Yes, you put the jars on the shelf and then Cole's mom is going to come along and take it off the shelf . . . Look at me. Why does she take it off the shelf? . . . Because she wants to . . . Look at me. Why does Cole's mom take the peanut butter?

S: Cole's mom's taking it.

T: Right, because she wants to buy it. [Moves on.]

In this situation, Barbara had to fight for Curtis' attention, and she was not successful at getting him to answer even the simplest questions. Under the circumstances (time was running out and Curtis was not very responsive), she decided to simply give the answer and move on.

She was more successful in eliciting acceptable responses from the same student in other situations, although she frequently had to shift from free response questions to choice questions or provide some other support to enable him to answer. For example, one day she enlisted her students in providing advice to her and her husband about how they should complement the steak they were intending to eat for dinner that night in order to compose a balanced and satisfying meal. During this segment, she was asking the students to suggest what type of potatoes to have, and explain why.

> T: Curtis, what kind of potato should we have?
> S: Mashed potatoes.
> T: Why?
> S: [No response.]
> T: Do you think I could make them fast?
> S: No.
> T: Do you think they don't cost very much?
> S: Yes.

In this situation, her open-ended why question did not yield a response, so Barbara suggested possible reasons until she elicited a yes response from Curtis, then moved on. A similar sequence occurred later in the lesson when Barbara was reviewing homework responses explaining what the family had to eat for dinner last night and why this meal was chosen. After noting that Curtis' response sheet indicated that the family had turkey the previous night, Barbara asked:

> T: Do you know why mom picked turkey? . . . Is turkey healthy?
> S: Yes.
> T: Yes, that's one reason why mom picked turkey. Look at me. Right here. It's your turn. You need to listen. Do you guys like to eat turkey?
> S: Yes.
> T: You're right, and that's another reason she picked turkey.

Once again, the student could not respond to an open-ended question, so Barbara shifted to simpler yes/no questions. In this case, she also had to admonish him to look at her and pay attention, because he was drifting off.

Still later in this same lesson, Barbara asked students to identify restaurants where they like to eat. All of her students except Curtis quickly named several restaurants. Unable to elicit a response to this open but very easy question, Barbara tried to help by suggesting potential answers (i.e., naming restaurants). However, Curtis answered no to all of her suggestions, and she never did succeed in eliciting either the name of a restaurant or a yes answer to a suggested restaurant.

On another day, Barbara was reviewing the food pyramid. After several questions about the fruit group, she shifted to the meat group. After establishing that the meat group has protein, she asked Curtis for an example of a food from the meat group. He responded "strawberries" (perseverating from earlier discussion of the fruit group). Rather than try to elicit an improved response in this situation, Barbara simply told Curtis that strawberries are not in the meat group and then told him to look while she pointed to the meat group on the food pyramid. She used such visual illustrations with him when possible, because his visual processing was better than his verbal processing.

When Barbara does extend interactions with autistic students, they sometimes flow in unexpected directions. In the following exchange, Barbara was eliciting examples of personal transportation and adding them to a list she was developing.

> T: Howell, what did you think of?
> S: My mom drives a van. [Ordinarily, Barbara would have noted
>   that vans were already on the list and asked the student to name
>   a form of personal transportation that had not been listed yet.
>   With this student, however, she chose to honor the response.]
> T: A van. It belongs to your family, and mom's the one who drives
>   it, so it is personal transportation.
> S: I have a bike and a little wagon. [Surprisingly, the student spon-
>   taneously added to his response. Bikes had been mentioned
>   already, but wagons had not, so Barbara seized the opportunity
>   to sustain the interaction.]
> T: A wagon. Does it belong to you?
> S: Yes.
> T: Who uses it?
> S: Me.
> T: So that is . . . your personal . . .
> S: Transportation. Why do I need transportation?
> T: Why do you need transportation?
> S: So I can get from one place to another.
> T: From one place to another. Or maybe with a wagon, you could
>   move your things from one place to another. [Moves on to
>   another student.]

The student surprised and delighted Barbara in this situation by supply-ing an acceptable response in the first place, then spontaneously adding to it, then continuing to respond to follow-up questions, and eventually asking a question of his own. Striking while the iron was hot, Barbara sustained the interaction over several exchanges and even succeeded in getting the student to answer his own question by repeating it back to him rather than answering it herself.

An example of a special accommodation for an autistic student occurred during a culmination activity for a unit on childhood through time and across cultures. Barbara asked each student to draw something that he or she had learned about childhood during the unit, using a standard-sized square piece of paper. She planned to combine these squares into a "quilt" which would be displayed as a memento of the unit and summary of its big ideas. Most of her students were eager to participate, but an autistic student who was strongly resistant to having his work displayed did not want to contribute a square to the quilt. Barbara accepted this, although she did require him to do the initial assignment of drawing a representation of something learned during the unit. She felt that it was a shame that he would not be represented in the quilt, but the whole point of the quilt was to be celebratory and reinforcing, and if requiring his participation would have the opposite effect on him, it made sense to honor his wishes and leave him out.

Barbara also uses "social stories" to help low-functioning, autistic, or other special students to remember what they are supposed to be doing and how to do it. These stories spell out the rationale for the desired behavior (within the appropriate setting) and the steps involve in carrying it out. Students keep the stories in a binder and reread them periodically as needed. These readings are coupled with assessments of how well the students are doing with regard to the behavior in each story.

Barbara makes allowances and provides special help for special needs students, but she does so within the larger context of helping them to succeed as learners. She wants these students to meet the learning goals established for the class as a whole, or at least as many of them as possible given their limitations. She makes sure that all of her students understand that she will not demand the impossible, but she does expect them to consistently pay attention and put forth reasonable effort, so as to make the progress they are capable of making.

To the extent that they do not do this on their own, she will push them to do it, although usually informally and relatively covertly. If students do not often volunteer to participate in lessons, she calls on them directly. If she believes that they are capable of answering a question more fully or precisely than they did in their initial responses, she will push them for more (but be prepared to help them if necessary).

Chapter 9

Planning

We have noted that Barbara's class maintains an almost continuous academic focus, with only brief and smooth transitions between each lesson or activity and the next. Creating and sustaining this kind of learning environment takes a great deal of planning and preparation. The same is true of other prominent features of her curriculum, notably its integration, connectedness, and personalization to individual students' life experiences and home backgrounds. This chapter explores Barbara's planning and preparation work, which she views as an ongoing part of her teaching role.

Yearly Planning

Like most teachers, Barbara begins her planning by blocking out the year as a whole, then planning at the unit level, and then shifting to the daily (lesson and activity) level. Her planning for a given school year begins the previous year, as she monitors and reflects on how well things are going. Her reflections include implications for structuring the next year's curriculum. For example, the health curriculum contains a safety unit that could be taught almost any time during the year, and Barbara originally taught it somewhere in the middle. However, one year she realized that, "I was putting out little fires that, if I had taught my safety lessons earlier, I wouldn't be needing to address now." So, she made a note to schedule the safety unit very early during the following school year, and found that it worked really well to do so. Consequently, she has taught the safety unit early in the year ever since.

When Barbara begins formal yearly planning during the summer, she starts by filling in a *curriculum map*—a grid printed on larger-than-legal-size paper that has a box for each of the weeks in the school year. To block out the year as a whole, she begins by entering the literacy and mathematics components of her curriculum that will be taught every day. Within the blocks of time assigned to these subjects, she also plans the general sequence of content development. Much of this is the same from year to year, although sometimes Barbara will make adjustments based on problems encountered with particular lessons or activities. Also, she does not select particular poems at this time. She prefers to wait until she has blocked out the entire curriculum, so she can select and sequence poems that connect with other things being taught at the time (in science or social studies).

The instructional materials that Barbara uses for literacy and mathematics are already packaged as year-long curricula, but blocking them into the yearly curriculum map is a more complicated process than just transferring from one curriculum outline to another. In mathematics, for example, Barbara's school does not use certain units because they do not match the state's standards. Also, previous experience with her instructional materials has led Barbara to make adjustments such as changing the order in which units (or lessons within units) are taught or substituting her own lesson content or learning activities for parallel components in the instructional materials that she has found to be problematic. Finally, her planning has to take into account the time required to meet the objectives of each component. One unit may have 13 lessons, but the next might only have ten. Two units might each contain ten lessons, but one might require more time allocation because several of its lessons are complicated and will require two days instead of just one.

After blocking out the literacy and mathematics components that she teaches every day, Barbara allocates the remaining time slots to units on science, social studies, health, or community building/character development. Rather than try to cover all four of these curricular components every day in very short lessons,

> I only teach one of those things at a time. So, if I'm doing a science unit, I'll do science every day for three to four weeks until that whole unit is completed. This way, we can go deeper. We can connect it to the rest of the curriculum. We can focus on that topic until the end of that unit and then switch to social studies, rather than doing science Monday to Wednesday and social studies Tuesday to Thursday.
>
> So, for example, during the first four weeks of the year, my extra thing was community building and character education. We went into that in depth until the children had connected understandings across all the different areas of community building and character education. Then we moved to health and did a safety unit for two weeks. We talked about keeping yourself safe in two ways—how to stay safe and what to do if something happens. We connected this to literacy by reading books that touched on safety themes. Now we're into social studies, studying families in depth. We connect it to things we've already learned and to other things taught at the same time. This will continue for about five weeks. Then in January when we do

our science unit on liquids and solids, we'll just do science. We'll do five weeks of in-depth, connected science lessons that include active, hands-on activities. Many of these will connect to literacy or integrate with what we are teaching in math, and during those weeks the classroom will be stocked with books and resources tied to those particular topics. So looking across the year, I spend about the same amounts of time in each of the main subjects as other teachers, but I teach them one at a time and go deeply to connect with other things and integrate with other areas.

Unit Planning

Most units last for four or five weeks, although some health, safety, or character education units are much shorter. For Barbara, unit-level planning means much more than just slotting the unit into her curriculum map and then shifting attention to its lessons and learning activities. Her unit planning begins with attention to the characteristics of the unit as a whole. She focuses on the unit's big ideas and their potential implications for establishing key vocabulary to use throughout the unit, and on making connections with things taught elsewhere in the curriculum or with her students' lives outside of school.

As illustrated in detail in Chapter 11 of our companion volume on social studies teaching (Brophy, Alleman, & Knighton, 2008), part of Barbara's approach to establishing and developing big ideas is not just to explain and emphasize those ideas clearly, but also to establish a basic vocabulary that she will use consistently throughout the unit as a way to support understanding and communication. She selects these key vocabulary terms carefully, emphasizing terms that a) her students already know or can easily learn and remember, b) suggest imagery or carry connotations that she would like her students to acquire as part of their basic understandings of big ideas, and c) at the same time, are not likely to stimulate misconceptions or carry connotations that might distract from the big idea as she wishes it to be understood. She says:

> What I do most often is look to create a chunk of common understandings, experiences, terms, and definitions—a common set of data or information that we then will use throughout the rest of the unit. So at the beginning of the solids and liquids unit in science, we look at examples of solids and liquids and we learn how to describe them in scientific terms that bring out their different properties. We create definitions for each of these things and then move on to extensions and applications that call for synthesizing or figuring things out. For example, after developing basic understandings about solids and liquids, we move on to questions such as how can you manipulate

solids, how can you manipulate liquids, how can you use them, how can you break up a group of solids and then assemble them back into their original groups such that each group has its own identity rather than containing a mixture of things. During that phase, we also explore tools that will help us work with these substances.

The same thing happens in social studies. I think of the first lessons as building blocks to create common understandings. I make sure that I have good chunks of time blocked out for these introductory lessons, and I do a lot of assessment to make sure that kids have clear understandings and have mastered the common terms I want them to use. I make sure the kids get lots of opportunities to see the same basic information brought up in books, used in creating posters together, used in writing assignments, used in my own questions and in their answers to my questions—getting that beginning chunk of information down really solid.

As another way to support learning and generate opportunities to make connections, Barbara seeks to develop content in logical sequences, not only within each curriculum component but across the curriculum as a whole:

I look for connections across units and then try to put the units together in a logical sequence. For example, I am teaching the food unit this year in social studies, and I scheduled it right after the living and non-living unit in science. So I started with consideration of living versus non-living things, then did the food unit, and then finished the sequence off with the human growth and development unit from health. They tie together because the sequence starts with the "umbrella" idea that there are both living and non-living things, then focuses on living things and what living things need. Food is one of those things that living things need. Then I finish off with the piece on human growth and development that talks about how life starts. This "ties the bow" on the idea that human beings start life and then need to be nurtured and cared for, and one of the ways we care for them is to provide them with food. This kind of planned sequencing allows me to make connections across units in different curriculum areas even when I am not teaching them at the same time.

When I taught second grade, I would teach the clothing unit and the shelter unit in social studies on either side of the science unit on weather. This was because during the clothing unit, we talk about reasons why people wear clothing and about special clothing for special needs. Then when we get into the science unit about weather, we can make ties back to, "Remember, there was special clothing that we wore—what kind of clothing would you need for this particular temperature?" Then we would move on to the shelter unit and talk about how there are places in the world where they do not need heaters in their homes: "Why do you suppose that is . . . Well, because of the climate. Where they live, heating is not needed because the weather is so warm."

As I plan the year, I know that I will need three weeks for this unit or four weeks for that unit, and where I clump units together I will need longer blocks of time. For example, I knew that I needed a good chunk of two solid months to complete the clump involving the living/non-living science unit, the food unit in social studies, and the human growth and development unit in health, so I planned these for April, May, and the beginning of June.

After placing these bigger chunks into her curriculum map, she then fills in the rest with leftover units, typically units that are smaller and less well connected to other parts of the curriculum (such as a required health unit on drugs). She also reserves four to six weeks at the beginning of the year for community building and character development (as part of establishing her class as a learning community), and she tries to reserve two weeks at the end of the year for finishing-up activities. These involve looking back and celebrating what has been learned during the year, as well as making connections to next year's learning.

Barbara's district provides her with basic textbook series and sup-plementary instructional materials such as sets of small books to use in reading groups and tutorials, as well as "big books" useful for science and social studies activities. She identifies additional materials during her planning and makes sure that they are available and ready for use when needed. Some of these are things brought from home, to be used when introducing new topics with examples from her own life. With the help of the school's librarian, she compiles potentially useful children's literature sources relating to the unit's topic. She typically incorporates some of these into her actual lessons (books with text or illustrations that relate directly to the big ideas she plans to develop), selects a few more to be read to the class during reading time, and makes most of the rest available as topic-relevant options for students to read on their own during literacy choice time. If suitable videos are available, she may include a few of them, too. She finds that videos are especially useful for days on which she has to miss the class for some reason.

Assessment

Barbara also includes assessment points in her curriculum map for the year. These include externally mandated and district-wide assessments in reading, writing, and mathematics; mandated building-level assessments;

and additional assessments that she includes for her own purposes. For example, she builds in periodic assessments of individual students' progress toward the personal education goals that she has established for them. At these times, she confers with the students individually (and sometimes with their family members as well) to review progress and consider dropping or adding goals that reflect the child's current status.

Some of the evaluations that Barbara has developed for her own purposes include *rubrics* used for assessing the completeness and quality of students' work on major assignments. However, she does not use rubrics merely as post-facto methods for generating scores to be used for grading purposes. Instead, she develops the rubrics in collaboration with her students prior to the activity in which they are going to be used, then scaffolds her students' use of the rubrics to guide their planning and responses during the activity itself, and then applies them (again, often in collaboration with her students) to evaluate the work and plan improvements.

Barbara has developed rubrics for both writing and drawing. The writing rubrics are checklists that subsume both writing mechanics (capitalizing, complete sentences, correct spelling, etc.) and qualitative criteria such as the number of ideas included in a composition, whether it is likely to be interesting to readers, its flow or structure, and so on. Students use these rubrics as self-checking mechanisms to assess early drafts and plan improvements before turning in a final product.

The drawing rubrics guide students in judging where their artworks fit on a scale from one to four that progresses in complexity. These rubrics are used only for pictures meant to be published. Barbara scaffolds her students use of the rubrics to judge where a given version of a picture fits and what might be done to make it more closely approximate a level-four version. Barbara finds that these uses of rubrics enhance the effectiveness of her feedback and other scaffolding of students' writing and drawing progress, because they help students to see why the better examples are better.

Weekly Planning

An overview of each week is included in the yearly curriculum map that Barbara prepares as she begins her planning. Later, she elaborates her weekly planning with the help of a five-day *weekly grid* containing boxes for entering notes about each period in her daily schedule. As she fills in her weekly schedule, she already has a mental outline and related imagery allowing her to anticipate how each lesson or activity will play out (unless she is teaching something for the first time). In addition to reactivating those plans and images, she includes any adjustments she has decided to make based on prior experience with a lesson or activity (e.g., add more hands-on experiences, more time for review, or more connections or applications). She also searches for specific integration opportunities.

In the past, she used a binder containing a separate sheet for each day, but she has shifted to the weekly grid because it makes it easier for her to see connections. In any case, each day follows the same schedule, making it very predictable for both herself and her students. This provides support for students "who feel most comfortable knowing what comes next and knowing the inside track. . . . It's a motivator, or at least a comfort level, for kids diagnosed in the autism spectrum. Schedules and predictability are really comfortable for them." The predictable schedule also is helpful for the class as a whole on days when Barbara cannot be there, because her students know that their daily routine will be the same even though they have a guest teacher for the day.

One basic integration move is to correlate the texts or poems read to students with content taught in other subjects. For example:

> The day I introduced the food unit, my morning read-to was *Eating the Alphabet: Fruits and Vegetables from A to Z* (Ehlert, 1993), because then in social studies, I was going to introduce the food pyramid, and I wanted them to have a good idea of what fruits and vegetables were before I got to that lesson. Later that week comes a healthy snacks lesson, and the morning read-to is about a little boy who eats too much. Then we were working with money and coins in math, and when I did the math lesson that involved buying stuff at the store, I depicted the items being purchased as food items.
>
> The weekly grid is laid out so I can see the whole week at once and look for those connections, and find ways that I can either foreshadow or support something elsewhere in the curriculum. That's also when I put in my homework for the week. I make sure that I do not have more than one special homework assignment going home at a time, and I try to make the homework supportive of the big ideas taught during the week.

When doing weekly planning, Barbara finds it helpful to review the previous year's curriculum map in conjunction with the previous year's weekly planning sheets for the same place in the curriculum. The curriculum map indicates what she anticipated would happen, whereas the weekly planning sheets show what actually happened (for example, when she ended up taking two days for a lesson that she only expected to take one day).

Lesson Planning

Barbara's teacher education program featured a specific lesson planning model that she was required to follow in her student teaching. She acknowledges that this was helpful at the time, but she no longer blocks out lessons in anything like the detail that the model called for. In part, this is because such detailed planning is no longer necessary when she has taught a lesson several times already and has very clear images of what she will do, in what order, and how her students are likely to respond. Even when planning a lesson that she will teach for the first time, she does not go back to the model she was taught because she finds that it focuses too much on procedural specifics and not enough on big ideas:

> The first time I go to teach something, *I always start with the big ideas*. Then I block out the lesson in terms of time—how much time do I want to spend with the transmission piece of it, how much on an activity or review, or on an application activity. If there is a practice piece that goes along with it or an assessment that needs to be done that day, I will need to take that into account as well. I block all that out in terms of how much time it is going to take and how it is going to flow: what I will do first, what next, and so on. Am I going to read the book first or go into an activity first? How is it going to be set up?
>
> There are some things that I do naturally in every lesson, so I don't need to detail these aspects of my plans. But I do write down much more detail than usual if I'm going to teach a new lesson or develop a new unit. For example, I am going to have to develop a science unit on magnets, because magnets have been placed into the first grade in the new state curriculum. That unit will be broken into individual lessons, and when I go to teach those lessons for the first time, I will break them down by posing the key questions that guide my planning. What are the big ideas? What do I really want the kids to understand and be able to do when I'm done? Am I going to use a book? Other resources? Manipulatives? When and how are we actually going to use magnets? Am I going to begin with explanation and modeling, then have the kids work with the magnets independently, and then bring them back together to share understandings and negotiate conclusions, or are we going to stop in the middle and have them make guesses and then test them out? What will be the general flow of activities, and how will the students likely respond? Almost all of the time, however, I will follow my same basic structure of explaining and modeling first; then scaffolding guided practice using student models; then continuing guided practice with everyone participating individually, with a partner, or in a small group; and then moving on to independent practice.
>
> If I'm grappling with a new curriculum, I do more special planning. For example, last year we began a new phonics curriculum, and in addition to my regular weekly grid for the curriculum as a whole, I developed a separate weekly grid just for phonics, breaking down the

lessons and activities in detail. In addition to noting big ideas and vocabulary phrases that I was going to emphasize, I developed lists of words that would be suitable examples for the phonics concepts taught in each lesson. When the lesson dealt with the short ŭ sound, for example, I had a list of short-ŭ words ready to use, prepared ahead of time.

Daily Rehearsal and Reflection

In addition to constructing and reviewing written plans and notes, Barbara's typical day includes a great deal of prior rehearsal and subsequent reflection relating to the day's lessons and activities. Most of the rehearsal occurs in the morning, at home and especially during her commute to the school. It focuses on introductions of new topics or other basic information presentations that will occur that day, especially presentations that she has not made previously or has decided to change:

> One of the things that is always going on inside my head on the way to school and prior to different chunks of the day is rehearsing particular pieces of the dialogue that I'm going to have with the kids. For example, I have a vivid memory of the conversation that was going on inside my head when I taught the food unit the second time and got to the lesson on farming. Because of some confusion experienced the first time, I wanted to make sure that I had a really clear definition of what a farm is. So, part of the conversation going on in my head on the way to school was picturing myself in front of the kids and saying, "OK, today we're going to talk about farms. A farm is . . ." And then the definition that I planned to use. And then I would look at that definition and think, "Where will all the anomalies fit within that?" For example, if you say that a farm is a place with animals and plants, there are some farms that don't have animals. There are some farms that don't have plants. So I can't use that. So how can I change the definition so that it fits all farms? OK, "A farm is a place where you grow plants or raise animals for people to eat." Well then, how does a Christmas tree farm fit into that? So I thought about anomalies and tried to anticipate potential questions. Also, how will the definition connect with what the kids already know? So I was having that kind of conversation in my head, thinking about how I was going to present the concept to kids and spending a lot of time thinking about the lesson—where they are going to get confused or where things might go wrong.
>
> I have a similar conversation in my head when I'm going to be teaching something new. For example, today's math lesson involved taking the number 100 and breaking it into two chunks that are both

multiples of 10, as in 20+80, 30+70, or 10+90. So, I was imagining talking to the kids about the terms or phrases they will need to know and understand. How would I explain these to them? What have we already done that connects with this? Gee—this reminds me of when we were counting dimes, so I could tie it back to that and use counting with dimes as some of the examples. I am always looking for things that they have done before—skills they have already learned that they will use in today's lesson. And I'm looking again for ways that the lesson could go awry—concepts or vocabulary that lend themselves to confusion.

I also think about the materials I will use and how to set them up in ways that might match something they have done before. Also, is there anything about the materials that might make it difficult for them? The lesson itself calls for using little plastic links to connect into long chains and alternating colors—ten red ones, ten blue ones, ten red ones, ten blue ones, etc. So, part of my thinking was about reminding them of how we counted dimes and how each of these chunks is just like a dime. Also, connecting to the idea that we have used Unifix cubes in groups of ten, which is just like the chunks of plastic links in the chain. But also, thinking about foreshadowing and moving them away from the links (because they aren't always going to have links with them), to thinking about what tool they might use the next time. And how problems could arise if they break their chain in the middle of a color instead of between colors, or do not end up with multiples of ten.

I also think about elaborations. What can I do for kids who get it reasonably easily? Maybe let them break the chain in odd places to see what kinds of numbers they come up with. Also, what will I do for the little one who is still struggling to count to 20? How is she going to be able to handle this task that calls for counting by tens?

So, the big thing for me—probably the three big things I think about, are what do I really want them to know or be able to do when I'm done, what are the words that I'm going to say (I actually rehearse them in my head, and when I first started this kind of rehearsing I would say them out loud), and how might this confuse them or create misconceptions. I mostly rehearse the things that I have taught the least or the things that have not been as successful in the past as I had hoped. For example, there's a math lesson where the idea is to get away from numbers—like numbers in the number chart—but still see patterns. The students are supposed to make a grid and then write their name on it, so my grid would be Barbara-BarbaraBarbara . . ., until all the squares were filled up. You are supposed to enter the letters continuously, starting each new row as a continuation from the previous row. But the first time I taught it, about half of the class would finish a row and then start their name all over again at the beginning of the next row. This defeats the purpose of the lesson, because after you finish filling out the squares, you are supposed to color in the first letters of your name and, depending on how many letters are in your name, you will see a pattern. Students whose names have the same number of letters will have the same pattern. Well, the first time I taught it, it was frustrating because too many students filled out the grid wrong, so they couldn't compare patterns [in the way intended]. Most of the time was spent talking about properly flipping the names down to the next line of squares instead of comparing and discussing patterns that you might see in a 100s chart.

So the next year, I did the name writing and coloring in of charts the day before the discussion, working with small groups while the rest of the class did a different math activity. This worked much better, but it made the lesson take a lot more time than I was willing to spend on it. So in the third year, I conducted a time/cost analysis as I was driving into school.

I decided that the lesson was not worth spending two days on, so I asked how I might give the directions so as to avoid the problem experienced in the first year. I'm thinking, "How do I get them to see that when they get to the end of the line, it's not the end of their name—that it's going to keep continuing down to the next row? What do we already do or what have we already done that might help them with this?" And I got to thinking about the calendar in our room that we use all the time. In teaching them about how a calendar works, one of the things that I emphasize is that you go to the end of the row and get to a Saturday, but the month does not stop there—it keeps going on the next row. Also, the month usually doesn't start on a Sunday and end on a Saturday—it might start in the middle of the row on a Wednesday and end on a Friday. And I realized that this calendar concept matched what I was trying to teach about filling out the name grids. Because your name is not always going to stop at the end of the line like on the Saturday—it might stop in the middle but then you continue it on the next line. So that third year, when I gave directions, I talked about how this is just like a month on the calendar: how you keep going—it's not always going to stop at the end of the row, how you're going to have to go down to the next row to finish your name.

This worked much better, but upon reflection afterwards, it occurred to me that I could pave the way for this lesson the next year by tweaking my teaching of the calendar at the beginning of the year. So when I taught the calendar at the beginning of the next year, I made sure to use a standard phrase in talking about how you observe or count the days in a month ("You don't just stop at the end of the row—you go on to the next row."). I emphasized that standard phrase when I taught the calendar because I knew I was going to use it later when I got to the math lesson using name grids.

Being able to do this kind of foreshadowing and tying back was one of the reasons that I loved looping [teaching the same cohort of students for two years in a row, in both first grade and second grade]. Because so much of what we do in second grade builds on what they learned in first grade. Knowing this, when I taught first-graders something that they would need to know in second grade, I emphasized the aspects that they would be using later and sometimes established certain key phrases to be repeated in the future. Even now, when I am no longer looping, one of the things I keep in the back of my mind during planning and reflection is, "How might I use this in the future?"

In addition to rehearsing lessons prior to teaching them, Barbara reflects on them afterwards, often on the drive home from school that day. During these times, she thinks about, and "files away" for future reference, what went well and what went poorly in the day's activities. She focuses in particular on any problems she encountered, and what she might do to avoid them in the future. For example,

One math activity that came right out of our math curriculum had to do with "fact families." It called for taking a bunch of number sentences, cutting them up, and then pasting them together in fact families. The first time I taught this lesson, it was just chaos. Kids lost pieces, cut pieces in half that weren't supposed to be cut in half, and so on. While driving home, I'm thinking, "OK, what do I want them to know and be able to do when they're done? . . . I want them to be able to look at two number sentences and tell me whether or not they are from the same fact family. OK, and what were they thinking about most as they did this activity? . . . Cutting, pasting, not losing their pieces, sharing the glue, getting them all cut out, figuring where to glue them on, doing it quickly, and so on. They weren't thinking at all about fact families and what they are supposed to be able to do at the end of the lesson. . . . Probably I should just junk this lesson and move on, but one of my big year-long "umbrella messages" is that you finish what you start. But in this case . . .

Continuation of reasoning about this dilemma led Barbara to decide to abandon further cutting and pasting. Instead, she brought the lesson to closure by leading a summary conversation the next day about families of number facts. She introduced it, however, by sharing her thinking about the dilemma: "It's really important to finish what you start and get your jobs done, but sometimes you need to take a look at what you are doing and figure out if it's working. And if it's not working, it's OK to abandon it and move on."

Nor did Barbara repeat that lesson in the future. Instead, she carefully analyzed what the lesson was intended to teach and devised a better way of teaching this to her students. In other words, she retained the goal (intended outcome), but replaced the lesson and related activity that came with her instructional materials. She is quite comfortable making such changes as long as she believes that her substitute activity is at least as successful as the adopted curriculum's activity for enabling her students to attain the intended outcomes. She even shared this aspect of her thinking the next day when she introduced the substitute activity with her students:

> I sat the little guys down on the second day and I said to them, "Everything we do, we do for a reason. There's something that I'm thinking in my head that I want you to know when we're done. I think, "When we're done with this job today, I want you to be able to look at two number sentences and know that they're in the same fact family. Do you think when you're done with the job that you're doing today, you are going to be able to look at two sentences and know if they're in the same fact family?" And the kids are all looking at me like, "No." Shaking their heads, going no. "Are you worrying more about the cutting and the pasting, or are you worrying more about the fact families?" And they are all like, "Cutting and pasting." So I say, "Here's the conversation I was having in my head about the work that we were doing at school yesterday. You know, I think about school all the time, even when we're not here. I'm guessing that some of you do that, too. That's what great learners do. Anyway, I just don't see any reason for us to keep doing this cutting and pasting, because we aren't learning what we need to learn from it. I've got something much better for us to do that will help us learn this. So what do you suppose we should do with these?" And they're all kind of looking around at each other, until one brave little kid says, "I think we should throw them away." And I say, "You know what? That's brilliant. Go get the garbage can." And they were looking like, "Really?" Because they were hating this thing. And I say, "Yes, really." So we brought over the garbage can and everyone ceremoniously dumped the cutting and pasting into the trash. Then we put the can away and started on the new job.

Incorporating Standards and Benchmarks

In developing their cultural universals curriculum for social studies, Jan and Jere started by assembling lists of big ideas—identifying what they believed to be the most fundamental and powerful ideas to teach to primary students about each cultural universal. Standards and benchmarks (published by the National Council for the Social Studies and by the State of Michigan) were taken into account in developing the units, but the units were not developed around them from the beginning. Instead, the units were developed around big ideas, and the standards and benchmarks then were used as checklists to make sure that the units addressed all of the important content that should have been addressed.

Barbara plans and develops units and lessons in other content areas in a similar fashion. Their purposes are to develop the big ideas and associated major skills that provide the rationale for including the units or lessons in the curriculum in the first place. So, her planning always begins by asking what are the major intended outcomes of the unit or lesson, and then proceeds accordingly. Whether she is developing curricula herself or adapting provided curricula, she is always asking how she can help her students to attain the intended outcomes, and evaluating in terms of the relative success of a lesson or activity for accomplishing this agenda.

She then uses the state's standards and benchmarks—the Grade Level Content Expectations (GLCEs)—as checklists for criteria by which to assess the completeness of her plans. She typically finds that units developed in this manner address most of the GLCEs effectively, although not always in the same order in which they are listed in the state's documents. Concerning the order, she says:

> I think about the GLCEs in terms of which part of the year I should emphasize them or where I think the kids ought to be able to handle them, developmentally speaking. There are some that you need to do before others. For example, in the word/phonics ones, some GLCEs talk about kids needing to be able to identify the beginning sounds of words and get the sound/symbol/letter relationship stuff taken care of, and others talk about being able to do word endings. Naturally, the former should come before the latter, so I think about which part of the year I should try to emphasize word endings.
>
> Another GLCE talks about approximating poetry [exposing students to poetry and scaffolding their initial attempts to compose poems of their own]. There is no particular point in the year when I think, "Alright, it's time to approximate poetry." But studying the GLCE, I find that there are some ways in which I already do that, so if I just continue to do the things that I have always done, I will hit that GLCE several times during the year. As another example, one of the

social studies GLCEs talks about past, present, and future time perspective. I do that in lots of different ways, and not just in social studies (during poetry time, calendar time, when reading books in guided reading groups or reading the *Scholastic News* or *Time for Kids*). So with these GLCEs that I know I hit many times across the year, I put them out of my head and do not worry about them. But some of them, I think about the specific time of year when it would be best to emphasize it—it might fit well with a certain unit in one of the subjects, for example. But I do make sure that the GLCEs are covered one way or another.

For example, there are a few math standards that our math program does not include. One of them is double digit addition without regrouping. The program touches on it briefly, a few problems in a single lesson, so what I do is identify that and other standards that are not in the curriculum (e.g., telling time, counting money) and create little mini-units that I embed in between the regular math units throughout the year. So for example, in January, in between two math units, I do a mini-unit on identifying coins. And I add a section to a math unit on addition that gives the kids more experience with double digit addition, having them add problems like 20+30. This was the logical place for adding that mini-lesson. For coins, I embed a mini-unit on dimes and pennies at the end of the math unit on place value, because that matches up with content about tens and ones. And I teach about nickels later in a math unit that includes a lesson on counting by fives. So again, my curriculum with respect to the GLCEs doesn't look at all like you might imagine from reading the GLCEs, but if you study it you will find that the GLCEs are all covered sufficiently in one way or another.

Based on her years of experience in teaching at the grade level, Barbara has developed a good sense of first-graders' trajectories of development in different areas of knowledge and skill. This has enabled her to create benchmarks that help her assess progress and individualize instruction throughout the year. For example, she knows that, by a certain point in the school year, her students ought to be able to read a certain number of sight words, create and report sentences of specified length and complexity, be able to write a certain number of sentences on a topic, or be able to write a paragraph that includes a beginning, middle, and end. She generates specific benchmarks for reading, writing, and mathematics skills, and then uses these to determine which students can meet them and which still need instruction and opportunities to practice specific skills.

Barbara publishes these benchmarks on posters displayed in the classroom and sends them home to parents in newsletters and report cards. In January, for example, she posts a list of expectations that will apply every day, to every assignment. She also posts and gradually adds to a "no excuses" list that includes leaving your name off your paper, writing a sentence without a capital letter, and writing numbers backwards.

Besides identifying and following through on individual remediation needs, Barbara uses her personal benchmarks and expectations lists as input to decisions about integrating her curriculum, especially when the integration involves using skills learned in reading, writing, or math to carry out assignments in science or social studies. So, when planning a content area activity or assignment that calls for writing, she will keep these guidelines in mind when deciding the task's level of complexity (What are her students ready for at this point?) and when assessing their responses (What levels of performance should she expect at this point from the class as a whole and from each individual?). Where appropriate, she also might include literacy or math goals along with science or social studies goals, as when requiring that answers to questions be written in complete sentences.

Making Connections and Integrating the Curriculum

As just noted, Barbara's curriculum planning considers both sequencing within subjects and connections across subjects. Rather than view curricular integration as a potential add-on after the curriculum is basically developed, she looks for ways to integrate the curriculum right from the beginning of her planning. She says:

> I don't have separate conversations in my head or separate plans for integration, because I look at things much more holistically than most other teachers do. I don't weed out things and say, "This would be good for integration." Instead, when I am planning activities, and throughout the day when I am teaching, I always keep in mind what I am doing that day, that week, and during that part of the school year. I am always looking for connections and ways to get double duty from some of my activities—design them so as to promote progress toward important goals in two different subjects. So this is not just about integration for me, it also is about getting the most out of my time and activities—it's about cost or time management, not just integration.
>
> For example, a big part of first-grade literacy is learning and practicing printing. I need to give the kids instruction in how to print letters and then opportunities to practice printing the letters we worked on. But I want to get as much out of that printing practice as I can, so I use the words from the current sight word list as the content base for printing activities in any given week. Also, as part of

developing independent work expectations for the kids early in the year, one of those expectations is that as they come in in the morning, they should quickly put their things away and then get to work independently. One of the two jobs that they will work on during this time is printing.

Later, during the morning meeting after making announcements, we read together the sentences explaining what we will be doing that day. These sentences then become the content base for their handwriting practice. Reading them together first puts meanings to the words, so they are not just copying something that they can't read. Furthermore, the sentences connect to later activities, such as what we might be doing in science or social studies. For example, the sentences might say, "Today we will talk about food. We will get to eat bread." So as they are getting handwriting practice they also are thinking about what is coming later in the day. Also, the sentences use words that they will need to know how to read.

So to me, this is what integration is all about. I usually do not think to myself, "Gee, we're having a social studies lesson about bread today, so I think I'll have the kids write five sentences about bread because that would be a good literacy activity, too." Instead, I think, "OK, I'm doing a lesson about bread in social studies, and we recently worked on describing words in science. I want the kids to keep thinking about describing words and practice using them, so today I will ask them to describe their favorite breads." Rather than make up something, I think about the things I already have done or want to do, and try to get the most out of them. That's where integration happens for me.

In fact, that particular lesson integrated mathematics as well, because we had been working on using tally marks in math. For the lesson, we tasted different kinds of bread and generated a list of words or phrases describing their flavors or characteristics. We also listed the different breads that we tasted. As the activity continued, the students took turns coming up to the bread list, placing a tally mark next to the name of the bread they enjoyed the most, and then giving a reason for this preference. Some of the things they said were, "I liked this kind of bread because it's soft because it has yeast in it," "I like this bread because it was made from rye flour and I like that flavor," or "I like this bread best because it was chewy, so they must not have put as much water in it." To complete the lesson, we made a pictograph depicting our bread preferences, because understanding pictographs is one of the state's GLCEs for the grade level. So in just that one day, they had their sight words in sentences in the morning that they wrote about eating bread; they had handwriting practice; they had a couple of math GLCEs in the tally marks and counting by fives of the tally marks and the pictographs; and they had a little oral language practice—answering in complete sentences as opposed to just giving one- or two-word answers. These kinds of integrative connections flow through all of the things that I do, but I don't say to myself, "OK, I want to create an integration activity that combines tally marks and social studies" and then think of something.

Indeed, connections like these do pervade Barbara's teaching. For example, a brief strand in her math curriculum focuses on sorting, combining, and recombining. Following lessons that developed basic concepts and provided initial practice on these skills, Barbara introduced a subsequent practice activity by reading a book entitled *Grandma's Button Box* (Aber & O'Rourke, 2002). As she began reading, she told her students to look for ways that the buttons were sorted in the story (by shape, color, number of openings, thickness, and shiny versus dull). She then used this information as the basis for a math activity calling for estimating, counting, and sorting into various frames.

Recurring examples of integration involve the poems that Barbara selects to read to her students and use as the basis for follow-up activities. These poems usually are chosen because they connect well with something taught elsewhere in the curriculum. For example, the literacy curriculum includes lessons on ellipses, a topic that can be challenging to teach to first-graders because the ellipses themselves are symbolic, their meanings are abstract, and they do not lend themselves to authentic activities. However, she found a poem entitled "Maytime Magic," that depicts a child growing a plant in the springtime. It talks about what the child would need to do to nurture the plant successfully, in couplet lines that end in ellipses ("A little seed for me to sow, a little earth to make it grow . . ."). Barbara got lots of extra mileage out of this poem because at the time the students were learning about plants and living things in science and about using ellipses in writing. In addition, the poem nicely fit state standards related to poetry, and many of its words were on the list of words that her students were supposed to be learning to recognize on sight.

As a final example, Barbara drew on what her students had been learning in writing to develop an assessment activity in science. This activity occurred at the end of the science unit that involved raising mealworms (feeding them, tracking their progress, etc.). Meanwhile, in writing the students were learning about using transition words (first, next, then, last). After several mini-lessons on transition words and associated brief application exercises, Barbara decided that she wanted to assess her students to make sure that they understood the main points she was teaching about transition words and could use them in an organized way. She emphasized this because one of the important GLCEs in writing involved being able to write a story with a beginning, middle, and end.

Her students had watched the mealworms long enough to know that they begin as larvae, then turn into pupae, and then the pupae break open and what eventually become beetles emerge. They had observed and discussed all of this, so she knew they had an experience base to enable them to respond successfully to an assignment calling for them to describe the development of a beetle. And, in fact, most of her students did produce stories along the lines of, "First, there was an egg. Then it hatched into a larva. Next it became a pupa. Then at the end it became a beetle." A few of them even added, "And then . . . there was another egg," putting to use what they had learned about ellipses and showing awareness that the life cycle starts all over again.

Barbara emphasizes that she included this activity because it was a perfect fit (she needed to assess her students' ability to write stories that included clear beginnings, middles, and ends, and the mealworm–beetle life cycle was a perfect content base for such a story). Rather than generate something "extra" and artificial, she built on what she was already doing because "it was a really natural, cost-efficient fit."

Many of her integration activities occur at the independent practice phase of a lesson cycle, and involve using familiar content to provide a base for application of recently learned skills. This provides a level of challenge that most of her students can handle, whereas most of them might become confused if the assignment called for using newly learned and only partially mastered skills to process or apply relatively unfamiliar content:

> I don't want them grappling with too much new at once. For example, when they are writing practice sentences on the board, I make sure that the words in these practice sentences are mostly familiar words—words from their sight word list that they can read and access easily. So for literacy integration, I want them using familiar, comfortable skills. If I'm going to integrate something, I'm not going to integrate two new things. I'm going to integrate something that's familiar and comfortable with something new that they're practicing.

Barbara believes that, to integrate successfully, teachers need to be very knowledgeable about their curriculum as a whole (including where students have been, where they are now, and where they are headed), as well as carefully assess and monitor their students' learning (their current strengths, weaknesses, and needs) and their own teaching (what they have already taught in depth, what they have not yet introduced or just mentioned in passing without systematically explaining). They then need to process this input in the light of their overall goals and priorities.

Barbara adds that making connections between what is taught in school and students' lives outside of school (and helping students to see these connections themselves) ought to get at least as much attention as across-subjects curricular integration. She explains:

> I think a huge piece of integration that people don't see but that matches a holistic model is pointing out connections to kids throughout the day. Not just pointing them out, but teaching them to look for them. This is a huge key to helping kids become lifelong learners. Everyone loves to "trot that pony out and pet it," but they usually do not have a good idea of what it really takes to teach kids to be lifelong learners.
>
> To become a lifelong learner, you've got to learn to become a self-sustained inquirer. It is easy to begin this with first-graders because they easily become obsessed with things they learn. For example, if they are not yet really seeing words as units and you teach them how to look for a word (identify a word they recognize), then they start to see it everywhere. When we teach them about ellipses and talk about what writers use ellipses for, the kids begin to see ellipses everywhere in everything they read, at least for a few days. You have taught them about ellipses in a mini-lesson in writing, and suddenly they're finding ellipses in poems, in books, on signs, and so on. You can capitalize on these experiences to teach them to generalize the expectation that what they are learning in school will have applications to life outside of school. Then they can begin noticing things and making connections themselves. So, in summary: know your curriculum, know your personal priorities within the curriculum, know your students (where they are, what they have mastered and what they haven't, what they need extra practice with), know your own teaching (monitor what you have so far taught well versus not at all or not so well), and look for connections. Point out those connections and teach the kids to do so themselves. Then begin to expect it from them. That's what holistic teaching is all about.

Holidays and Special Events

Barbara has to stretch her already tight schedule to accommodate time for holiday-related activities and special events. She tries to minimize the degree to which these activities disrupt her academic curriculum, and to the extent possible, designs her students' participation around activities that will connect with some of the big ideas she is emphasizing in her teaching:

> We are required to do some things, such as the constitutional activities during the week of Constitution Day. The state standards prescribe what we need to do for patriotism in first grade, so I squeeze in those

activities during that week. But activities related to special days usually are not mandated, so I include them or not depending on the importance of the day and the degree to which I can connect it with my curriculum. For example, I do not do anything special for Mother's Day, because it is not mentioned in the state standards and it doesn't match or connect well with my units or outcome expectations.

A different kind of example is the diversity fair that our school holds every year. I'm required to have a class contribution to the fair, so I look at what I am going to be doing anyway and what I am required to do, and look for a match. We were required to come up with some sort of display to put up here in the building as part of the diversity fair, and to show how we talk about diversity within our classroom. Well, one of the conversations we have during the food unit is about how everyone around the world eats bread—that bread is something that we all have in common, but different cultures make very different kinds of bread from the same basic ingredients. This lesson was already in my curriculum, so I just recreated that activity for the diversity fair. I put the big ideas onto posters. Then in class, the kids try different kinds of bread from all over the world (baguettes, bagels, croissants, pita breads, chapatti, tortillas, and so on). We talk about the kinds of grain that the flour is from, the different ways that people make the bread, and how they might use this kind of bread themselves at home. During the diversity fair, my display included samples of the different kinds of bread for families to try. So rather than create something just for the diversity fair that would add onto an already full curriculum map, I looked for something I was already doing.

Another option used in the past connected with the family unit I teach in the fall. Part of this unit talks about immigration—how they and their ancestors came here to Michigan from somewhere else. I have used that as the basis of a display for the diversity fair. Also, the family unit includes a lesson about celebrations—everyone celebrates but different people celebrate different holidays and celebrate in different ways. I've used that as a display for the diversity fair. One year, instead of going the social studies route, I went the math route. All year long we had created different graphs about the personal preferences of students or their families (Do you like pizza with cheese or pepperoni? Would you rather go to the beach or a carnival on vacation? What holiday do you like to celebrate the most? etc.). We created quite a collection of graphs displaying the variation in responses to these questions, so we used these graphs as our diversity fair display.

In general, whenever these kinds of requirements come down from above, I always look to connect it with our curriculum so it will be more meaningful and authentic for the kids. This way, when the kids come to school with family members for the special event, they can show the family members the poster and say something like, "Here are things I know: I know that all bread is made from flour and water but the flour is different because it comes from different grains. People in different countries use different flour because they grow different grains there, because not the same grain grows everywhere. And people cook bread in different ways, but everybody needs bread because it's part of the grain group." I also hope that they would point out the doughnut example and say, "This isn't as healthy as the bagel because this one was cooked in fat and the other was boiled in water. And boiling in water is healthier than cooking in fat." And I hope they point out the tortilla and the piece of white bread and say, "The reason this one is fluffy is because it has yeast in it and the reason this one is not fluffy is because it's made of flour and water but doesn't have yeast in it." The items on the poster connect with the big ideas we have talked about during the unit, so this provides students with authentic opportunities to talk about the displays with family members.

Here in Chapter 9 we have described how Barbara conducts her instructional planning, proceeding from the yearly through the unit and weekly to the daily levels. We also described her daily rehearsal and reflection activities and her approaches to incorporating standards and benchmarks and to making connections and integrating curriculum. In Chapters 10 to 12, we describe her teaching of the major subjects of literacy, social studies, mathematics, and science.

Chapter 10

Curriculum and Instruction in Literacy

An overview of Barbara's first-grade curriculum, as conveyed in the materials that she provides for families at the beginning of the school year, is shown in Chapter 3. That material also includes an outline of an average day in her classroom, which is reproduced below:

An Average Day:
- Math skill-building & catch-up time
- Morning meeting & Calendar
- Sight Words or Spelling
- Writer's Workshop
- Poem Books
- Recess & Snack
- Literacy Choice Time & Reading
- Lunch
- Quiet Reading Practice
- Math
- Student of the Week or Story & Surprise box
- Social Studies/Science/Health
- Specials (Art, music, gym, library)
- Home

As the outline illustrates, Barbara, like most first-grade teachers, concentrates on teaching mathematics and (especially) literacy. Mathematics appears twice (during a skill-building and catch-up time scheduled as the students filter into the classroom at the beginning of each day, and during a mathematics lesson taught early in the afternoon). Literacy appears five times. Following the morning meeting and calendar discussion (also designed in part to serve literacy goals), her students experience a word analysis or spelling lesson, a writer's workshop, and time spent reading or writing about poems. Following recess, they engage in literacy choice time activities while Barbara teaches reading lessons to small groups of two to five students. Finally, the first period following lunch is spent reading silently or quietly reading aloud to a partner. A later period during the afternoon scheduled for miscellaneous activities (e.g., student of the week, surprise box) also frequently includes reading a story to the students—another literacy activity. Some of these activities routinely include home assignments or take-home products, so her students experience interactions that support progress toward literacy and mathematics goals at home as well as at school.

Literacy Instruction

In Barbara's classroom, literacy is not only a formal part of the curriculum but a way of life. Summarizing several days of observation there, Jan noted:

> This class is incredibly literacy rich. I felt like I was in an environment with an ongoing conversation throughout each day. Children have multiple opportunities within the day to spend moments with Barb, moments with the aide, moments in talking to their peers during table talk or pair share, moments to take the lead during the morning rug meeting, moments to be leaders at their tables as they monitor and bring supplies or chat with their table mates, and moments within literacy choice time. There are all kinds of opportunities for talking, listening, reading, and writing. I was very impressed with the literacy richness and the balance between teacher talk and student talk.

Barbara also thinks about literacy as developed within four major curriculum strands of reading, writing, speaking, and listening. However, she speaks of thinking/listening, rather than just listening. She socializes her students to listen actively, processing what they are hearing to connect it to their prior knowledge, make sure that they understand it, and react to it in ways that may lead them to ask a question or make a comment. This is part of her overall emphasis on thinking and metacognition in her teaching of every content area, even to the newest first-graders.

Morning Meeting

Barbara thinks of her daily literacy instruction as beginning during the calendar discussions that occur as part of each day's morning meeting. As the school year begins, she uses some of this time to model for her students how to ask questions and elicit complete answers. For example, after posing the question, "What day is today?" she might lead the class in examining the posted date (e.g., Monday, October 19, 2009), and applying the phonics knowledge they are learning: "We break it down to a word level and look at letter cues." She also notes that the numerical date can be found on the calendar, so "we can look at the sequence of the week and figure out what day it is." Eventually, they work together to develop the complete answer (e.g., "Today is Monday, October 19, 2009."). This emphasis on working at the word level but then putting it all together holistically pervades Barbara's literacy teaching.

Especially at the beginning of the year, she may extend this activity by asking, "What will tomorrow be?" Again, she will help the students to look for cues at the word level and perhaps use other information to figure out what the answer is, then formulate it into a complete sentence. In addition to calendar time, she takes advantage of other curricular opportunities that arise during the day (not just during literacy activities) to pose questions, elicit response components, and then help the students to "put it all together" in a complete sentence that is verbalized aloud. She believes that this helps her students see the connections they need to see in order to grasp and retain the meaning of the complete thought.

Word Work

Formal literacy teaching begins with word work time, during which Barbara leads her students in word analysis and phonics activities focusing on letter-sound correspondences, onsets and rhymes, word endings, and other aspects of parts of language. For example, she might ask her students to identify words that end in "an." As they do so, she will list them on the board and verify that they do in fact end in "an." If a nominated word is incorrect (e.g., sand), she will take advantage of the teachable moment by writing the word on the board and providing informative feedback ("This one's a little different. Listen real closely. People have a hard time hearing the ending sound . . .").

Some of Barbara's teaching during word work time takes the form of relatively formal lessons. For example, in a lesson on the short ĕ sound, she wrote the words "elephant" and "egg" on the board, referring to the short ĕ sound as a "baby e" and pronouncing it to illustrate that it has a "little bitty" sound, in contrast to a long sound. She then wrote four more words on the board (ten, pen, den, when), noting that they all have a baby e in the middle. One student asked why these words all sound the same, then Barbara explained that this is because they all have the same letter in the middle, and went on to give more examples.

In addition to more formal lessons, word work time frequently includes games such as Hangman or informal challenges such as, "I'm thinking of a word that has two letters and the first letter is a vowel." Barbara also teaches her students rhymes and raps to perform as a way to help them remember key ideas or facts (e.g., A-E-I-O-U).

As the year progresses (especially after the holidays), word work activities shift focus from word analysis to spelling. Once again, the time is divided between formal lessons, spelling practice activities, and challenges such as examining words to determine whether they are spelled correctly or whether a letter is missing (and if the latter, to supply the missing letter).

To elicit home reinforcement of what she is teaching, Barbara encourages her students to engage in word work games and challenges at home with parents or other family members. For example, she might first model the giving of clues ("My word has two tall letters in it.") and invite her students to identify the word, then shift to a version which the students themselves give the clues, and then encourage them to play the same game at home ("Think about who at home would be good to play this game with . . . How will you explain it to them?").

Writer's Workshop

When teaching individual words (or facts, basic skills, etc.), Barbara emphasizes words that the students will be using, preferably right away. Consequently, the earliest words she teaches are words that students will want to use during their writing activities, and she schedules writer's workshop immediately after word work time to give them a chance to do so: "The very next part of the day is the writer's workshop, because I want them to take those building block tools they have just learned and use them immediately. Those word work skills—sounds, letters, 'if you can spell hat, you can spell cat'—are things I want them to use during writing time. So, it's the building-block chunk followed right away with the application chunk. I do a mini-lesson at the beginning of writer's workshop and include a little bridge building or connection making between what they did in word work that day and what they're going to do in writing."

As she does in all of her teaching, Barbara structures and scaffolds writer's workshop activities by not only explaining how to do the assignment but modeling the process herself, thinking aloud as she does so. She not only provides a concrete representation of the kind of product that she wants her students to generate; *she models the process by verbalizing the self-talk used to guide each step.* She says, "I try to build bridges between the different parts of literacy instruction (in this case, word work and writer's workshop). Then, during the writing time, I model for them. I actually write. And I use the same white paper that the kids use. A lot of teachers, when they model for the kids, they write on big, lined poster paper and then put it up on the wall. When I model for them, especially literacy work, I want the experience to be as close as I can make it to what they will be doing themselves" (Barbara's modeling is discussed in detail in Chapter 6).

After modeling, but before releasing the students to work independently, *she spends some time scaffolding their planning of the writing they will do on their own.* She will circulate during the writing time to guide students who need help, but she wants to make sure that all of her students begin with sufficiently clear plans and mental images to enable them to get a good start on their writing. Once she dismisses the students to begin working and they settle into the task, she circulates the room, focusing initially on students who appear to need help but then simply engaging students in conversations about their writing:

> I go table to table, and what ends up happening is that when I am talking to James who is right here next to me, the other two or three kids at the table stop writing and listen in on our conversation. I am OK with that because it gives them another shot at whatever important thing I'm working on, whether it's "stretch your story over three parts" or "find the sound and stretch it to find more sounds." Whatever it is that we have been working on or whatever I'm going to help James with, my guess is that everyone else at the table needs some support on this as well, so it won't hurt them to hear it. So, after I conclude my talk with James, I will chat with other students at the table about what they're doing. I might just say, "Tell me what you are doing as a writer." [To help develop her students' perceptions of themselves as readers and writers, she refers to them as readers and writers right from the beginning of the year. She characterizes them as people who already are readers and writers, but are developing and refining their skills—getting to be even better readers and writers.]

Barbara's conversations with students during writing time focus on the major goals she is working on during that part of the year. Early in the year, for example, her students work at composing very simple stories (often just a sentence or two) rooted in their personal experiences. Barbara scaffolds this by telling them to create stories that are personal narratives ("something about you—something that really has happened or will happen to you"). Other goals that might be emphasized at the same time include "add words to your story" (the earliest versions might be just a picture with a word or two of title, rather than a story containing words connected into sentences), and "find the beginning sound of every word that you attempt to write."

She frequently reminds her students that the whole point of writing is to communicate something to readers, and to do that, you need many words combined into sentences. She encourages them to keep at it and make the best use of their writing time: "Your writing time is precious. We only have so much of it in the day, and you have so many stories that you want to write and so many things that you would like people to know, so move from one story to the next. If you think you are finished, here are things that you can do: you can add more to the picture, you can add more to the words, you can start a new piece . . .".

This emphasis on self-regulation might lead to chaos in some classrooms, but *Barbara teaches her students to handle these responsibilities independently.* She uses her folder system as a way to keep both the students and herself aware of which writing pieces have been completed and which still need work. Having experimented with different approaches, she believes that this fluid process produces better results than attempting to move the class as a whole through a prearranged schedule that calls for everyone to spend a fixed amount of time writing stories, then another fixed amount editing them, then another fixed amount peer reviewing them, and so on.

To help her students be able to function independently for much of the time, Barbara builds in scaffolds and supports that they can use as resources. For example, a posted "word wall" can be consulted when students cannot remember the word they want to use or need to see how to spell it correctly. Other resources include posters and samples of previous writings by Barbara and their peers.

Barbara also includes independence and self-regulation in the modeling that she does as part of her lessons. For example, one year she decided to write a story about helicopters because the previous day she had spotted television helicopters hovering near her house, getting video for a news story. She explained this to her students and then did think-aloud modeling of the story planning process, including overcoming perceived barriers:

> I noted all of the things I wanted to put in my story and then I actually sketched it out. But when it came time to begin writing, I said, "Oh, wait. I can't write the word 'helicopter.' I don't know how to spell it. So there's just no way I can do this story. I guess I won't be able to write it after all." And then one of the kids said, "Oh no—you can't do that." And I said, "Well, if I don't know how to spell it for sure, what do you suppose I should do?" And after some discussion I segued into, "Well, you know what? Here's what I think I'll do." Then I broke it down into steps for them as to what you can do if you need words that you don't know. Then I modeled it for them: I was going to look for the first sound and write it as best I could, then go on to the next sound, and so on. I emphasized that, "You do the best you can and move on." This is a standard phrase that I use for that situation. Just like in any of the chunks of our day, I have standard phrases that I use so kids will know how to handle problems. Eventually, I want to get them to the point where they don't need me to say the standard phrase—they say it to themselves or it's in their heads.

I even have a poster for that one, because I know it is something that first-graders struggle with. The title of the poster is "Write Tough Words," and it breaks down the process. So if a kid says, "I don't know how to spell that word," I will say, "Well, what do we do when we get to tough words? Say it with me. Do the best . . ." If they are still stuck, I will refer them to the poster: "Take a look at the poster. What did we write down that you ought to do? . . . What do you do first?" . . . What do you do next? . . . What do you do last?" And if they're still stuck, I'll say, "Well, what did I do when I got to the word 'helicopter?' "

After modeling with her helicopter story, Barbara followed up with guided practice. She told her students to go through their own stories and find words they had struggled with, then follow the same process that she had used to see if they could figure out more sounds. She concludes:

I modeled it. I guided them through some practice. I prepared them to try it independently. Then I sent them off to do it. Then I gave them feedback about their independent work. So, modeling, guided practice, planning for independent practice, and feedback. I don't think teachers plan for independent practice or give immediate feedback about independent practice often enough. But, this is like jumping ship on them! You need to give your students opportunities to apply what you teach independently, and then check in with them to see how they are doing.

Reflecting the goals she is currently emphasizing, Barbara makes certain demands on her students during independent writing time. Otherwise, however, she grants them considerable autonomy in deciding what to do and how to do it. In the early weeks of first grade, for example, her primary goals during the writer's workshop time are building her students' capacities for working independently and both pressing and supporting them to add words to make more complete stories (if necessary). So long as individual students are making progress toward these two featured goals, she will not make other demands that she might make later in the year. For example, certain students frequently begin stories but then abandon them without finishing them. Also, some write three or four "stories" every day, in the sense that they write "I went to the store," "I went to McDonald's," or "I went to the mall," and then illustrate it with a drawing. Although not ideal, this is acceptable in the early weeks:

He feels like a really successful writer because he's knocking off stories, and they are true things happening to him. What's my goal?

That he moves through the process independently and uses words to tell the stories. Is he doing these two things? Yes. So now I am not going to push him, although occasionally I may suggest adding more words to the story. But I know that down the road we're going to get to a unit called Revising, and during that unit we will spend our time going back and adding more to our stories. The unit will include mini-lessons on adding details, such as by looking at your picture and using the details shown there to enhance your writing—to give you more words to put down. We also will have lessons about adding dialogue or adding feelings to your stories.

Many components of Barbara's approach to writing instruction involve *supporting students' confidence as writers and helping them to focus on communicating meanings rather than forming perfect letters.* Many years of teaching first-graders have convinced her that these students are typically eager and relatively uninhibited about learning to read, but much less confident and overly perfectionistic when learning to write. They often hesitate to make an attempt when they are not sure of how to form a letter or word, and when they make mistakes, they are obsessive about erasing and correcting them. This is why she encourages them to cross out mistakes and move on, rather than spending a lot of time erasing. If they need to create "perfect" versions to be displayed publicly or placed into a portfolio of accomplishments, she will provide the time and support needed to do so (and the job will be easier because they already will have "made their mistakes" as they worked on earlier versions).

Poem Books

In addition to stories and informational texts, Barbara reads poems to her students, three or four times per week. She also engages them in analyses of the poems' meanings, and in the process, rereads the poems several times. She then invites the students to write and illustrate their versions of the poems' meanings (as intended by the authors) or their own reactions to the poems. She scaffolds these activities with questions about the most important ideas in the poems and how these might be represented.

Literacy Choice Time and Reading Groups

Students are responsible for working independently on ABC jobs, reading jobs, or writing jobs during literacy choice time. Within established parameters, they are free to choose which jobs to do and exercise considerable autonomy in determining when and how to do the jobs. While this is going on, Barbara gathers small groups of two to five students for focused reading instruction.

When she began reading about centers—independent activities through which students rotate during working times—and observing in other teachers' classrooms, Barbara found that most centers fit within two major types, and neither was well suited to her purposes. She describes the first as activity based. These centers might have a unifying theme, such as a story that the class has read, but essentially they consist of a group of activities. Students work through one or two of these activities each day, completing them in a week or two. Then the center is replaced by a new one. Barbara viewed these activity-based centers as very labor intensive for teachers, who need to create or adapt activities, prepare them (often involving a lot of cutting, pasting, and so on), and then provide enough scaffolding on each of them to enable the students to do them independently.

For example, she recalled developing center activities connected to a book about peanut butter and jelly, in which the activities included making a list of foods, matching pictures with foods, writing a recipe for making a peanut butter and jelly sandwich, putting the steps in sandwich-making into the right sequence, and rearranging the letters in "peanut butter" to make different words. Besides preparing the centers for each of these activities, she needed to divide her class into color-coded groups, make a schedule indicating when each group was supposed to be at which center, deal with the management problems that arose when certain activities took longer than others, find time to clue in individual students who had been absent when she explained about the new centers, and restructure the groups periodically if they began to develop "sibling rivalry" issues (one member was bossy, another would not share, etc.). Another problem was that the activities seldom allowed for students at varying achievement levels to participate at different levels of challenge.

The second type of center that Barbara observed frequently was associated with a particular subject matter or curriculum strand. For example, a writing center might contain writing materials and call for students to complete writing activities; an ABC center might have magnetic letters, foam letters, or whiteboards and markers to be used in alphabetic activities, and so on. There might be a reading center, a listening center, a science center, a math center, or an art center, and perhaps also a sand or water table. Barbara was not impressed with most of these centers because, although they provided students with opportunities for choice and involved them in activities of varying curricular value (counting blocks, painting pictures, playing at the sand table, etc.), they did not involve much practice or use of the literacy skills being developed throughout much of the day. Also, they entailed many of the same labor-intensive preparation and management challenges seen with activity-based centers.

Literacy Choice Time

Over time, Barbara developed the center activities that occur in her class-room during what she calls Literacy Choice Time. They are designed to support her students' progress toward literacy learning goals, but in ways that avoid many of the time and management demands associated with more typical learning centers. Her approach ultimately empowers her students with a lot of choice and autonomy during independent work times, but it begins with structuring and scaffolding that prepares the students to exploit these opportunities productively.

Near the beginning of the year, Barbara's students learn that literacy choice time is scheduled at the same time each day and follows the same structure (first rereading books, then engaging in self-chosen activities). The students begin by rereading books that Barbara has read with them, including the "name stories" constructed to help them learn about one another. Near the beginning of the year, these books are very short, and students are required to reread all of them before they move on to other jobs. One of Barbara's goals at this time is to build up her students' "reading stamina."

Book boxes soon begin to fill up, however, because Barbara keeps add-ing new books, along with other reading material such as poems, songs, and posters or other graphics developed during science or social studies lessons. Consequently, students' jobs at the beginning of literacy choice time shift from reading all of the books in the book box to reading a selection of these books for a specified number of minutes. To enable them to determine on their own when the required rereading time is up, she teaches her students to conclude their rereading when the time shown on the wall clock matches the time she has set on a simulated clock located in the learning center. At this point, they shift from rereading to self-chosen activities.

The activity choices involve ABC jobs, reading jobs, or writing jobs. At the beginning of the year, she devotes a week to each of these types of jobs, scaffolding heavily as the students learn and practice them. As the year progresses, the ABC center is expanded to include spelling and phonics activities. For example, to illustrate that words are composed of letters, an early reading lesson involved using words chopped up into puzzle-like pieces that needed to be assembled properly to spell the word. After using these materials during a lesson, Barbara placed them in the ABC center for students who might want to repeat the activity. The ABC center also included a "word finder" activity that called for students to find particular words in a book, poem, or other piece of writing.

Along with book choices, the reading center included leftover copies of the periodicals *Scholastic News* and *Time for Kids* that previ-ously had been read in class, copies of previously read poems and previously constructed posters, and other reading material selected to reinforce or complement the main ideas emphasized in Barbara's curriculum (in all subjects, not just literacy). The center also included four "book phones" constructed of curved PVC pipe. Holding one end of a book phone to their ear and the other near their mouth, Barbara's students can listen to themselves as they read. Book phones are a popular choice when students are using the reading center. They provide the students with forms of feedback about their oral reading that they do not get from more typical situations.

Within the menus provided, Barbara's students are free to choose the jobs they do during literacy choice time. One year, for example, one of her students loved songs and nursery rhymes, including reading about them and drawing pictures based on them. Throughout the year, he picked jobs involving songs or nursery rhymes just about every day (which was feasible because Barbara kept adding more songs and nursery rhymes used previously during lessons). She did not mind this because, "Every single day, he's looking at those words, he's finding the same words, he's figuring out which nursery rhyme is which . . . We know kids need repetitive practice with the same texts to become good readers. We know they need to make a personal connection with literacy tasks to become better at them. And because they're selecting the tasks themselves, they're much more likely to be very engaged and to pick something that's right at their level." As other examples, she noted that one fall she had one student who got out the magnetic letters and put them in alphabetical order every day, and another student also got out the magnetic letters every day, but used them to make words. She viewed each of these activities as appropriate given these students' respective development of reading skills at the time.

Occasionally one of Barbara's students will invent a literacy choice time activity that she not only approves of, but views as valuable and incorporates into her menu of choices. For example, one day one of her students took a set of magnetic letters over to a table facing the word wall and began using the letters to make selected words from the wall. Barbara viewed this as a useful activity for many of her students, so she called attention to it publicly: "Oh look, kids. Antonio is sitting by the word wall with the magnet letters. He knows exactly how to spell those words now. How many words have you got, Antonio?" He responded, "Five." Barbara concluded the interaction by observing, "Yeah, when you use the magnet letters next to the word wall, you know just how to spell the words."

If students finish the first of the jobs they have selected, they put the completed work in the "done" side of their folder and select another job. If literacy choice time ends before they have completed the job they are working on, they put the paper in the "still going" side of their folder and resume working on it the next day. Once this system is in place, Barbara does not have to deal with management issues that arise when students complete work and do not know what to do next, and her students do not have to worry about rushing to finish a job before the end of the period. Barbara checks their folders regularly, both to identify any learning gaps or confusions that will need individual attention and to track her students' individual interests (which she may follow up by referring to them during lessons or by suggesting new books or activities that individual students are likely to enjoy).

Barbara periodically holds conferences with individual students to review the quantity and quality of their accomplishments during literacy choice time. She suggests (partly individualized) norms for how many jobs each student ought to be able to accomplish during this time (e.g., two to three per day), but also emphasizes that she is interested in the level and quality of their work, not just the quantity ("If you are only doing quick jobs, maybe you aren't doing very much."). She also helps them think about sensible choices ("Get first-grade perfect first, then move into second-grade cursive."). She also reviews their folders with them, helping them to understand the meaning of quality work and to begin to assess their work accordingly.

Ad Hoc *Groupings*

Some of Barbara's independent work activities call for students to collaborate in groups of three or four. She uses *ad hoc* groupings in these situations, having determined that it is not worth the trouble to form groups that will stay together for weeks or months, because of absences, student turnover, and behavior problems that sometimes develop when group members have been together too long. When groups are needed, she forms them quickly, but tries to make sure that each group includes an academic leader and no more than one student who may have difficulty understanding or may present a behavior problem. Also, if she knows that two students do not work well together (even though they may be friends socially), she assigns them to separate groups.

In one such lesson, for example, Barbara modeled and led discussion of preparation-for-reading activities such as drawing inferences about the probable contents of the book by examining its title and cover and then paging quickly through it to get an overview. These activities included studying the cover carefully to look for clues about probable contents, thumbing through the book to note the pictures and speculate about what happens in the story, and formulating questions about the story that might be answered through the reading. She then had the students take turns reading pages from the book, focusing her questions and feedback on using story context clues to identify and infer the probable meaning of unfamiliar words.

When students had difficulty even pronouncing these words, she would scaffold their application of already learned decoding skills ("Put your finger on the first sound . . . What is it? . . . Now the next sound . . .", etc.), continuing until the students could generate a guess. After having them reread the sentence with the guessed word included, she would ask if this word made sense. If it did, she would tell them to move on; if it did not, she would resume scaffolding of word analysis. By working back and forth between the word/sound level and the story/meaning level, she helped her students not only to get the meaning of the current story, but to build their skills for reading with comprehension independently in the future.

Quiet Reading Practice

Following literacy choice time and reading group activities, Barbara's students go to lunch. Then they return for 15 minutes of quiet reading practice. During this time, they are free to read books of their choice, including books checked out from the school's library. Early in the school year, she works with her students to co-construct posters to help them identify appropriate books to read.

For example, one year the poster was entitled, "How Do You Pick a Great Book?" Under this was a subtitle, "What kind of book is this?" Barbara elicited answers to this question and added them to a running list: funny, chapter, X-Men, cartoons, animal, fiction, non-fiction, ocean, cookbook, unicorn, mystery, fairy tales, etc. She concluded this part of the discussion by noting that one criterion for book selection is the genre, content, or general nature of the book: is this something that I find interesting and would like to read about?

She then elicited responses to a second subtitled question, "How Can I Choose?" Suggestions included: ask a teacher or friend; look at the pictures; familiar book, author, or character; share it with others; try reading it (is it too easy, too hard, or just right?); finish an unfinished book; look for a specific topic; learn something new; read or listen to advertising about it. As students generated these suggestions, Barbara would elaborate on them. For example, in response to a student who reported that he usually reads books that others suggest to him, Barbara said, "A fancy word for that method is 'recommendation.' " Based on these discussions, Barbara later developed a laminated chart summarizing the best ideas about questions to ask oneself when choosing books for personal reading.

Literacy Unit Completion Celebrations

A pervasive aspect of Barbara's teaching is her attempt to encourage her students to value learning and build self-concepts as efficacious learners.

One of the most noteworthy ways in which she does this is to structure and scaffold *celebrations at the completion of each of her instructional units*. For these celebrations, both she and her students don the special tie-dyed T-shirts that she prepares for these occasions. Then they celebrate what they have accomplished during the unit.

For example, one of the first celebrations experienced by her first-graders culminated a unit on writing first-person narrative stories (i.e., "stories about things that happened to you."). Barbara sat with her students in a circle, reviewed key ideas about personal narratives, and then had each student in turn read the title of his or her story. As each title was read, she rang a chime as a form of celebration. After all the titles were read, she scaffolded a discussion in which students talked about which stories they wanted to hear first (based on the titles) and why. Then students were directed to go to the table of their choice, listen to peers read their stories, and then talk about the stories. Then they rotated to another table. After this, she noted that all of the stories would be available for reading during literacy choice time, and encouraged her students to read all of their classmates' stories. She concluded by introducing the concept of toasting during special occasions by distributing plastic glasses of "bubbly" and then leading the class in sharing a toast in celebration of their great stories.

A more elaborate celebration was held a few weeks later, following a unit on "small moment" stories:

> T: Now you know something more about how to be a great writer. That's why we're having a writing celebration today. I know that at some time today, somebody's going to look at you and say, "Hey, why are you all wearing the matching shirts?" And what will you say, Jerod?
>
> S: Because we're celebrating our writing.
>
> T: We're celebrating our writing. He's absolutely right. We're celebrating our writing today. Well, one of the ways that you celebrate is to say exactly what you learned to do. That helps your brain learn to do that more. So that's part of our celebration today. We're going to make a list of the things we have learned to do, because we want to make sure that tomorrow and every day after that you do the things that we know great writers do. So, Small-Moment Stories [writes this as the title of the poster] ... Now, are small-moment stories true stories about things that really happened, or are they made-up stories?
>
> Ss: True.
>
> T: Small-moment stories are things that have really happened to you. Charlie, is your story about something that really happened to you?

S: Yes.

T: Rachel, is your story about something that really happened to you?

S: Yes.

T: Your story is about going to the . . .?

S: Dentist.

T: Did you really go to the dentist?

S: Yes.

T: So, it really happened to Rachel. That's what small-moment stories are. True stories. Now, one of the things that I notice when I look at your stories today, compared to our last writing celebration, is that these stories have more pages to them. These stories start at the . . .

S: Beginning.

T: At the beginning, you're right. At the first thing or the beginning. And then they tell the . . .

Ss: Middle.

T: And then they have an . . .

Ss: End.

T: Yes. Our small-moment stories have a beginning, a middle, and an end. Now, another thing we talked about that would make a great small-moment story is that we practiced . . .

Ss: Zooming in.

T: We did practice zooming in. We practiced zooming in to tell one small part. Tomika, what is your story about?

S: The haunted house.

T: And did you tell everything about our school's spooktacular, or did you zoom in on one part?

S: I zoomed in on one part.

T: Do you remember that she had a story where she told all about the spooktacular? But then we said, "just like a camera," small-moment stories zoom in to one part, and the one part that she picked was the haunted house. So, a small-moment story will zoom in and tell that one part. We also said that a small-moment story wouldn't have just the outside details of everything that happened, but it also will have . . .

Ss: The inside details.

T: The inside details. When I was reading Derek's story, he was telling about being at Caesarland. Turn to the second page of your story, Derek, and read the last sentence to us. I . . .

S: I really was happy.

T: I was happy. That says something that you can't tell by looking at him. That's something that's . . .

Ss: Inside.

T: Inside. You're right. It's something that tells us how he was . . .

Ss: Feeling.

T: So, small-moment stories often have an inside part . . .

Ss: And an outside part.

T: And an outside part. The inside part might tell your feelings or something that you were thinking. So let's see what we have learned about small-moment stories [leads students through review of main ideas on poster, then shifts to next activity]. . . . When you get up to celebrate your story today, I want you to tell me one thing that you did that is true about small-moment stories. I'm going to show you how it will look by using Taylor's story. I'm looking over Taylor's story and I'm thinking about these small-moment parts . . . Hmmm . . . OK, if I were Taylor, I would stand up and say, "In my small-moment story, I had a beginning, a middle, and end." And then I'd go back and sit down. So think about your small-moment story. What was something you did to be a great writer this time? It might be that you said, "It's true, it really happened." Maybe you say you have a beginning, middle, and end. Maybe you say that you zoomed in or that you told one part or that you have some inside feelings or something you were thinking. So, look over your stories again and think about what you are going to say about your small-moment story. Go ahead and start thinking. Be ready to tell me what makes it a great small-moment story. When you have your answer ready, give me a thumbs-up. [Begins calling on students to respond.]

For the next activity, Barbara passed out post-it notes that students would use in a subsequent pair-share activity in which they would take turns reading their stories to their partners, who then would write feedback reactions on the post-it notes. She then modeled the process herself, indicating that the feedback notes might say that the story was great, had good ideas, was fun to read, etc. Following this activity, she concluded the celebration as follows:

T: I think that you have learned so much about writing great small-moment stories, and it sounds like the kids in the class think so too. As I was going around, I saw that you have lots of notes from other kids on your stories, telling what they thought about them, and I heard comments like, "I really like this book," or "This part was great," or "It was a great story." You are becoming even better writers all the time. When we go to write tomorrow, think about the things you did that made your stories great. Think about making it true. Putting in a beginning, a middle, and an end. Zooming in. Telling things on the outside details and the inside details. Feelings, the things you were thinking. I hope that you all looked at each other's stories so that you can be an even better writer tomorrow. Now, here's what will happen with the books that you have right in front of you. I'm going to make a copy of each of your books, and the copy will go out on the bookshelf in the project area for kids in our room to read and the kids in the class next door to read. Then, I'll let you take your story with all of the post-it notes home to share with your families. I'm even going to send home a couple of post-it notes, so when Taylor reads her story to her mother, her mother can write a message and stick it right on Taylor's story, like you did today.

Barbara's literacy teaching illustrates how, just as with her general classroom management and expectations for student self-regulation of behavior, her subject matter teaching consistently emphasizes goals, rationales, and self-regulation of learning. Instead of disoriented bits and pieces, her students are learning connected sets of knowledge and skills that they use for authentic purposes (in the case of literacy, reading for meaning and writing to communicate their experiences and ideas to others). This helps them to appreciate the value and applicability of what they are learning, and to use it with metacognitive awareness of their goals and strategies for doing so.

Chapter 11

Curriculum and Instruction in Social Studies

This chapter highlights a few of the most important features of Barbara's social studies teaching, most notably her sustained focus on big ideas. A much more complete and detailed analysis can be found in Brophy, Alleman, and Knighton (2008).

Much of the content that Barbara teaches in social studies is drawn from units that she selects from Jan and Jere's cultural universals curriculum (Alleman & Brophy, 2001, 2002, 2003). These units provide for systematic instruction on food, clothing, shelter, communication, transportation, family living, childhood, money, and government. The units involve teaching networks of connected content structured around big ideas, developed with emphasis on their connections and applications.

Focus on Powerful Ideas

The importance of structuring content around powerful ideas has been recognized at least since Dewey (1902, 1938), who viewed them as the basis for connecting subject matter to students' prior knowledge in ways that make their learning experiences transformative. *Transformative learning* enables us to see some aspect of the world in a new way, such that we find new meaning in it and value the experience (Girod & Wong, 2002). When students explore in depth the concept of biological adaptation, for example, they begin to notice aspects of the appearance and behavior of animals that they did not notice before, and to appreciate the ways in which these observed traits have helped the animals to adapt to their environments (Pugh, 2002). They get more out of trips to the zoo, notice things about their pets that they never appreciated before, and so on.

Others who have addressed the classical curricular question of what is most worth teaching have reached similar conclusions. Whether they refer to powerful ideas, key ideas, generative ideas, or simply big ideas (Smith & Girod, 2003), they converge on the conclusion that certain aspects of school subjects have unusually rich potential for application to life outside of school—most notably, powerful ideas developed with focus on their connections and applications.

Powerful ideas have several distinctive characteristics. First, they are fundamental to the subject area in general and the major instructional goals in particular. They tend to cluster in the midrange between broad topics such as transportation and particular items of information such as the fact that the fuel used in airplanes is not the same as the fuel used in cars. Most are concepts, generalizations, principles, or causal explanations. Examples within transportation include the categories of land, sea, and air transportation; the progression from human-powered to animal-powered to engine-powered transportation; the importance of transporting goods and raw materials (not just people); the role of transportation in fostering economic and cultural exchange; and the development of infrastructure to support a given form of transportation once it gets established (e.g., roads, service stations, traffic control mechanisms).

Powerful ideas are embedded within networks of knowledge and connected to other powerful ideas. Teaching about an object, tool, or action principle, for example, ordinarily would include attention to propositional knowledge (what it is, why and how it was developed, etc.), procedural knowledge (how to use it), and conditional knowledge (when and why to use it).

Big ideas are more generative or transformative than other aspects of a topic and they provide the basis for worthwhile lessons and learning activities. It is not possible to improve parade-of-facts curricula simply by replacing their worksheets with better activities; one must first replace the knowledge component by shifting from parades of miscellaneous facts to networks of connected content structured around big ideas that can provide a content base capable of supporting better activities (if you doubt this, try designing worthwhile activities based on information about the states' flags, songs, birds, etc.). *Big ideas lend themselves to authentic applications, of which many will be generative and even transformative; trivial facts do not.*

Three Layers of Powerful Ideas for Teaching

Big ideas are multilayered. The most macro layer includes overarching cross-curricular and yearlong content. These ideas pop up frequently during planning and implementing of units and lessons. One such big idea that Barbara emphasizes throughout the year, for example, is, "When you encounter something new or unusual, keeping an open mind without making value judgments allows you the opportunity to appreciate the realm of possibilities and fosters curiosity." Another example at this macro level is the idea that logic is a powerful tool for making sense of the world and how it works. Often big ideas at this level exist without teachers being aware of how they influence their teaching.

The next level of big ideas applies throughout a unit of instruction. These big ideas should guide the structure and planning of a unit. Their absence at this level can lead to disconnected sets of lessons that focus primarily on activities. Examples of unit-level big ideas include: geography affects how you meet your needs; people are more alike than different; and people make choices based on personal preferences, economic resources, local availability of potential options, climate, etc.

The final level of big ideas applies to specific lessons. These ideas guide the teacher's decisions about discourse during lessons and related activities/assessments. Examples of lesson-specific big ideas include: trade is one way to get the things you need or want; it works best when each person has something the other wants; families change and adapt to changes; people pay money (called taxes) to the government to support its activities.

It can be challenging for teachers to keep all three levels of big ideas in mind as they plan, implement, and assess lessons. However, it enhances meaningfulness; is cost effective; and provides the most opportunities for powerful instruction in the time available ("If you don't know where you are going, how will you know when you get there?").

Barbara's Focus on Big Ideas

Through her collaboration with Jere and Jan, Barbara has become much more systematic in structuring her teaching around big ideas, both in her advance planning and in her decision making during lessons. Based on her experience, she believes that teachers go through four stages in developing expertise in structuring their teaching around big ideas. At first, they are "unconsciously unskilled" about big ideas, thinking that they already focus on them (often because they follow textbooks closely and assume that their content is structured around big ideas). However, if something causes them to assess their teaching critically in this regard, they become "consciously unskilled," recognizing that their instruction is more like a parade of facts than a network of content structured around big ideas. As they begin to work on the problem, they become "consciously skilled," being careful to maintain focus on big ideas when planning and teaching. Eventually, through repeated experiences teaching a given content network with emphasis on the same big ideas, they become "unconsciously skilled," highlighting and making connections among these ideas almost automatically, without much conscious thought.

Barbara was quickly sold on structuring content around big ideas once she heard the explanation for its importance and inspected lessons that had been designed accordingly. Consequently, she was highly motivated to implement this principle in her own teaching. However, she found it challenging to do so at first. For awhile, she resorted to jotting down the day's big ideas on index cards that she kept handy for reference during lessons. As she gained experience in using this approach, she became less reliant on these lists and eventually phased them out. She also became less mechanical in moving through the big ideas, shifting from going through them one at a time in a fixed order (checking items off the checklist) to making connections back and forth routinely. She has noticed that her students bring up big ideas more frequently now, and she has generalized the approach to her teaching in other subjects.

Barbara has found that students in the early grades have difficulty handling more than one or two new big ideas per lesson, so if lesson plans call for introducing more than that, she will either pick one or two as primary and treat the others as secondary or else spread the lesson over two days. Also, some big ideas are not the focus of any single lesson but are developed across a sequence of lessons, so they need to be articulated at an appropriate time. Much of what she emphasizes in a given lesson depends on what her students have learned in recent lessons and how well they have mastered it. She gives extra emphasis to big ideas that they find difficult and provides extra review when it appears necessary.

A clear focus on the lesson's big ideas helps Barbara make confident decisions about what to include, how to make connections, and when to pull students back toward the big ideas if they begin to drift away from them. For example, when she first taught about developments in transportation, she often felt that she was floundering—just putting out a lot of facts and examples without clear big ideas around which to structure her narratives. When she teaches this content now, she is more comfortable and focused, because she emphasizes the big ideas that inventions made it easier for people to travel from one place to another and subsequent innovations improved on existing inventions once people became aware of their imperfections.

Barbara also uses big ideas as the basis for deciding which children's literature selections to include in a unit, and for planning how to present and use the books. A book about the eating habits of animals can be used as a vehicle for talking about the food groups, for example, and in reading the *Little Red Hen* story, she emphasizes that you have to grow, harvest, and grind wheat before you can use it to bake anything. In fact, Barbara uses this story for different purposes in different subjects. In language arts, the story is read and discussed as children's literature, with emphasis on its literary characteristics and moral. In social studies, she reviews the story as a set-up for the land-to-hand story of apple pie, and in the process, inserts words such as harvest, dough, yeast, and mill that are not included in the book.

Barbara has several big ideas in mind as she and her students work together to create peanut butter during the food unit. She hopes that they will recall nutrition and food group information as well as understand the steps and careers related to growing peanuts and manufacturing peanut butter. She also helps them analyze the amount of processing that the peanuts go through to become peanut butter. Then, during the literacy portion of the school day, the class reads the fanciful book *Peanut Butter and Jelly* (Westcott, 1992) and compares the book to the actual steps learned in the social studies lesson.

Barbara taught a similar lesson in earlier years before she learned to emphasize big ideas. However, her goals then were simply to provide all the students with a shared experience and to sequence the steps in making peanut butter. Most of the lesson was spent shelling and cleaning the peanuts. Students were engaged and motivated, but they rarely carried any big ideas away from the lesson.

Barbara ordinarily includes four major elements in lesson segments that introduce big ideas: a) using herself as an example, b) using books, photos, or other instructional resources to provide examples, c) making personal connections to her students' lives or experiences, and d) making connections to the big idea and to previous lessons. She tries to weave these elements together, and she tends to come back to one of them if she hasn't included it for a while.

Both Jan and Jere in their development of units, and Barbara in her planning of instruction, struggle with the question of how far to develop a big idea, given limited time and the constraints on primary students' prior knowledge and learning capacities. All of us are comfortable with the notion of "knowledge of limited validity" (Levstik, 1986)—explanations that are comprehensible and accurate as far as they go but do not attempt to go beyond what is necessary to accomplish the lesson's goals.

For example, in teaching about developments in transportation, Barbara emphasized the invention of engine-powered vehicles as a quantum leap. To explain engines, she used the steam engine as an example, illustrating by drawing a fire under a pot of water, squiggly lines coming up from the water to represent steam, and a simple representation of a paddle wheel as something that the steam could turn. She was confident that this much of the idea would be clear to her students because of the drawings and an earlier lesson on hot air pushing up balloons. However, she was less confident of the cost effectiveness of attempting to present more of the basic idea, such as by using examples of water-powered mills to communicate the idea that once you get something spinning, you can convert that motion into energy to move something else.

Explanations of complex phenomena to young students usually are partial, ending in some form of black box. However, the students usually will accept this. Barbara's steam engine explanation left off with, "You need something that pushes it around and around and around. That's how you get your energy." At this point, a student asked how you would stop it, leading the discourse off into a different direction. Then another student wondered how boats could be steam powered because, "Wouldn't the water put out the fire?" Barbara provided an explanation in response to this thoughtful question.

Cost/benefit issues arise not only in connection with questions about how much to explain, but also when to explain it. For example, when teaching about developments in transportation, Barbara identified Henry Ford as a key contributor and talked about his inventions and innovative ideas (assembly line, making cars affordable). In doing so, she explained "just enough" about assembly lines to enable her students to follow the flow at the time, but withheld a more thorough explanation because she knew that assembly lines were going to be the focus of a future lesson.

Maintaining Focus on Big Ideas without Getting Sidetracked

Barbara maintains focus on big ideas in deciding what content to include and how to develop that content. For example, one of the food lessons emphasizes that people sometimes use special meals to mark special occasions. As an example, she talked about how she and her husband went to an expensive restaurant to celebrate their anniversary. However, she did not add the name of the restaurant, the fact that it is located at the top of a well-known building, the fact that it revolves slowly to offer a panoramic view, or any of many other details that she might have inserted at this point, because none of them were relevant to the big idea of eating in expensive restaurants on special occasions.

Similarly, when teaching about breads around the world, she gave the name of each bread that she introduced and located the country that it comes from on the globe. However, she did not emphasize remembering the names for each of the breads or the grains from which they were made. Nor did she introduce other geographical facts about each of the countries mentioned. Instead, she focused on the big idea that the three basic ingredients of flour, water, and yeast are used to make all of the different kinds of bread found in different parts of the world.

During a lesson on healthy foods, a student commented that a television ad for a popular cereal said that the cereal is healthy. In response, Barbara could have foreshadowed a lesson in the communication unit by noting that ads are intended to get you to buy a product rather than to give you balanced and accurate information. However, even though this is a big idea of some importance, it was not relevant to the ongoing lesson and would have derailed the intended flow. Consequently, she acknowledged the comment but refocused attention on the point she wanted to make (that you can find out what is in foods by reading the ingredients information on the container).

Techniques for Focusing Students' Attention on Big Ideas

In addition to using big ideas to guide her own planning and teaching, Barbara uses several techniques to help her students recognize the importance of the big ideas, remember them, and to see their connections and applications. In the first place, when she is ready to state the big idea initially, she does so with particular emphasis (e.g., prefacing it with group alerting statements such as, "Look me in the eyes," or "Here's the scoop.").

Then she restates it several times, often rephrasing it. For example, as part of making the point that farms in the past were small but modern farms are large, she pointed to an illustration and said, "Look at those big fields full of wheat. Lots of space. Lots of land."

If a cause–effect linkage is involved, she often articulates the linkage both forward and backward ("What things do we have because there are wheat farms? ... If we didn't have wheat farming, what wouldn't we have?"). These multiple repetitions and rephrasings in alternative formats help make sure that students both understand and remember the big ideas.

Barbara's responses to and elaborations on students' answers to her questions similarly re-emphasize the big ideas. If the response does not include the big idea she was hoping to elicit, she may ask follow-up questions or elaborate on the response in ways that express the big idea. During reviews, she elicits restatements of the big idea from the students themselves through purposeful questioning, and concludes the segment with her own final restatement.

For variety, she also uses other techniques suited to the situation. She often builds up to the big idea by introducing some basic information and then asking questions designed to stimulate the students to articulate it themselves. For example, as she showed and led discussion about toys and games used by pioneer children, she noted or elicited that these children did not have many toys, that the toys they did have were simple, and that many of their playthings were found objects or toys constructed from materials found near the house. Then she cued the shift to the big idea by asking, "What are you noticing about toys and games from long ago?" On occasions when a student responds to a question or makes a comment that articulates the big idea nicely, she sometimes will ask the rest of the students if they agree with this statement, as a way to reinforce their attention to it.

Cultural Universals

With first-graders, Barbara typically teaches units on three cultural universals—basic human needs and social experiences found in all societies, past and present. The intent is that the students will develop a basic set of connected understandings about how the social system works; how and why it got that way over time, how and why it varies across location and cultures; and what all this might mean for personal, social, and civic decision making. We do not reproduce the curriculum material here, but instead relate some noteworthy observations about the way Barbara develops these topics with her students.

Food

An early lesson in the food unit is built around a food pyramid poster that reflects guidelines for healthful eating. The pyramid begins with a small "other" category at the top, then expands to larger meat and milk categories, then still larger fruit and vegetable categories, then ends with the largest category (grains) spread across the bottom. In combination, the pyramid shape and the placement of these categories provide a visual illustration of the guidelines for healthful eating (i.e., eat more servings per day of the foods in the larger categories toward the bottom of the pyramid).

When Barbara first started teaching with the food pyramid, she would invite her students to decide what groups to talk about first and to suggest examples of each food group. However, these lessons tended to get chaotic and also usually left the "other" category to the end. Now, she leads her students through the food pyramid in a top-to-bottom order and shows foods that she has brought from home as examples from each category. Beginning at the top allows her to start by showing examples of foods included in the "other" category (fat, oil, sweets). Then she moves to the next two categories (meat/protein and milk/dairy) which are more familiar to her students and easier for them to talk about. Here, she engages them in suggesting additional examples.

Going through the pyramid in a top-to-bottom order also means that the latter part of the lesson focuses on the foods that people should be eating most frequently, which facilitates transition into the follow-up activity that involves assessing potential meals to determine whether they are balanced and healthful. In the process, Barbara gets into complications such as that certain vegetable proteins are included in the meat group and some foods span two or more groups (ice cream includes sugar; hot dogs and bacon include a lot of fat and oil; pizza includes bread, vegetable, milk, and meat products). She includes spices, even though they are not on the pyramid. She deliberately mentions calories but does not try to provide a scientific explanation of the term (this would not be cost effective early in first grade). She notes that processed versions of foods often are less healthful than raw versions, either because the processing (e.g., cooking) has eliminated some of the nutrients or because less healthful ingredients are added (e.g., sugar).

All instructional planning involves making decisions about what content to include, but this question is especially challenging when teaching young students with limited prior knowledge of the topic. Ordinarily, lessons focus on the purposes and goals of human activities related to cultural universals and the processes involved in carrying them out, without getting into extraneous details or trying to teach too much specialized vocabulary.

Barbara's decisions about whether to introduce a specific term are made mostly on the basis of her assessments of its importance for cultural literacy (i.e., the term will come up frequently in the future) and its unit- or curriculum-specific centrality (i.e., it relates to a big idea). For example, the lesson on advances in farming does not include the term harrow, and Barbara ordinarily would not introduce it. However, one year her teaching of this lesson included the following excerpt:

T: What do they do after they plow?
Ss: Plant.
T: They have to plant the seeds. Take a look [at an illustration in a book]. Here he is with the horse. And this back here, the seeds were in it, and the seeds would drop down into the . . .
S: (Inaudible) [Student asked something about the harrow.]
T: It's called a harrow. H-A-R-R-O-W [spells the term]. That name isn't important, but the job was to get the seeds into the ground . . .

As can be seen in the way that Barbara was proceeding before the student asked the question, she was not intending to introduce the term harrow when explaining the process of dropping the seeds into the plowed furrows. Because the student asked, she did supply the term, but then quickly returned focus to the processes involved in planting.

Earlier in that same lesson, a student asked a very good question ("How would you get a plow if you didn't know how to make one?") that is difficult to answer in a way that a first-grader could understand. A full explanation would get into concepts such as independent inventions, diffusion, and tool making as a specialization. However, Barbara provided a "just enough" explanation:

T: Somebody had to think of the idea. Somebody who was looking around and said, "You know, this would be much easier if I had a stick, or maybe if it had three sticks." And they did. Look, this has three sticks. [Pointing to an illustration of a primitive plow in a book.] And later someone said, "You know, I bet it would be easier if I put a big handle up here." And they put it together and tried it and it was better. And maybe they tried some things that didn't work. So somebody came up with the idea because they said, "How can I make this better?"

Even when they are not abstract, some things can be complicated to explain to young learners because doing so involves explaining several other things along the way. To explain about potting as an early method of food preservation, for example, Barbara had to explain the process of converting clay into pottery and also explain what lard is:

> T: They also did something called potting. They would take meat and pound it until it was like a mushy paste and then put it into a pot that was made out of clay. Clay was down in the ground and they figured out that if they made a bowl out of it and put the bowl in the fire, it would get hard. So they would take this clay bowl and they would fill it with the mashed-up meat and fill the pot up and then they would cover the top of it with what we call lard. Lard is just the fat that comes out of an animal. The lard would keep the germs from getting to the meat. Let me show you a kind of picture. They would take the meat and they would pound it into a paste and they would put it in the pot and then they would cover it. If you've ever seen . . . like if mom's ever cooked with Crisco—big white goopy stuff. It looks almost like a glue stick—a mushy glue stick. So that lard, that mushy stuff, they would pack it down on top of the meat and that would keep the germs from getting in. And that was called potting. Then later on they would scoop all of the lard off the top and they could get to the meat. It would be all kind of mushed and dry so they would add water to it and they might make soup or stew out of it.

The need to provide these inserted explanations conflicts with the need to maintain the continuity of the "story." Yet, it is important to include such explanations, because if a text passage or teacher presentation contains too many unfamiliar terms, it will not be coherent enough for students to follow (Beck & McKeown, 1988).

Barbara's focus on the big ideas relating to the purposes of activities and the processes involved in completing them can be seen in the following excerpt, in which she recaps the land-to-hand story of pasta elaborated in the previous lesson. She emphasizes choices, repeats the term pasteurized, re-uses a prompt introduced earlier to elicit understanding of what pasteurizing does, and ties back to material on food preservation taught in a previous lesson. Mostly, however, she emphasizes motivations and cause–effect linkages in talking about why the different steps in the process of manufacturing pasta are performed.

> T: I want to remind you of the story about pasta. First you grow the wheat, harvest the wheat, grind the wheat, take the flour to the pasta factory, then you mix the ingredients. All you need is flour, water, and eggs to make pasta. Sometimes you can choose to put other things in, like milk or tomatoes or spinach. You don't have to. You can. If you needed to make pasta, you could just use those three things to make pasta. Then to make the dough, you put all the ingredients in, you roll the dough, you pasteurize the dough—you get it really hot to kill the . . .?
>
> Ss: Germs.
>
> T: Then you cut the dough into strips for fettuccini or into corkscrews or into shells or into those funny little things we saw in the book called tortellini. So you cut the dough into whatever shape you're going to choose. Then, you can either have it fresh—nice and soft, or you could dry it. If you dry it, it will . . .?
>
> Ss: Turn hard.
>
> T: It gets hard. Why would you want to dry it? Who wants to eat crunchy pasta? Why would you dry it? Why would you do that, Arden?
>
> S: So the germs won't get in it.
>
> T: So the germs won't get back in there and the pasta will . . .?
>
> S: Last longer.
>
> T: Last longer. It's a way to preserve or save the food longer.
>
> S: You don't want to eat it.
>
> T: Yeah, I wouldn't want to eat it when it's hard and crunchy. You definitely need to boil it in water. Then you're going to put the pasta into a package, then put the packages into boxes so you have maybe 10 or 20 packages all in one box. You load those boxes onto your semi truck. The semi truck takes it to the store and then someone will take those boxes off of the truck. They put the pasta on the shelf, and someone comes along and picks it out. There's lots to choose from. There's red ones that have tomato flavor and green ones that have spinach flavor, and long skinny ones and curlicue ones and ones that are called bow ties because they look just like bow ties, or ruffled ones. Maybe you want to make lasagna with it, so the choice of what kind of pasta to buy depends on what you like and what you're making.

Clothing

Our interviews with children about clothing indicated that most of them knew a lot about the nature and functions of business clothes, work clothes, and play clothes, but most did not know that cloth is a fabric woven from threads spun from the original raw material (they thought it was a solid like plastic or leather). Consequently, the land-to-hand lessons near the beginning of the unit emphasize the processes of spinning threads or yarn and weaving fabrics. The first of these lessons tells the story of wool, because children can easily understand shearing sheep (using the haircut analogy) and can be shown the processes of spinning (twisting the fibers of combed wool into yarn) and weaving (the woolen yarn into a fabric).

It is relatively easy for children to follow this story because the wool used to spin yarn is transformed only minimally (cleaned, combed) from the raw wool sheared from the sheep, and because woolen yarn is coarse enough to allow the students to observe directly, or even participate in, the processes of spinning and weaving.

The next lesson provides the story of cotton. This is more challenging to explain to children because most of them are much less familiar with cotton plants than with sheep, and it is harder to demonstrate or scaffold participation in spinning and weaving processes because the fibers are much thinner. However, the students already learned about these processes in the previous lesson on wool. Teaching them about cotton requires detailed explanation of the processes involved in extracting fibers from cotton plants, but teaching subsequent material on spinning and weaving mostly involves tying back to familiar big ideas, not introducing these ideas for the first time.

The following excerpt illustrates Barbara's teaching of part of this lesson. Prior to the excerpt, she was reviewing responses to a home assignment calling for students to bring clothing items from home and talk about their functions. She saved a T-shirt for last, to facilitate the shift into the lesson on cotton.

> T: I have a T-shirt. Who brought the T-shirt? . . . Tell us about it.
> S: It communicates that I like rollerblading.
> T: OK. What else is it good for?
> S: Modesty.
> T: Why is it good for modesty?
> S: Covers your body.
> T: Keeps your body covered. Is that made out of wool, do you think?
> S: No.
> T: I think not. He's feeling it and it's smooth. If you look at it closely, does it look like the wool we looked at?

Ss: No.

T: The wool looked kind of rough and scratchy. The fibers looked really different, didn't they? This is made from cotton, and I'm so glad you brought it today, because guess what we're talking about today?

S: Cotton?

T: Cotton. We're going to talk all about cotton and we're going to see if we can figure out how to go from the cotton to this shirt. Can I hold on to it while I talk?

S: Yeah.

T: Alright. Thanks. What are you wondering, Mariah?

S: If you put cotton in a washer, it'll shrink.

T: Yeah. We'll talk about cotton and what to do with it and how to take care of it as we go. Wool comes from what?

Ss: Sheep.

Ss: Alpaca.

T: Sheep or alpacas or goats. Cotton, on the other hand . . . where does cotton come from, Darryl?

S: Trees.

T: Trees or plants. So cotton must not come from an animal. Cotton must come from . . .

S: Plants.

T: You can tell. You can see part of the plant right in there. So we're going to talk today about how cotton gets from a plant to a shirt. Does this shirt look like a tree?

Ss: No.

T: Does it look like a plant?

Ss: No.

T: Does it look like leaves?

Ss: No.

T: Does it look like something that's been growing?

Ss: No.

T: So we must have to do a lot of work to get from the plant to a shirt. More than likely most of you are wearing something cotton today. I know I have a cotton shirt on. If you're wearing blue jeans, blue jeans are made out of cotton. Mariah, I'm not sure if that's cotton. Can you feel A.J.'s shirt next to you instead?

S: Is mine cotton?

T: Yup. The way I'd know for sure, Mariah, would be if I checked the tag, because the tag tells us what it's made out of. This tag says 100 percent cotton.

TA: Ninety percent polyester, ten percent spandex. [An undergraduate student teaching assistant reads the label in Mariah's shirt.]

T: So that's not made out of cotton. Mariah, we'll talk about how we got that on a different day, but I think everybody else should have been able to feel something that you were wearing to know that it's made out of cotton. Where'd we say cotton first started out, Curtis?

S: A plant.

T: It starts out as a plant, so I wanted to make this cotton shirt. The first thing I'm going to have to do is . . .?

Ss: Grow it.

T: I'm going to have to grow it. I'm going to have to put a . . . [mimes planting]

Ss: Seed.

T: A seed in the ground. What do we call the person who takes care of the plants?

Ss: Farmer.

T: A farmer. Sure. A farmer's going to have to put the seeds in the ground, grow the cotton plant, and he's going to have to take care of it. He might need a tractor. He might need people working with him. He might need to water it. He might need to feed it. Some people choose, instead of growing food on their farm, to grow cotton on their farm. What they do is they have plants that look like this [shows illustration from book] . . . It grows nice and tall and then a flower pops out, the flower changes color, and then you end up with this big boll right here. Then on the inside of it, as it starts to die . . . you know how like right now our leaves are changing color because they're starting to die and the green that's in them is starting to go away so we can see the color? That's kind of what happens for the cotton boll too. The flower grows and everything's nice and green. And then it starts to die because the plant wants there to be more cotton plants, so inside here it makes seeds and it attaches those seeds to a white fluffy stuff. Now if I just left my cotton plant, eventually the seeds would float away with the white fluffy stuff and then the seed would land and then a . . .

S: A cotton plant.

T: A new cotton plant would grow, and that's how it used to be that they got a lot of cotton plants. Now we have farmers that get the seeds out of the cotton plant and put them in the ground themselves. That way they could make more plants than if that white fluffy stuff floats away. What do you think might make that go away?

Ss: Wind.

T: The wind would blow the cotton around.

S: Sometimes it moves a long way.

T: Yeah, if it was a nice hard wind. So, taking a peek at this cotton that's in here [shows raw cotton], you can see little bits of seed tucked in there. Where I'm looking on this side I can see. These are cotton bolls. What do you see?

Ss: Seeds.

T: Seeds. Look. I'm stretching it. Do you see the fibers? It's getting kind of stringy. Do you remember talking about fibers?

Ss: Yeah.

T: What do we do with the fibers?

S: Pull it.

T: Yeah, so do you have a guess already about what's going to happen down the road? This is a cotton ball [not a raw boll, but a manufactured cotton ball]. This is not really what grows in the plant. Do you see how it kind of looks a little different?

Ss: Yeah.

T: They've taken this [boll] and somebody in a factory has made this [ball]. This [raw boll] is real cotton and I can tell because it has little bits of plant and little bits of seed things in there. I bet if you take a look at this, you're going to be able to guess what our first job is going to be after we're done picking the cotton. So pass that around and give it a feel and take a peek at it. Does it feel like the cotton? What do you notice? It feels soft.

S: It feels like my shirt.

T: Kind of feels like your shirt?

S: It feels funny.

S: Where would you go to get cotton with seeds on it?

T: If I wanted cotton that had seeds, I would go to a place where cotton grows . . .

S: I mean how did you get that?

T: This is Dr. Alleman's. She must have gone to a cotton plant, broken off a piece of it and put it in her jar. Cotton needs to have a warm place to grow. Here in America, in the United States, cotton can grow down south in states like Mississippi, Alabama, Georgia, down closer to Florida where it's nice and warm. It can't be too wet. It needs to be warm and a little bit dry for cotton to grow. So, the first job was what?

Ss: Grow it.

T: To grow it. You've gotta grow the plant, plant the seed in the ground and grow it. Next, somebody has to get this cotton off. Look at that cotton field.

S: It's full.

S: That's a lot.

T: It looks like maybe even there's snow on there or somebody's glued cotton bolls to all those plants, but that's just the way it grows in the field. It looks just like that does in the jar. The farmer's next job is to get just the cotton off of the plant. Now, today we have machines that help pick the cotton, and those machines leave the cotton plant there and just get the cotton off of it, because you want the plants to grow for next year. [At this point, Barbara detours from the main storyline to talk about hand picking cotton and slavery, then resumes the land-to-hand story.] . . . OK, let's go on to what the steps are. The first thing you gotta do is . . .?

Ss: Grow it.

T: Grow the cotton. Then you have to . . .?

Ss: Pick the cotton.

T: Pick the cotton. Looking at that cotton, what do you suppose we need to do next to it? What do you think, A.J.?

S: Clean it.

T: Clean it. We've got to wash it clean, and what did we say was in that cotton?

Ss: Seeds.

T: Seeds, so we've got to get out the seeds, and there's dirt and twigs. What do you think, Mariah?

S: You have to weave it.

S: Stretch it.

T: You have to weave it, but before you weave it, like you said, you pull it, you stretch it . . . Now that I've got long fibers of cotton, what am I going to do?

S: Weave it.

T: You're going to weave it into . . .?

S: Yarn.

T: Fabric. After you weave it, it's called fabric. [From this point, Barbara leads the class twice more through the basic steps of growing the plants, removing the bolls, cleaning them, stretching the fibers, twisting them into threads, weaving the fabric, and then manufacturing the garment by dyeing, cutting out fabric parts, sewing them together, adding buttons, etc.].

The next lesson tells the story of silk. Barbara knew that her students were much less familiar with this fabric than with wool or cotton, so she began by talking about its look, feel, and other characteristics that motivate people to continue producing it even though it is time consuming and expensive to do so. She talked about her wedding dress as one example and was prepared to cite others, but then noticed that Jan was wearing a silk blouse that day. Ordinarily, Barbara made no mention of the fact that Jan was sitting behind the students taking notes on the lesson, but on this day she seized the opportunity and asked Jan to circulate among the group and allow the students to feel her blouse. She then launched into the land-to-hand narrative, using a book on the topic that included good illustrations of each stage. The book was not a children's literature story but a book about fibers that was beyond her students' readiness, so Barbara told the story in her own words without reading from the text.

After her students had learned about three natural fibers (wool, cotton, and silk), Barbara was able to teach them "just enough" about synthetic fibers to support learning with understanding. The challenging part was teaching about the raw materials, which Barbara approached by regaling her students with stories about how scientists had figured out ways of processing and combining surprising raw materials such as oil into fibers that could be spun into thread. After that, the rest of the story was familiar (thread is spun from raw material, fabric is woven from thread).

Other Social Studies Curriculum Components

Barbara supplements the cultural universals with the traditional social studies "holiday curriculum." The holiday curriculum features lessons and activities (dramatic recreations, etc.) associated with Columbus Day, Thanksgiving, Presidents Day, Martin Luther King Jr.'s birthday, and other holidays that have special historical or civic significance.

Much of her social studies teaching is done within the whole-class lesson format. Social Studies lessons often extend for longer time periods than her lessons in other subjects. However, little of this time is spent in traditional lecture mode. She does do a lot of explaining and modeling, but most of it is incorporated within her characteristic narrative style, as illustrated in Chapter 5. Other aspects of Barbara's curriculum and instruction in social studies are analyzed and illustrated in considerable detail in the companion volume to this one (Brophy, Alleman, & Knighton, 2008).

Chapter 12

Curriculum and Instruction in Mathematics and Science

Barbara's approaches to curriculum and instruction in mathematics and science follow the same general principles that guide her literacy and social studies teaching. Key features include clarity about goals and intended outcomes, developing and connecting big ideas, modeling skills, and teaching for independent and self-regulated learning.

Mathematics

Barbara prioritizes two major goals in planning her mathematics teaching. First, she wants to make sure that her students acquire the knowledge and skills reflected in the state's standards and benchmarks for her grade level. In first grade, these include capacities such as being able to count to 100, fluently add two numbers, extract information from graphs, create or extend patterns, and know the names of basic geometric shapes. In the process of teaching basic knowledge and skills, she also emphasizes her second goal: helping her students to "see the logic and the sense and the underlying patterns in mathematics."

For example, in addition to memorizing that 2 + 3 = 5, she wants her students to develop "a good sense of what it means when you add two things together." She wants them to understand that they can "take two of these and three of these and put them together," "start at three and count on two more," or "break five things into two piles, such that I will have three things in this pile and two things in the other pile." Elaborating on this point, she explains:

> During math lessons, I am not just thinking about how to get them to the right answer; I'm thinking about "What knowledge do they need to go along with this skill that will help them apply it—help them to see where it comes from, how it connects to other math problems, and how it is usable?" For example, I want them to learn the basic skill of counting by fives with fluency, but I also want them to see connections and applications. You use that skill when telling time, so

learning to count by fives is also helping you to learn to tell time easily. You also count by fives when you count how much money you have with nickels. And counting by fives and telling time and counting nickels are a lot like the bundles we use when we make tally marks. We go one, two, three, four, and then cross it to make a bundle of five tally marks, which is like a nickel and also like one chunk of a clock.

So, I want them to see the connections between different concepts in mathematics, how we use them, and how skills in this area can help them solve problems. I've had kids who used clocks to help them solve addition problems. And I will make other connections, such as that a clock is a lot like a timeline and also a number line. I want them to see that tools can be used in more than one way, that problems can be solved in more than one way, and to understand where the answer came from. Instead of just thinking, "The answer is five because it's five," I want them to understand where the concept comes from and how it is connected to other things they have done.

Standard Teaching Procedures

When planning mathematics instruction, Barbara incorporates the same basic procedures that she uses throughout her curriculum. After initial instruction focused around big ideas, she models skills or assignment responses herself, then has one or more students model, then scaffolds guided practice, and then releases the students for independent practice. During independent practice, she circulates to make sure that students are on the right track:

> For example, today they were given ten pennies and asked to partition them into two groups and then write the addition problem represented by the partitioning. So, if they put two pennies in one group and eight in the other, they were supposed to write down 2 + 8 = 10. I guided them through a whole sheet showing all of the different ways to break ten into two groups. I modeled the activity, holding my paper up as an example and leading discussion about each partition and addition problem. As we agreed on each answer, I wrote it down on my paper and then they copied it on theirs. We did that whole sheet together as guided practice. Then, for independent practice, they did the same activity with nine pennies. As they began the activity, I checked to see who had successfully transitioned from the first activity into the second—who knew what they were doing and could keep doing it independently. I also identified five students who needed additional instruction, so I gathered them into a small group to provide it while the others continued to work independently.

After completing the small-group reteaching and getting these students started on successful independent work, she checked the work of the other students, certifying that they had done the second task correctly or identifying places where they needed to make corrections. The class would build on that activity the next day, this time partitioning ten pennies into three piles and writing longer addition problems. To help make connections, she would remind students of an earlier assignment in which they analyzed an illustrated outfit that had a jacket, a shirt, and a pair of pants, to determine how many total pockets the outfit included. This also involved adding three numbers together. She would draw the connections by saying, "This is like something you have done before, when we had three different things and you put them all together. Today, it's the same thing, only backward. We've got these pennies and we're going to break them into three parts. Last time we put them together, but this time we're breaking them into three parts."

Promoting Understanding and Higher Order Thinking

Barbara's mathematics teaching includes several components designed to insure that her students understand and reflect on what they are learning. For example, she makes sure to include multiple representations of the concepts and procedures that she teaches.

Multiple Representations

Reflecting what she was taught as an undergraduate, when Barbara first began teaching she took pains to make sure that she introduced any new mathematical concept or procedure by beginning with concrete materials, then moving to pictorial representations, and only then moving to symbolic representations. She no longer believes that this sequence is always necessary, but she does recognize the importance of making sure that her students understand the connections between these different levels of representation:

> So, when we were talking about the pennies, I made sure that the kids could see the pennies and the numbers together, so they would understand the connection between three pennies that were in the pocket and the number 3 that we wrote on the paper. We also used pictorial representations, like in the math paper that the kids did for practice. Lately, we have been using a lot of blocks and then writing addition sentences about them. Today's math assignment called for using pictures of blocks rather than actual blocks. Their next assignment uses just squares to represent blocks, rather than actual pictures of real blocks. I make sure that they are comfortable at the concrete level

using objects before I move them to the pictorial level on a worksheet that they are supposed to do more independently. They still need these concrete and pictorial representations—they're not ready yet for a math paper that just has 3 + 2.

Metacognition and Self-regulation

Besides using multiple representations, Barbara frequently incorporates metacognition and strategy teaching into her mathematics instruction. This begins with the thinking out loud that she does during her own modeling of the processes involved in analyzing and solving problems. It then continues with the kinds of questions that she asks as she scaffolds student modeling and guided practice. During a lesson on potential partitions and alternative representations of the number 23, for example, a student suggested reorganizing a collection of buttons to create tens frames. Barbara nodded to communicate tentative acceptance of this response, but then asked, "So how will that help?" . . . "How do you know that that's 23?" Her students soon become accustomed to such elaboration and explanation questions, realizing that they are not indications that their answers have been incorrect, but requests for explanations of the rationales that underlie them.

To help her students recognize equivalent alternative representations and become more comfortable with working at the pictorial and symbolic levels, Barbara will articulate the relevant connections during her own explanation and modeling. When distributing the worksheet showing pictures of blocks, for example, she might say, "Oh, look. These are pictures of the blocks. Just like when we had the real blocks. So, this is just like counting blocks, except that you count the pictures." Later when she introduces worksheets, she will say something like, "Oh, look— instead of pictures, this one has squares. The squares look like blocks and they stand for blocks."

To help move her students toward self-regulated learning, she will inject observations that help them to figure out what they need to know. For example, she might say, "You know, the better you get at adding, the less you will need the blocks with you," or "Perhaps you don't need the blocks—you could just draw pictures of the blocks." Then she teaches them how to do that, and later how to make it even easier by using just dots to represent the squares that represented the blocks. Later she might observe that, "You've gotten so good at adding 3 + 2 that you know it in your head, so you don't even need those dots anymore. You can just look at 3 + 2 and say, "Put three in my head and count on two: three, four, five." This kind of teaching not only familiarizes students with multiple levels of representation, but provides them with thinking tools to use in analyzing and solving problems.

Authentic Applications

Another support to learning with understanding is providing students with opportunities to engage in authentic applications of the knowledge and skills they are learning. For example, rather than requiring her students to complete numerous worksheets containing disconnected tally mark exercises, Barbara incorporates a lot of their tally mark practice into authentic activities that also include practicing graphing. For example, every day she writes a question on the board that includes several answer options. Each student is asked to come up and place a tally mark next to the answer that reflects his or her own thinking or experiences. Questions might include: Do you like rain (or scrambled eggs, etc.)? (yes, sometimes, or no), Do you have a dog? (yes/no), or What do you like on your pizza? (several choices given, with multiple responses allowed). When everyone has responded to the question, the tally marks are counted and converted to Arabic numerals, and the results are graphed and discussed. Similar data are collected through home assignments such as asking students to tally and then total the numbers of tables, chairs, windows, and lamps in their homes.

Story Problems

Barbara frequently engages her students in analyzing and solving story problems as another way to promote mathematical thinking and provide authentic applications. When introducing story problems, she does a great deal of modeling and strategy teaching. For example, one early problem begins with three rats sitting together on a mat, but then, "Two rats ran away. How many rats are left?" To model ways to analyze and respond to such problems, Barbara proceeded as follows:

> When I hear that story, I start to make a picture in my head of what's happening in the story. So, in my picture I've got a mat. And how many rats are on my mat? [Students answer three.] So, calmly, in your head right now you should have a picture of a mat—that's like a rug—with three rats sitting on it. So I have that picture in my head but then two of the rats run away. So now, if I draw a picture of a rug with three rats sitting on it, I can't make them run away on the paper, so what do you suppose I could do so that people would know that those rats ran away? ... You know, I could draw two arrows showing two of them running away. That's one idea. But, usually if something goes away or I get rid of it, I just cross it off with a big X. So, on my picture, I've got the three rats, but I'm going to cross off two of them, meaning that they ran away. Now I can look at my picture and figure out what do I have left in the picture.

The first couple of times that her students were confronted with such problems, Barbara modeled by actually drawing the picture on the board (to represent the picture in her head), then drawing it on paper. She talked them through each of these actions as she performed them, "focusing on the specific actions I do as a mathematician." Later, during guided practice, she scaffolded application of these strategies by asking questions such as, "What do mathematicians do when they hear a math story?" [Make a picture in their head.], and "Now that you're done making a picture in your head, what are you going to do?" [Draw it on the paper.], and commenting "Right, because that's what mathematicians do. They take the pictures from their head and draw them on paper." Gradually, she guides her students toward independently reading and solving problems. If they get stuck, she scaffolds by asking cueing questions ("What did you see me do?") or repeating her modeling ("Here, I'll solve this one . . . What do you see me do as a mathematician? . . . What do you see me do as a thinker?").

A Typical Lesson

Barbara's reflections on a typical math lesson reveal both the standard framework from which she operates regularly and the ways she adapts it to the situation. The lesson called for using a shopping scenario to support students' early development of the ability to write number sentences. "Prices" were allocated to objects that the students would "purchase," working from a budget of ten pennies. Barbara chose to use familiar, everyday classroom objects for this lesson (scissors, glue sticks, crayons, pencils, markers, etc.) because she wanted to keep her students' attention focused on the mathematical concepts and operations, not the objects. She had seen another teacher attempt this lesson using toys given away as "prizes" from McDonald's, and noted that the students focused on the toys rather than the point of the lesson.

The activity called for deciding which items to purchase, withdrawing the numbers of pennies corresponding to their prices from the original pile of ten pennies, and forming separate piles. Then students would write the appropriate number sentence (e.g., $6 + 2 = 8$) and determine how much money they had left over. Barbara began by modeling the activity herself, thinking out loud as she inspected the items to determine which ones she might want to buy, estimated whether she could afford them (i.e., their prices would total 10 cents or less), and then made her tentative selections. Next she removed the appropriate number of pennies to create separate piles (counting aloud and making other comments explaining what she was doing and why). Then she modeled verifying that the number of pennies in each pile was correct and entering these numbers in a number line sentence ("I have two cents and four cents, so $2 + 4 = 6$.").

She finished by modeling the process of checking her answer against the piles of pennies she had created.

After completing modeling and discussion of the first example, she modeled again on a second example. In the process, she began establishing a four-step "mantra" which her students could use to guide their thinking on this type of problem ("Pick the objects, pick the pennies, put them together, count it out."). Her modeling and scaffolding of steps in a process often includes such mantra-like self-regulation formulas, especially if the process will be repeated across several lessons or is intended to be applied in life outside of school.

Having modeled the entire process twice herself, she then ran through it four more times using students as models. As she usually does at this stage in her teaching, she picked four of her struggling learners who would likely have the most difficulty working independently. In each case, she scaffolded their work as needed and frequently repeated the four-step mantra.

The next lesson involved a similar scenario and task, but now the students were allocated 15 pennies rather than just ten, and were expected to move into independent work much more quickly. This time, Barbara noted that the activity was similar to the one done the previous day, only with more pennies. Also, she modeled the process only once and scaffolded guided practice with only one student model before releasing students to work independently. To help insure that the independent work was successful, she frequently repeated the four-step mantra. She also assigned her students to work in pairs rather than by themselves, making sure that each student who was likely to struggle with the assignment was paired with a student who was likely to handle it successfully. From previous training about how to function during paired activities, her students understood that each member of each pair was expected to complete the work independently and learn what the activity was designed to teach, but they all were free to help their partners understand anything that they were not clear about. As her students settled into the task, Barbara circulated the room to monitor progress and provide additional scaffolding where needed.

Addressing Diversity

Barbara refers to the math curriculum as "structured and homogeneous" in ways that make it more confining to teach than reading or writing. In the literacy subjects, her whole-class lessons tend to be relatively short, so much of her teaching is focused on the special needs of small groups or individuals, and students spend a lot of time working independently according to their individual needs and interests. She tracks their progress and makes sure that each student gets whatever special instruction or practice he or she may need, but at any given point in time, students will have progressed to different levels in different areas and will spend their time working at a variety of somewhat individualized assignments and self-chosen activities.

Barbara finds that this approach is not feasible for mathematics, at least not with the mathematics curriculum guidelines and instructional materials she is expected to use. Instead, her mathematics teaching follows a lock-step sequence, in which much of her instruction is given during whole-class lessons, followed by independent practice time during which all of her students work on the same assignment. Under these circumstances, she finds it more difficult to pull together *ad hoc* small groups for targeted reteaching or provide one-to-one help to individuals. She notes that it is difficult to keep the class together when:

> I've got a handful of kids who are already adding fluently and easily. I've got a middle chunk who are developing the skills and beginning to see the connections and the strategies they can use to add and remember some addition. And then I've got some kids who look at me when they count up their pennies and go, "Oh, what does a 7 look like?" They don't know what a 7 is or how to write it. I even have one who doesn't get the same answer when she counts the pennies twice because she doesn't have one-to-one correspondence yet. So, students are at different spots on the spectrum of where they are and what they need, and yet we are all expected to have the same lesson in math.

Despite this rigidity, Barbara makes time to provide extra support to her struggling students. After she releases the rest of the class to work independently, she keeps these students with her to provide additional instruction and guided practice. Meanwhile, students who finish the assignment quickly understand that they are expected to select or create other mathematical jobs with which to occupy themselves during the remaining independent work time:

> Today, I kept my five real struggling kids here with me. Everybody is working on the same assignment, but I have these five here with me. The kids that finish quickly and easily (because this is something they're already fluent with) know that then their job is to get something from the math materials corner and recreate a similar job using something other than pennies. They could get, say, the pattern blocks. Or, sort out some triangles, sort out some hexagons, and then write down the addition problem that goes with how many triangles and hexagons you ended up with. So, they are still working on addition problems using different manipulatives, but creating the problems themselves and recording what they are doing. Meanwhile,

the kids who are more in the middle of the road have just enough time to finish the whole assignment. The kids that I kept to work with me only got through three or four items out of the ten, but I know that they got those three or four done accurately because I sat here with them while they did it. And with some, we worked on writing the numbers the right way. Besides showing them how to write a 7 when they needed a 7, I reminded them of resources we have in the room that they can consult to figure out what a 7 looks like if they are working independently.

On some days, instead of keeping the struggling students with her and expecting the highest achievers to create their own additional math jobs, she will pair the struggling students with selected higher achievers (those who are among the most prosocial and able to understand and implement her instructions about providing struggling students with prompts and other assistance but not doing the tasks for them). Two of her students are pulled out for special instruction on kindergarten math skills during Barbara's math time. Otherwise, all of her students are present. Given the lock-step sequencing and the undesirable consequences that would ensue if students missed the formal mathematical instruction that she provides each day, she makes sure that none of her students are pulled out of her classroom during math time (for anything other than mathematics instruction).

Overall, Barbara feels very constrained by the mathematics guidelines and expectations put forth by the state and her school district. In addition to the lock-step curriculum already described, she finds that her ability to address individual needs is limited by the fact that the Grade Level Content Expectations (GLCEs) and associated assessments are far more numerous and specific in math than in other subjects. For example, the GLCEs for literacy call for students to learn to read fluently in different genres, but the GLCEs for math specify competencies such as counting by fives to 100. Also, she has more than two hours allocated each day to teach literacy, but only 45 minutes to teach math, so this further restricts her opportunities for individualization.

Ironically, despite math's more numerous and specific standards and more "objective" assessments, Barbara feels more confident in her knowledge about her students' progress in reading and writing than she does in mathematics. By routinely hearing them read in a variety of genres and monitoring their work on a variety of writing assignments, Barbara has pretty clear ideas about each individual's current status, general level of progress relative to grade expectations, and needs for specific remedial instruction and practice opportunities. The mathematics program, however, relies much more on "objective" tests, in which students need only to select among provided responses rather than generate their own responses or show their thinking. This makes it possible for students who are good test takers or even just lucky guessers to appear more proficient in mathematics than they are, so it is not uncommon for Barbara to find that certain students struggle with the same mathematical issues late in the year that they struggled with earlier in the year. She wishes that she had both more time and more flexible district guidelines to enable her to monitor her students' mathematics learning and address their individual needs more comprehensively.

Science

The first-grade science curriculum is very basic, focusing on developing vocabulary and fundamental skills. Barbara does most of her science instruction during whole-class lessons, with the format being similar to social studies. Her introductory presentations incorporate the narrative style illustrated in Chapter 5 when possible (this is more difficult to do in science than in social studies because of the focus on inquiry and experimentation). When she shifts from knowledge to application, she follows her typical sequence of modeling, guided practice, and independent practice.

Most elementary science programs that schools use are commercially produced and typically focus on hands-on experiences for students. Units are often packed with separate experiments and activities designed to provide a range of learning opportunities. However, tying the experiments and activities together with major goals or focus questions (which frequently are not included in the teacher materials) can improve the effectiveness of the science unit:

> When I think and plan for science instruction, I try to go beyond just providing my students with experiences and hands-on opportunities found in the kits or manuals. I create major goals for each unit and then make sure that everything I have planned matches those goals. For example, during the Solids and Liquids unit, my goals include: learning a set of questions to sort objects into solids and liquids as well as being able to describe objects with a variety of words.

Another goal for early elementary science is introducing students to the idea of scientific thinking. During the sand and silt Earth Science unit, Barbara frequently has her students make educated guesses and then use the experiments and hands-on activities to gather data to prove or disprove their hypotheses. Students maintain a science journal in which they draw pictures, add labels, and record information. These activities provide a foundation for future science classes that address and use scientific thinking.

An additional important aspect of Barbara's science units is providing students with opportunities to use knowledge from class in the world outside the classroom. As part of a weather unit, she asks students to work with their families to find and evaluate sources of weather information and forecasts. The class then works to determine which are the most accurate, efficient, and quickest places for people to look when they need to know about the weather.

Barbara uses hands-on activities and experiments with her students, but does so very thoughtfully. "I always try to balance the amount of time the activity takes with the gains made towards my unit goals and big ideas. If the activity doesn't significantly help my students understand the big ideas better, I either change the experiment or delete it altogether. There are so many demands on our class time that I can't afford to spend time on experiments that aren't efficient." For example, the unit on solids and liquids calls for the class to spend two days preparing for an activity where students sort different-sized beans from a soup mixture. Barbara determined that this took too much time away from instruction, so eventually she reorganized the experiment to be a one-day event that was more focused on big ideas such as:

- The properties of solids (size, flexibility, texture, color, shape, etc.) help us to work with materials.
- When you describe a solid, you look for properties that are common and unique.
- When you use trial and error, you take what doesn't work to figure out what will work.

Another technique for making experiments more time efficient is to break them into small chunks that fit into the odd parts of the day. Prior to starting the Plant Unit, Barbara's class planted seeds and cared for them during the 15 minutes between their specials class (gym, library, etc.) and lunch. Therefore, when the plant unit started two weeks later, the plants were already growing, and the students had a good amount of background knowledge and common experiences (as well as familiar plants) to discuss.

The big ideas that served as the foundation for the early experiments included: plants need water, nutrient-rich soil, and sunlight to grow; the plant cycle begins with seeds that become sprouts, and finally plants; and a plant has many parts including root, stem, and leaves.

Lesson on Descriptive Words

As mentioned earlier, a major knowledge goal for early elementary science is developing vocabulary that students can use to describe objects and provide a basis for activities calling for comparing, categorizing, or sorting objects. Throughout a sequence of lessons designed to build descriptive vocabulary, Barbara co-constructs with her students a running list of "describer words." During one lesson that was recorded and transcribed, Barbara was expanding a partial list developed in earlier lessons.

She began with a guessing game that allowed her students to review both the meanings of the words already on the list and the process of using them to describe objects. Having assembled a collection of small objects found in the room, she then invited students to take turns choosing one of the objects and using some of the listed words to describe it to classmates, who then would try to guess which object it was. The describer word list already contained words for substances (e.g., wood, plastic, metal) and paired adjectives describing their properties (e.g., smooth versus rough). Consequently, the first student called on said that the object she was thinking of was metal and smooth. Applying these clues to the objects included in the collection, the class soon determined that she was thinking of the spoon. Barbara held up the spoon and asked about other describer words that applied to it. She then shifted to the major goal of the new lesson, which was to add additional paired adjectives to the list. A student provided her with a natural opportunity to segue into this agenda by observing that the spoon was reflective (without using that term, which hadn't yet been taught):

S: You can see something in the metal.

T: *Ah. That's a whole different word! Let me tell you that word. That's a great* science *word, so I'm glad you thought of that one, Jermaine. Sometimes people use the word shiny, but there's a real fancy science name for it. The science word for shiny is reflective. Reflective: reflection is when you can see your face or you can see yourself when you look at this object. Like a mirror. When you can see your reflection, it is reflective. Reflective. So, a mirror is reflective. The spoon—when I look at the spoon, I can see myself, so the spoon is reflective, too.*

Barbara then continued to introduce other descriptive pairs such as flexible versus rigid, sharp versus dull, and opaque versus translucent. In the process, she added complications, such as that a pencil can be both sharp (at the writing end) and dull (at the eraser end).

For a follow-up application activity, Barbara paired off the students and provided each pair with a bag containing descriptive words printed on separate pieces of paper. Then, as she held up an object, each pair would draw one of the descriptive words out of their bag, confer briefly as to whether it did or did not describe the object, and then be prepared to answer yes or no when called on.

After completing this activity, Barbara made a follow-up assignment:

> T: Tomorrow, here's what your job will be. We're going to look around our room for things that are dull and flat and sharp and pointy and flexible and curved and metal and bumpy. Because tomorrow you'll get a turn to find some things in our room that all match one of these words. Your partners will have to see if they can figure out what words you were using. So, tomorrow you might find in our room three things that are rigid and bring them back to your table and say to your partner, "What is the same about all of these?" And your partner will go, "Oh, this one is shiny but that one is not, so it can't be shiny. And this one is pointed but that one is dull, and this one is soft but that one is hard. But oh, all of them are rigid. I think you picked them because they are all rigid."

She added that during literacy choice time the next day, students should spend part of the time going around the room looking at objects and thinking to themselves about their properties (smooth, rigid, etc.). Then later, during science time, they would play the guessing game with their partners. Before concluding, to make sure that they knew what to do, she told them to "Look around the room right now. Find one thing with your eyes and be ready to tell me one describing word for that thing." She then called on several students who identified objects in the room and correctly stated applicable description words.

Scientific Tools and Procedures

Along with big ideas and other science content, Barbara introduces her students to basic tools and procedures used to carry out scientific investigations. For example, a mid-year lesson taught to first-graders involves using graduated sieves and sifters to separate and analyze the contents of a mixture of solids. In this case, the mixture included corn meal, rice, lentils, navy beans, and lima beans.

Barbara began by reminding students of a previous lesson that used these five food items. She then elicited their names, observations about their relative sizes, and the fact that all of the lima beans had been together in one plastic tub, all of the navy beans had been together in another tub, and so on. She then segued into the new lesson using a story that she had concocted to inject a much-needed air of authenticity (and to amuse herself in the process):

> T: . . . so, I was cleaning out the tubs and putting some bags together—scooping out the navy beans and the rice and the

lentils, because the mice will come along. But at the same time I was chitchatting with Mrs. Johnson, and suddenly I realized that I had taken the stuff and put it . . .

Ss: In the bag!

T: . . . all together in the same bag. Then I got to thinking about the kids from next year, and I said, "Well, next year . . .

S: How are you going to use that?

T: . . . because it's all mixed up together!" So your job today, for each table, I have a big bag and your job at the table will be to sort out all the different parts. Now the lima beans and the navy beans and the lentils and the rice all can go into these little cups. The holes in the bottom of these won't work for the . . .

S: Corn meal.

T: Corn meal. So, I'll get you a cup that doesn't have any holes for you to put the corn meal in. But when we're done, I need to have a cup with . . .

S: Lentils.

T: And then a cup with?

S: Rice.

T: And then a cup with?

S: Corn meal.

T: Corn meal. And a cup with?

Ss: Lima beans.

T: Right. There should be cups with five different things because there are five different things in this bag that got all mixed up together. So that's going to be your job—sorting this out.

At this point, Barbara distributed tubs to the tables and assigned students to tables to work together in small heterogeneous groups. She also reminded them about working well together and cautioned them to keep the sifting tools over the tubs, so that what emerged from the sifters would go into the tubs and not spill out onto the table. She also demonstrated use of the tools, emphasizing their differences in the grain sizes of the materials they would let through:

T: Yesterday, Jaalen noticed that when he put a mixture into the funnel, everything went through except for . . . two things; what two things were left?

S: The lima beans.

T: The lima beans, because they're the biggest. And what else wouldn't go down the funnel?

S: The navy beans.

T: The navy beans. So the big bean and the next big bean wouldn't go down. So if you use the scoop and put a mixture of things in here, a little at a time, the big things will stay in the funnel but the little things will go through. Now, what will happen if we use the screen?

S: The squares are too small.

T: The squares are too small. What will go through them?

Ss: Corn meal.

T: What else? Will the rice go through the screen?

Ss: No.

T: So if I put this little screen on top of the tub and pour, what's the only thing that's going to get through?

Ss: The corn meal.

T: None of it goes through except for the . . .

Ss: The corn meal.

T: I'll put some on . . . and then we're going to . . .

Ss: Shake.

T: Shake it a little, just like we did the other time [does so]. The only thing that went through was . . .?

Ss: The corn meal.

T: So if I do this with my mixture, what will I be sorting?

Ss: The corn meal.

T: [Shifts to a different screen with larger holes.] What if I put this screen over a tub?

S: Everything will go through.

T: Did the lima beans go through?

Ss: No.

T: Did the navy beans go through?

Ss: Yes.

T: So now I can sort the beans because the navy beans go through but the lima beans do not.

At this point, Barbara allows the students to begin working through the activity on their own (in small groups). As they do so, she circulates, intervenes where necessary, and takes note of things that she wants to bring out later in the reflection portion of the lesson. Because the goals of the lesson focus on the nature and use of scientific tools, Barbara emphasizes the students' tool use in leading the reflection segment. She does not, for example, emphasize the properties of the food items except for their relative sizes.

T: One of the things I noticed was that each group had a cup of lima beans, so it must have been pretty easy. Why do you think sorting the lima beans was easy? What made it easy, Chris?

S: You could sort them right in there . . . they were easy to pick out.

T: They were easy to see, weren't they? But I noticed that lots of groups had a tub of corn meal. Tad, was the corn meal big enough to pick up and put in a tub?

S: No.

T: No, it wasn't. What made it easy to sort the corn meal, do you think? The lima beans were the biggest, so that made them easy to sort, and when you used the little strainer and poured the mixture into it, what did you notice?

S: It went through the holes.

T: What went through?

S: The corn meal.

T: What else? Did the rice go through the little bitty strainer? . . . No. The only thing to go through the little bitty strainer . . .

Ss: Was the corn meal.

T: Was the corn meal. So the corn meal was easy to sort because you had tools—the only thing that would go through that tool was . . .

S: The corn meal.

T: So once you started using the tools, the corn meal was pretty easy to sort, too. Now Maurice and I sorted some rice. [Barbara worked with Maurice as a partner during the activity.] Maurice, do you remember what we did to sort the rice?

S: We used a medium-sized tray, and when we put the mixture on . . .

T: The medium-sized tray. When we poured the mixture on, the rice was the only thing to go through, because the corn meal was already . . .

S: Sorted.

T: So when you took the mixture that was left, the rice was the only thing to go through the medium screen. So by doing it in order, it made it easy to sort out different things. If we did the medium screen first, we would have had both corn meal and rice in the tub, and that would have made it a little bit harder. But by finding just the right order . . . and what did you do as scientists that made it so you could find the right way? What did you do, Greta, that scientists do?

S: We had tools to use that would sort.

T: You used tools, scientists use tools. Here's another thing you did today that scientists do: scientists look at their tools, and then they look at the experiment, and they make really smart guesses. Yes—scientists look at their tools and they look at their experiments and they make smart guesses and then they try it. Did you try one thing or more than one thing? . . . More than one thing. Did some things work great? . . . And did some things work not so well? I know when Maurice and I were trying one experiment, a lima bean got stuck. But we tried it again and it worked fine the next time. That's what scientists do—they look at their tools and figure out something to do to make it work. They look at their tools and look at their experiment and try to see what will work.

Time was rapidly running out, so Barbara concluded the lesson relatively abruptly. She was more comfortable doing so than she might have been under other circumstances, however, because she knew that the same general theme of scientific tool use would be continued in subsequent lessons, and she could begin the following lesson with a reminder about and continuing reflection on this lesson.

Using District-Provided Instructional Material as Part of a Larger Set of Resources, Not the Whole Curriculum

Barbara is adamant about the importance of teacher content knowledge. When she first begins to teach a unit in science, for example, she uses the materials that are provided to her as a resource to gather content knowledge herself. She reads through all the books; she reads through all the experiments; she reads through the tests; and she takes the tests and quizzes herself. She tries to make sure that she has as much knowledge about the topic as she can. Then, using the content that she now knows, along with whatever state benchmarks or content expectations there might be, she formulates her big ideas for the unit. Once she has formulated those big ideas, the district-provided materials become a resource. Instead of thinking, "I have to follow them in the given sequence," she looks at what she wants her students to know and uses what she knows about the topic to pick and choose the experiments, activities, books to be read, and how she wants her students to use their science journals in relation to this unit. She does all of those things with those goals and big ideas in mind.

She then can also identify useful parts of any tradebooks the district might have given her, so she can look at those as resources and use the pieces that match (rather than feeling like she needs to read them all in their entirety whether they match or not). Again, she takes what she knows about the topic and takes the materials that the district has given her and then uses those two resources as tools to help her figure out how to get her students to learn what she wants them to learn from the unit.

As with her teaching of other subjects, Barbara's teaching of mathematics and science is guided by her goals (intended outcomes). The content is organized around big ideas and developed with emphasis on their connections and applications. This supports both understanding of the learning and appreciation of its value.

Chapter 13

Making Good Teaching Better

In this book and its companion volume (Brophy, Alleman, & Knighton, 2008), we have used Barbara's teaching as a basis for offering numerous principles, supported by richly detailed and analyzed examples, of unusually coherent and powerful teaching of first and second grade students. Jere and Jan find Barbara's teaching remarkable, among other things, for its establishment of home-school collaborations, maintenance of productive learning communities, coherence of instruction around big ideas linked to major goals phrased as intended student outcomes, emphasis on connections within and across curriculum components and between the curriculum and life outside of school, combination of interesting information presentation segments with social constructivist segments (whole-class discussions and collaborative independent work done in pairs or small groups) to systematically develop and apply big ideas, and incorporation of the inclusion philosophy and a great deal of personalization and individualization within ongoing whole-class instruction.

We could see that teachers in general, and primary teachers in particular, would have much to gain by learning about Barbara's teaching, so we began to write articles about it. The more we learned about Barbara, the more we realized that very little of what occurs in her classroom is accidental. Her teaching reflects plans that are both richly layered in their complexity and remarkably well coordinated to exploit connections and support student progress toward major goals. Jere and Jan eventually concluded that, although articles on particular components of Barbara's teaching were helpful, readers would get much more out of a book-length analysis that outlined the big picture and showed how various components fit within it. As it turned out, there was so much to describe and analyze that two books were required.

This brief chapter concludes our analysis. In it, we focus on one last aspect of Barbara's approach to teaching that Jere and Jan find remarkable: she constantly monitors and reflects on her teaching, objectively evaluating its strengths and weaknesses and generating and following through on plans for improvement. Jere and Jan periodically questioned

Barbara about these self-monitoring and improvement aspects of her teaching. Taken together, her responses reflect an inspiring philosophy of what it means to constantly renew oneself and grow as a professional. The highlights of this philosophy are presented in the rest of this chapter.

Whenever Barbara wants to socialize her students toward becoming lifelong learners, it is easy for her to draw examples from her own life and professional career. She assesses and reflects upon her teaching every day, looking for ways to improve the things she already does. In addition, she reads professional literature, attends presentations and workshops, and "talks shop" with other teachers to acquire new ideas and learn about methods that she may want to try with her students.

She talks about supporting herself as a learner in order to continue her professional development as an educator. Part of this is reacting systematically to opportunities that come along, such as taking what she learns in district-sponsored inservice workshops and thinking about whether and how it might be applied in her classroom. But much of it is more proactive, beginning with her systematic goal setting.

Setting Goals for Improvement

Barbara's goal setting is informed in large part by her daily reflections on what went well or poorly, and why. Her analyses of reasons for disappointing results usually carry implications for change in the future, either in the lesson or activity itself or in the way she structures and scaffolds it with her students. Occasionally, however, she determines that a lesson or activity that did not go well in the particular year nevertheless is fundamentally sound and appropriate for the grade level, and that the problem she experienced that year had more to do with something unique to that group of students than to her implementation of the activity. She applies this reasoning to her more general goal setting as well:

> When I do goal setting I try to avoid thinking about a particular class or year, because I don't want to get into the habit of making reactive decisions like that. You're never in control of the students you have from one year to the next, so something that worked fine until this year might start working well again next year.
>
> So I look for trends. For example, when I first started teaching, I made a concerted effort to make a lot of family connections. I developed several ways of doing so and institutionalized many of them, such as my weekly newsletter and publishing my phone number and e-mail address. But in reflecting on family connections this year, I realized that I was doing a number of things automatically but had drifted away from looking for new and different ways to communicate. That's why I chose to make family communication my

big goal, my big focus this year—because I hadn't done anything new with it in a long time. So part of goal setting is paying special attention to aspects of my teaching that I have not really questioned or changed in a while.

I also look closely at areas that have been frustrating for me, where I find myself consistently experiencing the same disappointment. Last year, one of my major goals was improving writing instruction, because I was seeing a pattern of being frustrated by the same things every year, no matter what the group of kids was like. So that is when I went out looking for inservice training on writing instruction, because I was not happy with the way my teaching was turning out. And I knew it was something about the instruction itself, not something unique to a given group of kids, because I was running into the same frustrations every year.

A third source of input to goal setting and adoption of new practices is the input I get from other professionals and from information sources for teachers. I try to keep close track of what is happening in my district—what am I seeing going on in other classrooms, what trends are emerging over time, and what implications might these have for my classroom. I explore professional magazines and websites, looking for something that makes me think, "Boy, that's something I could incorporate in my room." So, I look for new trends, I look for what's happening around me in other classrooms and in the district, I look at how things have been to see if there are places where things are not going as well as I hoped, and I look for areas where I have been doing the same things for many years, just to re-examine them and make sure I still think they are sound practices.

For example, I recently visited a classroom that had lots of pictures of the kids' families posted in places where kids could see their families all the time. I decided that I wanted to incorporate this in my class this year. It connects to the whole idea of communicating with families, which is something I really wanted to do more of this year, and it also connects to our social studies unit on family living and to my community-building goals.

Just like I use posters as reminders for the kids, I use signs to remind myself about new things that I am trying out or things that I want to remember to do frequently. I post reminders of things like my big goals that I want to keep in the front of my brain all the time. And with this year's class, I noted early on that as a group they were unusually whiny or dependent, always saying things like, "You need to do this for me" or "This is too hard." And I had read a research report indicating that one of the things that successful teachers do is maintain an attitude of "you can do it" with their students all the time, and that the better you are at maintaining that attitude, the more successful the kids will be. If you see them as being successful, they will begin to see themselves as capable and successful. So that's why one of the signs I have on my teacher wall says, "You can do it," and another says, "I will not give up on you." These are things that I want to keep saying to them all the time.

Finally, I always go back to my overarching, umbrella-type goals. Am I meeting those? Am I staying true to the things I believe? Am I still making sure that the kids are building relationships? Do I really feel that they're getting a solid literacy block? Is my classroom a safe place? Are students continuing to be independent? Are they developing a sense of self-efficacy—feeling like they can function well? I keep these big questions in mind when I review my teaching and establish goal priorities for the year.

Active Assessment, Reflection, and Planning

In identifying areas in need of analysis and possible change, Barbara pays close attention to assessments of students' progress and goal attainment, at both the general class and the individual student level. She views assessment data as carrying information not only about students' progress but about her own success as a teacher. So, besides noting the relative level of success achieved by the class as a whole and identifying any students who will need additional instruction and practice, she asks herself questions such as: "Do I need to change how I teach (e.g., telling time)? Do I need to spend more time on it? Do I need to teach it in a different way or at a different time in the school year? On a daily basis, she does similar reflecting at the individual lesson or activity level, routinely after completing these activities but sometimes even during her implementation of them:

> You don't have to be formal about it, but you have to pay attention and remember anything that will be important for future reference. As I was finishing a math lesson a few days ago, I was thinking to myself, "You know, you did a great job modeling and you did a great job having some kids come and model, but you didn't do a very good job with the guided practice, and now that the kids are in independent practice, it's not going so well." When I see these kinds of problems, I try to find the disconnect. What didn't I do well? In this case, what didn't I do during guided practice that made it difficult for the kids when they got to independent practice? So as I'm going from group to group to monitor their progress and provide help to individual kids, I'm already thinking, "The next time you do this lesson, or even the next time you want the kids to work independently on something like this, you need to be more specific about each step. You didn't break it down into specific steps well enough for them."

Often these are things that I can fix on the spot, so in that situation, I would interrupt independent practice and break down the steps more specifically for them, like I should have done in the first place. I make it a point to remember these experiences and take them into account in the future. Usually filing away a "mental note" is enough, but if I want to make sure that I remember something especially important, I will summarize it on a post-it note and attach it to the section of the teacher's manual that outlines the lesson. But the main point is that I'm always thinking about my teaching while I'm teaching and also when I finish teaching. And I remember those things and think about them before I teach again. One of the really big things you have to do to grow as a teacher is not just assess your kids but assess your own teaching and ask whether and how it could be made more effective. Is there a way that I could do this better the next time?

Additions Require Deletions

Barbara often has to accommodate additional curriculum specifications from the state or district that make additional time demands on an already full schedule, and her own decisions about strengthening her teaching often involve additional time commitments as well. Adding new strands to the curriculum or budgeting additional time for existing strands creates a need to reduce time budgeted for other strands. This need is part of what motivates some of Barbara's curricular integration (i.e., when she finds ways to make a single lesson address GLCEs in two different subjects). Other deletions result from cost/benefit analyses:

> For me, deletions come in the form of, "What am I doing that doesn't meet either my basic overall goals or my special goals for the year?" For example, I always used to do a hands-on art project once a week, but a couple of years ago I decided that this wasn't meeting any of my goals. It was taking more time to do than it was worth.
>
> As another example, for several years in a row there, the kids and I would create/make/cook a snack together once a week. This began during one of those years in which I focused on new ways to build community, and I always felt that if you sit down and eat together, a certain amount of community building results. So I did that for a few years, but again, I found that it was taking too much time—to get parents to contribute the ingredients and then assemble them and make the meal. It was procedurally complicated and not yielding enough payoff for community building to make it worth the time.
>
> Anything I do in the classroom, I'm doing it for specific reasons—to meet a need or a goal. So if I find that the activity isn't meeting the goal or giving me the benefit I expected from it, or if conditions have

changed so that it no longer is as important or effective as it used to be, I will get rid of it or replace it with something else. Often I do not delete something, but I change it to make it more efficient or make it so that it meets needs or fits my goals better.

Barbara Creates Her Own Organizational Supports

To help keep herself organized, Barbara maintains a teacher area in her classroom that is much more than the typical desk containing in- structional materials and a few personal knickknacks. It is an unusual and salient enough feature of her classroom that visitors typically notice it and spend some time inspecting it. Barbara describes it as follows:

> It's a combination of things. Much of it is information. For example, I keep student schedules there, and my calendars for the current month. Also my calendars for the following month, so I have plan- ning stuff there. It's got pictures. It's got information that a guest teacher might need.
>
> It also has lots of reminders for me, about my overall goals, my special goals for the year, and anything else that I want to keep in the front of my brain. I also keep lists. For example, I have a list of all the poems that I have planned out for the first several months. When I am sitting there and reviewing plans, I might be thinking about an upcoming social studies unit on family living or about how we are going to be studying "s" endings in phonics, and I will look at that list of poems and try to identify connections I can make. So, another piece of it is keeping curriculum stuff there. I can look across the subjects and see that we're talking about plurals in phonics and about counting in math, and I could blend these together in a natural way by having the kids write sentences containing numbers or write answers to counting problems.
>
> Many of the posted signs remind me about exact words that I want to say to the kids. Like with this group, you will hear me say, "This is important" all the time. I put that on a poster because I want to focus on meaningful learning with them—letting them know that there is a reason why we're doing everything that we do.
>
> There are also reminders of things that I need to do. I keep the information we get from our principal there, because I want to make sure that I stay true to what my district expects from me. Having those reminders there helps me to figure out ways to weave what's important to the state and the district into what I already do. And it also is a window for kids, other teachers, parents, or visitors to see what is important to me. They get to know me by looking at what's

over there. Anyone who comes in here can walk over there and see my goals, see pictures of things that are important to me, see the thinking that underlies my teaching.

Collaboration with Colleagues

As a last piece of advice on growing as a professional, Barbara emphasizes that, in addition to all of the things that teachers can do primarily on their own, it is important for them to have conversations with others about teaching. She talks about her teaching with her husband all the time, and she seeks out colleagues who share her commitment to professional development. Early in her career, she was part of a group of colleagues who all were helpful to one another because:

> We were very aware of and desirous of being the best teachers we could be and getting better than we were currently. We were not bad teachers—we already were pretty good. But we all realized that we wanted to be better than we were, and we all had some idea of what that would look like. We didn't have formal meetings or shared planning time, but we would get together informally when opportunities arose. For example, on the playground, as we kept an eye on our kids, we would have conversations like, "Let me tell you what happened this morning . . . Here's what I tried . . . Do you think that was a good idea? . . . What do you think you might have tried?" Or, one of us might pop into another one's class after school and say, "Here's a book that I found that I thought was helpful, especially this part. Would you like to read it and see what you think?"
>
> On some days, we would hang around for half an hour or so after school to seek advice and share observations. For example, I have a vivid memory of four of us sitting in my room one day after school and talking for half an hour about what you might do if you have a kid that just really can't sit still on the carpet. What about letting them stay at the back of the group on their knees—would that work? What would be an alternative? Is there any research on this? What might be going on with that kid? Questions like that. Often it was more general. Someone would say, "I would like to get better at X." And then we would talk about it—what getting better at X might mean and some examples of what it would like in the classroom.

Although Barbara acknowledges the value of talking about teaching with colleagues, she emphasizes that these discussions need to be focused on coping and problem solving, not complaining. She notes that everyone needs to be able to let off steam, but you should not get mired in feeling sorry for yourself if you want to grow as an educator. To the extent that the focus is on problems, it should move beyond identification of the problems to ask, "How can we make things better?" And instead of focusing only on problems, collegial discussions should include a lot of growth stimulation ("Here's an idea I am thinking about trying in my class . . . What do you think about it?").

Barbara has found her collaboration with Jere and Jan to be very useful in supporting her own professional development, and especially in stimulating her to think about things that she might not have thought about on her own. As they review transcripts of her lessons together, Jere and Jan often raise questions about aspects of Barbara's teaching that she had never considered. Many of these questions help her to understand and analyze her own practice better. For example, when asked why she has done something (or done it in a particular way), Barbara often knows exactly why and can explain at length, but sometimes she does not have a ready answer and needs to think out loud as she develops one. These situations often lead to discovery (or at least, more clear formulation) of a principle that Barbara has been following tacitly without ever becoming conscious of it or articulating it clearly. She recommends that teachers find partners or small groups with whom they can collaborate in this kind of detailed analysis of tapes or transcripts of one another's teaching.

In this chapter we have focused on Barbara's remarkable approach to making her good teaching better. We hope that you have been inspired and desire to constantly monitor and reflect on your practice, objectively evaluating its strengths and weaknesses and generating and following through on plans for improvement. The appendix that follows offers an array of tools to assist you in achieving your goals.

Appendix

We hope that, as the result of reading *A Learning Community in the Primary Classroom*, you will develop an understanding and appreciation for what an accomplished teacher can create within the four walls. Our "up close" approach, robust descriptions, and fine-grained analyses are intended to help you become personally connected with Barbara and to the content, to carefully examine where you are in your development as a teacher, and to chart your course for expanding your practice using the principles and insights shared in this text.

This appendix offers an array of tools to assist you in processing the information found in each chapter. Whether you are reading this book on your own, engaging in a school or district-wide professional development initiative, or using it in a college class, you will need to process the information and apply it to your own teaching situation.

There are multiple ways to do this (speaking, listening, writing, mapping, drawing, charting, graphing, etc.) and many challenges involved in attempting to incorporate new practices into existing ones or replace ones that are not effective. Our hope is that getting to know Barbara through reading will lead you to examine your practice to find connections and disconnections with hers. Using the tools in this Appendix (or modifying them to fit your needs) should make it easier for you to self-audit, make changes, share your struggles and successes, and document your growth.

We begin with a review of the book's table of contents (see Table A.1), which provides an initial structure for comparing features of your own practice to parallel features of Barbara's practice as presented in the book.

Chapter 1: Introduction

Reflective Questions

1. Review the table of contents carefully. Then ask yourself, "Which chapters appear to offer the most, given where I am in my development? What specific questions do I hope will be addressed?"

Table A.1 Outline for Summarizing Results of Portfolio/Journal Assessments of My Own Teaching.*

Facets of a Learning Community	Principles of Good Teaching	Barbara's Thoughts and Techniques	My Current Thoughts and Practices	My Plans for the Future
Chapter 1: Introduction				
Chapter 2: Establishing the Classroom as a Collaborative Learning Community				
Chapter 3: Communicating with Families				
Chapter 4: Managing the Learning Community's Everyday Activities				
Chapter 5: Using Narrative to Build a Content Base				
Chapter 6: Modeling of Self-regulated Reasoning and Learning				
Chapter 7: Motivating Students to Engage in Learning Confidently and Thoughtfully				
Chapter 8: Individualizing to Meet Students' Needs				
Chapter 9: Planning				
Chapter 10: Curriculum and Instruction in Literacy				
Chapter 11: Curriculum and Instruction in Social Studies				
Chapter 12: Curriculum and Instruction in Mathematics and Science				
Chapter 13: Making Good Teaching Better				

* One page per chapter

Note: We encourage you to co-construct this journey using a portfolio/journal to document what you learn from Barbara, what you currently do, and what changes you will enact in the future. Adding evidentiary materials (student work, classroom photos, community building activities, supportive articles, etc.) can create a personalized and growth-producing experience, ultimately producing an exemplary learning community in your classroom.
    We encourage you to co-construct with students visuals that can be displayed in your classroom. They can serve as powerful reminders of the practices you are implementing to insure the success of all students within a safe, engaging, and growth-producing environment.

2. Also ask yourself, "What chapter topic represents an area I have considered only nominally in my practice? What are my initial questions about this topic?"

3. Ask yourself, "What goals do I hope I can achieve as the result of reading *A Learning Community in a Primary Classroom*?" Write these goals down and review them often. If you achieve some of them early, identify others.

4. What questions do you have regarding the Brophy, Alleman, and Knighton collaboration?

5. What are compelling reasons for engaging college professors and teachers in studying classroom practice? Do you see any drawbacks?

6. As a classroom teacher, would you be willing to collaborate with college professors in learning more about practice? Why or why not? Explain.

Activity

Imagine, as a classroom teacher, collaborating with a couple of college professors in an attempt to learn more about your practice. Sketch out a plan establishing whom you would want to collaborate with, under what conditions you would launch the study, the initial questions you would investigate, etc. Share your ideas with peers. Revise accordingly. Consider seeking a collaborative opportunity with a former or current professor.

Check Out Your Practice

Surf each chapter and generate a series of questions you will address as you read the text, have conversations with peers, and study your own practice. See how many you can get answers to as you participate in the professional development initiative.

Chapter 2: Establishing the Classroom as a Collaborative Learning Community

Reflective Questions

1. This chapter offered many insights about learning community for students in the early grades. What was a real "aha!" for you?

2. How is Barbara's learning community similar to other classroom communities you have observed? Different? Which aspects of Barbara's approach do you think would be easy to adopt? Why? Which would you find most challenging? Why?

3. How might an uninformed observer react to what he/she sees and

hears during a first visit to her classroom at the beginning of the year? Explain the reasons for your response.

4. How might parents unfamiliar with Barbara's approach to learning community react to what they see and hear during their first visit to her classroom at the beginning of the year? Explain the reasons for your response.

5. What is your reaction to Barbara's decision to emphasize learning community activities during the first few weeks of school? How do you think she would respond to a principal's concern about "getting to the content sooner"?

6. Barbara spends a lot of time early in the year helping students acquire self-monitoring/self-regulating skills. How would you address this topic with families?

7. How do you propose balancing the desire to develop a learning community within the classroom with the push toward teaching content and preparing students to be successful on standardized tests?

8. Which of the self-regulation strategies would be easiest for you to adopt and apply to your practice? Why? Which would you be hesitant to adopt? Why?

9. What is your reaction to Barbara's practice of having students self-monitor and assess their own work? Will you consider adopting this practice? Why or why not?

10. Barbara has been very successful in using social stories to teach behavior control and decision-making strategies. What is your reaction to this approach? What is one new insight you have developed about social stories? If you were to create one for your class, what would it be about, and why?

11. Barbara encourages you to imagine that you are on stage when presenting rules and routines, to make them memorable and make sure everyone is connecting to your emotions. What is your reaction to this? Explain.

12. Barbara emphasizes personal responsibilities beginning the first day of school. What is your reaction to this? What evidence is there that this practice exists in your classroom?

13. Barbara's students are expected to participate in lessons and be prepared to respond thoughtfully, both when it is "her turn" and when it is "their turn." What challenges in your classroom are associated with this practice, and what can you do to overcome them?

Activity

Imagine that you have just observed Barbara's classroom with a focus on learning community. Spend an allocated amount of time jotting down notes or creating a visual depicting what you envision her learning community to sound like, look like, and feel like. Then, in pairs or triads, describe your experience. What features were new to you, quite remarkable, and ones you want to incorporate into your practice? What challenges do you envision and how will you address them? Discuss new questions that were raised for you.

Check Out Your Practice

Audiotape your class for a morning (or ask someone to observe and take field notes with an emphasis on learning community). As you listen to the tape or study the notes, use Table A.2 to assess your learning community. What seems to be going well? What needs attention? Guard against making this activity tedious. The intent is that you can become a better self-monitor and a more reflective practitioner.

Table A.2 A Look at My Learning Community

Teacher Behavior	Examples in My Practice
Provides Activities Focusing on Classmate Names/Personal Details	
Uses Sponge Activities to Elicit Information about Students	
Promotes Self-regulation Supports/scaffolds (e.g., day's schedule, visual displays)	
Engages in Teaching and Reinforcing Learning Community Norms (e.g., reinforces desired attitudes, assigns jobs)	
Engages in Teaching Self-regulation (e.g., asks students to tell what they have/have not done; restates expectations; models each assignment and posts own paper; uses social stories)	
Makes Rules and Routines Memorable (e.g., is expressive)	
Establishes Personal Responsibility (e.g., models what responsibility looks like; conducts formal checks on students' fulfillment of personal responsibility)	
Promotes Lesson Participation Responsibility (e.g., talks to students about listening carefully and thoughtfully, contributing)	

Construct a wish list focusing on hopes to be experienced in the classroom this year. Study the results and select an area you want to work on. Establish a plan and enact it.

OR

Create one or more social stories adapted to the needs of your students. Begin each social story with an explanation of how and why the topic is important to the class. Explain step-by-step what students should do, why they should do it, and what will happen if they do not. Finish with a summary of what students need to do to be successful. Enact stories one at a time and study the impact of each. Make adjustments as needed. Planned redundancy is important.

Chapter 3: Communicating with Families

Reflective Questions

1. What is your overall reaction to Barbara's approach to communicating with families? How does it compare to yours? What unique practices of Barbara's will you adopt first? Why?
2. Are there any of Barbara's practices that you would hesitate to adopt? Which ones? Why?
3. What practices in dealing with families do you employ that you would offer as suggestions to Barbara? Explain.
4. Imagine being a parent of a child in Barbara's classroom. What would impress you most about her practices? What might make you uncomfortable? Explain.
5. Imagine being a specials teacher in Barbara's school. What would impress you most about her practices? What might make you uncomfortable? Explain.
6. If you were Barbara and a parent of twins (one in her room) came complaining about the other child's teacher (e.g., a lack of communication with families), how would you respond? Would you attempt to do anything about it? Why or why not?
7. What is your overall reaction to Barbara's approach to homework? How would the families of your students react to it? Why?

Activity

Examine your year-long plan for communicating with families. If it exists only in your head, take this opportunity to put it on paper. After you have written it down, crosscheck your ideas with those reported by Barbara. Make any additions that you think will enhance your practice. Share your document with your principal. Look for evidence of impact of your actions. Building a team that involves families in the children's learning process is vitally important. It promotes both a sense of belonging and enhanced achievement.

Check Out Your Practice

A recent family communication goal for Barbara was to have at least eight interactions with each family prior to the first family conference scheduled after about three months of school. For the next month, document and monitor your interactions with families. What patterns emerge? Make adjustments according to your goals.

Chapter 4: Managing the Learning Community's Everyday Activities

Reflective Questions

1. What is your reaction to Barbara's statement, "Students want information! They want to know what is going on . . . It takes the mystery out of school—that's what kids worry about the most"?
2. To help her students retain a learning set as they carry out transitions or experience interruptions, Barbara's instructions often include content designed to keep students' minds focused on the curriculum. What is your reaction to this practice? How can it be realized more in your classroom?
3. What is your reaction to Barbara's "My Turn/Your Turn" strategy? What challenges would this practice pose in your classroom?
4. Which of Barbara's strategies for encouraging active student participation do you already use? Which are new to you? What needs to happen in order to incorporate the new ones into your practice?
5. What is your reaction to Barbara's approach to enforcing the rules? Why? How would you explain this approach to parents who punish their children when they behave inappropriately?
6. How do the last few days of your school year compare to Barbara's? Which of the disbanding strategies do you incorporate into your practice? Which new strategies would you consider adding? Why?

Activity

By now you have developed images of what Barbara's classroom learning community looks and sounds like, as well as her philosophical stance regarding student efficacy and how to develop it. As a class, describe and illustrate this stance, with special emphasis on socialization and students' potential for regulating their own learning. What new insights have you acquired from Barbara? What aspects would you challenge and why?

Check Out Your Practice

Audiotape, videotape, or ask someone to observe and take field notes focusing on your situational management strategies. As you study the tape or field notes (select segments), use Table A.3 to assess your management strategies. What seems to be going well? What needs attention? Are you more successful in one subject area than another?

Guard against this activity becoming tedious. The intent is that you become a better self-monitor, a more reflective practitioner, and better manager of your learning community's everyday activities.

Select a content area and monitor your performance. When you feel satisfied with your success, select another subject. Document your behavior. Are you equally successful?

Table A.3 Situational Management Strategies

Teacher Behavior	Examples in My Practice
Locating learning activities physically	
Maintaining awareness of who has the floor during lessons and what this implies about participation expectations	
Supporting understanding of the nature of the activity and what this implies about the questions or comments that are appropriate	
Maintaining or recapturing thoughtful attention to lessons	
Structuring students' group and individual work on independent learning activities	

Chapter 5: Using Narrative to Build a Content Base

Reflective Questions

1. Imagine that an observer was in your classroom to determine how your students develop social studies understandings. Describe what would be occurring. Would things look similar or different if you were teaching science? Math? Explain your response.
2. Imagine that you are planning one of the early lessons for your next social studies unit. How will it look? Describe one of your final lessons. Compare the two. Would the same pattern emerge if you were comparing your first and final lessons of a science unit? Why or why not?
3. Reflect on your last social studies unit. Describe how examples of conceptual change unfolded. Now, do the same thing with your last science unit. What did you learn from this exercise? What will you attempt to change in either the science or social studies unit next time? Explain.
4. Reflect on a recent or current social studies unit. What does it take to seriously build a content base with your students? Repeat the process with a science unit. Make sure you consider your students with special needs.
5. In what other areas of the curriculum might you use narrative to build a content base? Explain. What will you need to do differently to make this change? Would you expect any challenges in making the change? Elaborate.
6. How can the narrative format serve students with diverse backgrounds?
7. What aspects of your science, social studies, literacy, and/or mathematics curriculum are amenable to representation within narrative structures? Explain.

Activity

Bring to the session a lesson in the content area of your choice that lends itself well to the narrative format because it includes a robust body of new content. In small groups, present mini-lessons emphasizing the "story" and focusing on a few big ideas. What do you observe? What are the challenges associated with this approach? What are the payoffs?

Check Out Your Practice

Audio or videotape a lesson in a current curricular unit that needs modeling or explanations from you to provide grounding for subsequent discussion. As you review the lesson, what do you notice? Do your explanations feature informed narrative (storytelling) rather than formal lecturing? Does the narrative illustrate networks of connected ideas? Substantive coherence? Continuity? How and why is the content made memorable? What might you do differently to make this lesson even more powerful the next time? Explain.

Chapter 6: Modeling of Self-regulated Reasoning and Learning

Reflective Questions

1. Teaching cognitive processes and skills involves propositional knowledge, procedural knowledge, and conditional knowledge. Which of these do you think is easiest to teach? Why? Which is most difficult to teach? Why?
2. What do you view as most challenging about cognitive modeling? Why? What are some recent examples from your teaching that illustrate your use of cognitive modeling? What have you observed when you make a concerted effort to use it in your classroom?
3. Imagine that you were given the opportunity to team teach with Barbara. After reading and reflecting on the transcripts incorporated in this chapter, would you be excited about this assignment, or tentative? Explain.
4. What is your overall reaction to the emphasis Barbara gives to reasoning and decision making by early elementary students? Make sure you provide a robust explanation.

Activity

In triads, select a couple of empowering strategies that you would like to teach your students. Plan how you will teach them. Include three things for each one: propositional knowledge (what it is), procedural knowledge (how to do it), and conditional knowledge (when and why it is used). After your plans are complete, micro-teach for each other and elicit feedback regarding your effectiveness.

Check Out Your Practice

Select one aspect of modeling self-regulated reasoning and decision making from the chapter that really resonated with you and build it into your planning and instruction. Invite a peer, the principal, a student teacher or some other interested party to observe your enactment and provide feedback to you.

Chapter 7: Motivating Students to Engage in Learning Confidently and Thoughtfully

Reflective Questions

1. The best teachers rely on multiple strategies to motivate students, while avoiding behaviors likely to demotivate them. What specifically do you do to motivate your students?
2. What is your reaction to the expectancy x value model of motivation? How does it apply in your classroom? What is your biggest challenge in operationalizing it?
3. Do you find it more challenging to provide expectancy or value support? Explain.
4. What is your reaction to the routines that Barbara uses during individual response opportunities? How does her approach fit with yours? Which of her routines would you consider adopting? What is a routine that you would suggest to her?
5. What is your reaction to Barbara's de-emphasis on competition? Why?
6. Barbara is all about fostering student self-efficacy. What are the most compelling examples of this you have gleaned from this chapter?
7. What sorts of psychic or social rewards do you provide your students? What additional ones would you consider using as the result of reading about Barbara's approach?
8. Barbara leads her students to expect that interesting and important things will occur in her classroom. What do you do to ensure the same in your classroom? What techniques would you consider adding to your repertoire? Explain.
9. One of the most salient and observable features in Barbara's teaching is the frequency with which she notes connections between curricular content and the experiences of her students or their family members. What do you do to make sure this happens in your classroom? What could you do to make it happen more often? How could you acquire more information about your students that would promote this feature of your practice?
10. Barbara would tell you that she has fun teaching and truly loves her classroom role. What hints of this can you glean from the chapter?

Activity

In small groups, create visual representations of Barbara motivating students to engage in learning confidently and thoughtfully. In a large group, share responses. What patterns emerge? Discuss which strategic moves might be challenging to implement and why. Discuss what you need to do to begin working on them.

Check Out Your Practice

Ask a colleague to periodically observe you to determine how effective you are at motivating students (or simply use Table A.4 and Table A.5 on page 260 as tools for planning).

What patterns emerged? Where are you most successful? Are you more (or less) successful in specific subject areas? In different teaching situations (lessons, activities, assignments, tests)? What area(s) needs your attention?

Chapter 8: Individualizing to Meet Students' Needs

Reflective Questions

1. What are the most powerful insights you acquired about addressing students' individual needs as the result of reading this chapter?
2. How does Barbara's approach to special needs students compare to the one in your building? Explain.
3. Barbara initially focuses on students' assets as opposed to zeroing in on their deficits. What is your reaction to this? Explain.
4. As a parent of a special needs student, would you want this child to be placed in your classroom or in Barbara's? Provide reasons for your response.
5. Barbara describes herself as the "Buck Stops Here Lady." What is your reaction to this? Do you hold a similar view? Why or why not?
6. Barbara is viewed as exceptional in her ability to coordinate support staff. Imagine that you were one of those support persons. What would be your reaction to Barbara's approach? Provide reasons for your response.
7. Barbara is seen by the principal and parents of special needs students as very effective at socializing and teaching these children. Do you agree with their assessment? Why or why not? Use concrete examples to illustrate your reasons.
8. It's intriguing to observe Barbara addressing students' special needs "on the fly" during lessons. What is your reaction to the strategic moves described in this section?

Table A.4 Providing Expectancy Support

Expectancy Supports	Examples in My Practice
Making students aware that they are expected to learn and will be held accountable	
Articulating clear expectations about students' classroom conduct and learning efforts	
Attributing students' successes to their willingness to put forth their best efforts	
Encouraging students' efforts and praising their progress	
Encouraging students to take risks by accepting appropriate challenges	
Encouraging independence by expecting them to do as much as they can before asking for help	
Teaching students strategies for organizing their efforts and regulating their own learning	
Letting students know they can be successful on challenging tasks if they maintain their persistence	
Consistently scaffolding students' efforts to meet expectations and celebrate progress as they achieve	

Table A.5 Providing Value Support

Value Supports	Examples in My Practice
Communicating the importance of learning activities	
Providing engaging content	
Providing extrinsic rewards not as bribes but tools to extend learning (including games and playful activities to make lessons more enjoyable and concrete)	
Providing students with choices concerning certain aspects of their learning	
Consistently emphasizing the importance of acquiring and using knowledge taught in school	

Activity

Imagine that this chapter was the content featured by a keynoter presenting at a national conference on addressing students' individual needs. In small groups, plan 15-minute mini-sessions you would present to your faculty highlighting the most salient elements. Present them to your colleagues.

OR

Imagine that you are a parent of a special needs child. You have requested a meeting with Barbara. You have heard that she is skillful, but you worry that she may be too demanding. In small groups, plan role plays of the meeting. Then enact them in large groups and discuss the results.

Check Out Your Practice

Select a specific student (or students) with one of the special needs described in this chapter (Impulsive/Hyperactive, Shy/Hesitant, Speech Communication Problems, Autism/Asperger's Syndrome). Using your current strategies, plus additional ones Barbara uses, work to increase that child's level of success. When you feel adequately satisfied with the progress, select another area, etc. Small steps add up!

Chapter 9: Planning

Reflective Questions

1. How does your overall planning scheme compare to Barbara's? What do you do differently that Barbara might benefit from? What does Barbara do that you will consider adding to your repertoire? Explain.
2. Rank order your levels of planning from most successful to least successful. At your least successful planning level, what ideas from Barbara's approach can you add? How do you think that this might improve your instruction?
3. Barbara spends considerable time in daily rehearsal, focusing on three big questions: (1) What do I really want my students to know or be able to do when I'm done? (2) What words am I going to say? (3) How might this confuse them or create misconceptions? How does this approach fit with what you do? Explain.
4. Barbara is very willing to change or replace an activity, even one from a prescribed curricular package, if she thinks it is ineffective. What is

your reaction to this? Are you as willing to serve as the ultimate decision maker? Why or why not?

5. How are your views and practices regarding curricular integration similar or different from Barbara's? Explain. What is your biggest challenge associated with integration? What are you doing to address it?

6. What is your stance regarding holidays and special events as they relate to your academic curriculum? How does it fit with Barbara's? What new questions does her approach raise for you? What unique pressures do you feel regarding this matter in your district? What might you do to overcome them?

Activity

Reread the transcript beginning on page 174 of this chapter that addresses "Get away from numbers and still see patterns." Then, as a group, track Barbara's thinking. Select a "teacher" to demonstrate/replicate exactly what she did, so your group gets the visual as well as the auditory experience. What is the reaction to what she said and did? What can you learn from this? What new questions are raised for you?

Check Out Your Practice

Select an upcoming topic or chunk of basic information that caused problems the last time you taught it. Plan and enact a mental rehearsal focusing on the following questions:

(1) What do I really want my students to know or be able to do?
(2) What words am I going to say?
(3) What do I need to say to avoid confusion and misconceptions?

Tape this segment as you teach it. Critique it for its effectiveness, paying attention to both your explanations and your students' responses.

Chapter 10: Curriculum and Instruction in Literacy

Reflective Questions

1. "In Barbara's classroom, literacy is not only a formal part of the curriculum, but a way of life." What is your reaction to this statement? Could the same claim be made regarding your classroom? Explain.

2. How does an average day in your classroom compare to Barbara's?

Explain. If you were to make one change in your schedule, what would it be and why?

3. What is your reaction to Barbara's overall emphasis on thinking and metacognition in teaching her students in every content area? What evidences of these practices exist in your classroom?

4. Which of Barbara's literacy practices are most like yours? Least like yours? Explain.

5. Which of Barbara's literacy practices will you consider adopting? Why? How will you go about doing this?

6. Barbara's emphasis on self-regulation during writer's workshop (as well as during other activities) is quite remarkable. What is your reaction to her approach? Would it work in your classroom? Why or why not?

7. What is your reaction to Barbara's emphasis on poetry? Explain.

8. A pervasive aspect of Barbara's teaching is her attempt to encourage her students to value learning and build self-concepts as efficacious learners. What is your reaction to her approach? Is it something you are comfortable doing? Explain.

Activity

Bring to the session an accounting of all the literacy opportunities your students experienced during the current week (or a typical week). In small groups, decide whether or not your classroom would be characterized as literacy rich. What evidence is there? Could it be made more so? What would need to be removed? Use an opportunity cost model for your analysis (i.e., consider not only the benefits, but also the costs of any contemplated changes).

Check Out Your Practice

Select one aspect of your literacy curriculum, such as poetry or writer's workshop. Study it carefully. Tape class sessions if appropriate. How closely does it parallel Barbara's practices? What might you add? Delete? Based on your approach and successes, what would you suggest that Barbara consider adding? Explain.

Chapter 11: Curriculum and Instruction in Social Studies

Reflective Questions

1. What is your overall reaction to the importance of focusing on big ideas?

2. Which of the layers of big ideas is most challenging for you? What do you think you might do to overcome the issues associated with it?
3. Assuming that you, too, believe that teachers go through four stages in developing expertise in structuring their teaching around big ideas, what stage are you in? What evidence can you show?
4. What is your reaction to Barbara's use of big ideas as a basis for deciding which children's literature to include in a unit and for planning how to present and use the books?
5. Typically, Barbara uses four elements in lesson segments that introduce big ideas. Which one are you most comfortable with? Least comfortable with? What might you consider doing to increase your comfort level as well as your actual enactment of all four elements?
6. Barbara feels strongly about maintaining focus on big ideas without getting sidetracked. Are you equally determined to make sure the big ideas remain center front? Why or why not?
7. Barbara has developed several techniques for focusing students' attention on big ideas. Which of the techniques are new to you? Which will you begin incorporating into your lessons immediately?
8. Which of the techniques that Barbara has perfected for focusing students' attention on big ideas will you attempt to investigate further —and then probably incorporate into your practice?

Activity

Carefully examine one or more sections of the lesson transcripts provided in this chapter with an eye toward the development of big ideas. What specific "strategic moves" does Barbara make to keep her students focused? What are your overall reactions to her approach?

Check Out Your Practice

Take a careful look at your current social studies unit or an upcoming one. List the three levels of big ideas associated with the unit. We encourage you to make a concerted effort to consciously incorporate these big ideas throughout the unit/lessons as appropriate. Use some of Barbara's techniques to focus on the ideas. Audiotape one or more lessons. As you listen to them (in the car, on the way to school perhaps), ask yourself, "What do I notice?" "Do the lessons have more direction?" "What happens to the discourse?" "How do I feel at the end of the lesson?" "What happens for the students?"

Chapter 12: Curriculum and Instruction in Mathematics and Science

Reflective Questions

1. Key features of Barbara's math and science teaching include clarity of goals and intended outcomes, developing and connecting big ideas, modeling skills, and teaching for independent and self-regulated learning. How do these align with those featured in your math and science teaching? Explain.

2. One of Barbara's priorities in math is helping her students see the logic and sense of the underlying patterns. Is that one of your priorities? If so, how does it look in your classroom? If not, why not?

3. Barbara, perhaps like you, was taught to begin with concrete materials, then move to pictorial representations, and finally move to symbolic representations. She no longer believes this sequence is always necessary. Do you agree? Why or why not?

4. Barbara incorporates a lot of metacognition into her teaching. What evidence of this can be seen in your teaching?

5. Authentic application of content and skills is a high priority in Barbara's instruction. What challenges do you experience when trying to implement this practice?

6. How does Barbara's approach to story problems compare to yours? Explain. What new questions does this raise for you?

7. Barbara refers to the math curriculum as more structured, homogeneous, and confining than most of the other subjects. If your experience has been different, what recommendations would you make to Barbara?

8. How does your science curriculum compare to Barbara's? If you were to make changes in it, what would you do and why?

9. The format Barbara uses in science is typically whole class, very similar to what she uses in social studies. How does this compare to your approach? If different, what do you see as the tradeoffs? Explain.

Activity

Bring to the session a math or science lesson plan of your choice. In small groups, plan and present selected lessons, emphasizing the basic procedures that Barbara includes in a typical lesson: 1) initial instruction focused on a big idea or central question, 2) teacher modeling of skills or assignment responses, 3) students' model, 4) scaffolded guided practice, 5) student independent practice. Debrief. What new insights did you acquire as the result of this activity?

Check Out Your Practice

Audiotape or videotape a science or math lesson. As you listen or view and listen, what do you notice? Check for clarity of goals and intended outcomes, for big ideas, for modeling skills, and for independent and self-regulated learning. How do you rate yourself? What do you need to do to receive an even higher rating?

Chapter 13: Making Good Teaching Better

Reflective Questions

1. What are your views about constantly renewing yourself and growing as a professional? How do they parallel Barbara's? Explain.
2. Imagine if Barbara were to join your faculty. How would you and your colleagues react? What contributions would she bring to your workplace? Explain.
3. What is unique about Barbara's approach to continuously growing as a professional? Explain.
4. By now you realize that Barbara is very goals-oriented. Identify examples from the text to illustrate this. Are you equally focused on goals? If not, why not?
5. Visualize the "teacher area" in Barbara's classroom. Then check out yours. How do they compare? What would you suggest that Barbara might add to hers? What will you add after reading the description of Barbara's? Explain.
6. Barbara wants to have lots of conversations with others about her teaching, especially those who view the profession as dynamic, growth producing, joyful, and rewarding. Is this your practice as well? Why or why not?

Activity

As a group, brainstorm what can be done to facilitate teacher development in your building. We hope that Barbara's practices will trigger ideas for you and your peers. Then prioritize your ideas, and as a faculty, design a plan that will incorporate your top two or three. Submit it to your building leader for consideration.

Check Out Your Practice

Keeping in mind that you are a "work in progress" and want to make your good teaching even better, do a self-audit using the practices Barbara implements as your initial guide (see Table A.6). Add other categories that suit your personality and the vision you have established for yourself as a professional.

Table A.6 Assessing Your Practice

Teacher Behavior	Already Do	Will Incorporate This Year	Will Plan to Add Next Year
• Assess and reflect on my teaching daily			
• Do serious goal setting			
Pay attention to aspects of my teaching that I have not questioned or changed for a while			
Look closely at areas that have been frustrating me			
Consider adopting new practices based on input from other professionals and from information sources for teachers			
Revisit my overarching goals			
• Revisit student progress/achievement data			
• Review additional curricular specifications from the state and district			
• Do a serious cost/benefit analysis (e.g., what am I doing that does not meet either my basic overall goals or my specific goals for the year?)			
• Seek out family and colleagues for conversations about teaching that are inspiring			
• Other?			

References

Aber, L., & O'Rourke, P. (2002). *Grandma's button box (math matters)*. Bloomington, IN: Kane Press, Turtleback Books.

Ali, S., & Frederickson, N. (2006). Investigating the evidence base of social stories. *Educational Psychology in Practice, 22,* 355–377.

Alleman, J., & Brophy, J. (2001). *Social studies excursions, K-3. Book One: Powerful units on food, clothing, and shelter*. Portsmouth, NH: Heinemann.

Alleman, J., & Brophy, J. (2002). *Social studies excursions, K-3. Book Two: Powerful units on communication, transportation, and family living.* Portsmouth, NH: Heinemann.

Alleman, J., & Brophy, J. (2003). *Social studies excursions, K-3. Book Three: Powerful units on childhood, money, and government*. Portsmouth, NH: Heinemann.

Alleman, J., & Brophy, J. (2004). Building a learning community and studying childhood. *Social Studies and the Young Learner, 17*(2), 16–18.

Baker, J., Terry, T., Bridges, R., & Winsor, A. (1997). Schools as caring communities: A relational approach to school reform. *School Psychology Review, 26,* 586–602.

Barton, K., & Levstik, L. (2004). *Teaching history for the common good*. Mahwah, NJ: Erlbaum.

Beck, I., & McKeown, M. (1988). Toward meaningful accounts in history texts for young learners. *Educational Researcher, 17*(6), 31–39.

Beck, T. (1998). Are there any questions? One teacher's view of students and their questions in a fourth-grade classroom. *Teaching and Teacher Education, 14,* 871–886.

Bogner, K., Raphael, L., & Pressley, M. (2002). How grade-1 teachers motivate literate activity by their students. *Scientific Studies of Reading, 6,* 135–165.

Briody, J., & McGarry, K. (2005). Using social stories to ease children's transitions. *Young Children, 60*(5), 38–42.

Brophy, J. (2010). *Motivating students to learn* (3rd ed.). New York: Routledge.

Brophy, J., & Alleman, J. (2006). *Children's thinking about cultural universals*. Mahwah, NJ: Erlbaum.

Brophy, J., & Alleman, J. (1996, 2007). *Powerful social studies for elementary students*. Belmont, CA: Wadsworth.

Brophy, J., & VanSledright, B. (1997). *Teaching and learning history in elementary schools*. New York: Teachers College Press.

Brophy, J., Alleman, J., & Knighton, B. (2008). *Inside the social studies classroom*. New York: Routledge.

Brophy, J., Prawat, R., & McMahon, S. (1991). Social education professors and elementary teachers: Two purviews on elementary social studies. *Theory and Research in Social Education, 19*, 173–188.

Bruner, J. (1990). *Acts of meaning*. Cambridge, MA: Harvard University Press.

Cameron, C., Connor, C., & Morrison, F. (2005). Effects of variation in teacher organization on classroom functioning. *Journal of School Psychology, 43*, 61–85.

Comer, J. (1980). *School power: Implications of an intervention project*. New York: The Free Press.

Comer, J. et al. (1999). *Child by child: the Comer process for change in education*. New York: Teachers College Press.

Dewey, J. (1902). *The child and the curriculum*. Chicago: University of Chicago Press.

Dewey, J. (1938). *Experience and education*. New York: Collier Books.

Dolezal, S., Mohan Welsh, L., Pressley, M., & Vincent, M. (2003). How nine third-grade teachers motivate student academic engagement. *Elementary School Journal, 103*, 239–267.

Dorsett, C. (1993). Multicultural education. Why we need it and why we worry about it. *Network News and Views, 12*, 3–31.

Downey, M., & Levstik, L. (1991). Teaching and learning history. In J. Shaver (Ed.), *Handbook of research on social studies teaching and learning* (pp. 400–410). New York: Macmillan.

Egan, K. (1988). *Primary understanding: Education in early childhood*. New York: Routledge.

Egan, K. (1990). *Romantic understanding: The development of rationality and imagination, ages 8–15*. New York: Routledge.

Ehlert, L. (1993). *Eating the alphabet: Fruits and vegetables from A to Z*. San Diego: Harcourt Brace.

Evertson, C., & Weinstein, C. (Eds.), (2006). *Handbook of classroom management: Research, practice, and contemporary issues*. Mahwah, NJ: Erlbaum.

Girod, M., & Wong, D. (2002). An aesthetic (Deweyan) perspective on science learning: Case studies of three fourth graders. *Elementary School Journal, 102*, 199–224.

Glasser, W. (1965). *Reality therapy*. New York: Harper-Collins.

Glasser, W. (1990). *The quality school: Managing students without coercion*. New York: Harper & Row.

Good, T., & Brophy, J. (2008). *Looking in classrooms* (10th ed.). Boston: Pearson/Allyn & Bacon.

Hinitz, B. (1992). *Teaching social studies to the young child: A research and resource guide*. Boston: Garland.

Kennedy, M. (2005). *Inside teaching: Classroom conditions that frustrate reform*. Cambridge, MA: Harvard University Press.

Kounin, J. (1970). *Discipline and group management in classrooms*. New York: Holt, Rinehart & Winston.

Leming, J. (1989). The two cultures of social education. *Social Education, 53,* 404–408.

Levstik, L. (1986). The relationship between historical response and narrative in the classroom. *Theory and Research in Social Education, 14,* 1–15.

Marker, G., & Mehlinger, H. (1992). Social studies. In P. Jackson (Ed.), *Handbook of research on curriculum* (pp. 830–851). New York: Macmillan.

Mitchell, M. (1993). Situational interest: Its multifaceted structure in the secondary school mathematics classroom. *Journal of Educational Psychology, 85,* 424–436.

Noddings, N. (2005). *The challenge to care in schools: An alternative approach to education* (2nd ed.). New York: Teachers College Press.

Pianta, R. (1999). *Enhancing relationships between children and teachers.* Washington, DC: American Psychological Association.

Pressley, M., Dolezal, S., Raphael, L., Mohan, L., Roehrig, A., & Bogner, K. (2003). *Motivating primary grade students.* New York: Guilford.

Pugh, K. (2002). Teaching for transformative experiences in science: An investigation of the effectiveness of two instructional elements. *Teachers College Record, 104,* 1101–1137.

Purkey, W., & Novak, J. (1996). *Inviting school success: A self-concept approach to teaching, learning, and democratic practice* (3rd ed.). Belmont, CA: Wadsworth.

Rogers, C., & Freiberg, H.J. (1994). *Freedom to learn* (3rd ed.). New York: Merrill.

Shaver, J. (1987). What should be taught in social studies? In V. Richardson-Koehler (Ed.), *Educators' handbook: A research perspective* (pp. 112–138). New York: Longman.

Smith, J., & Girod, M. (2003). John Dewey and psychologizing the subject-matter: Big ideas, ambitious teaching, and teacher education. *Teaching and Teacher Education, 19,* 295–307.

Stanley, W. (1985). Recent research in the foundations of social education: 1976–1983. In W. Stanley (Ed.), *Review of research in social studies education: 1976–1983* (pp. 309–399). Washington, DC: National Council for the Social Studies.

Thornton, S. (2005). *Teaching social studies that matters: Curriculum for active teaching.* New York: Teachers College Press.

Toplis, R., & Hadwin, J. (2006). Using social stories to change problematic lunch-time behaviour in school. *Educational Psychology in Practice, 22,* 53–67.

Westcott, N. (1992). *Peanut butter and jelly: A play rhyme.* New York: Penguin.

Wubbolding, R. (1988). *Using reality therapy.* New York: Harper-Collins.

Wubbolding, R. (1991). *Understanding reality therapy.* New York: Harper-Collins.

Wubbolding, R. (1996). *Reality therapy training* (9th ed.). Cincinnati: Center for Reality Therapy.

Index

CPSIA information can be obtained
at www.ICGtesting.com
Printed in the USA
FFOW03n2116210417
34799FF